AF575778

THE GREAT HORNED OWL
AN IN-DEPTH STUDY

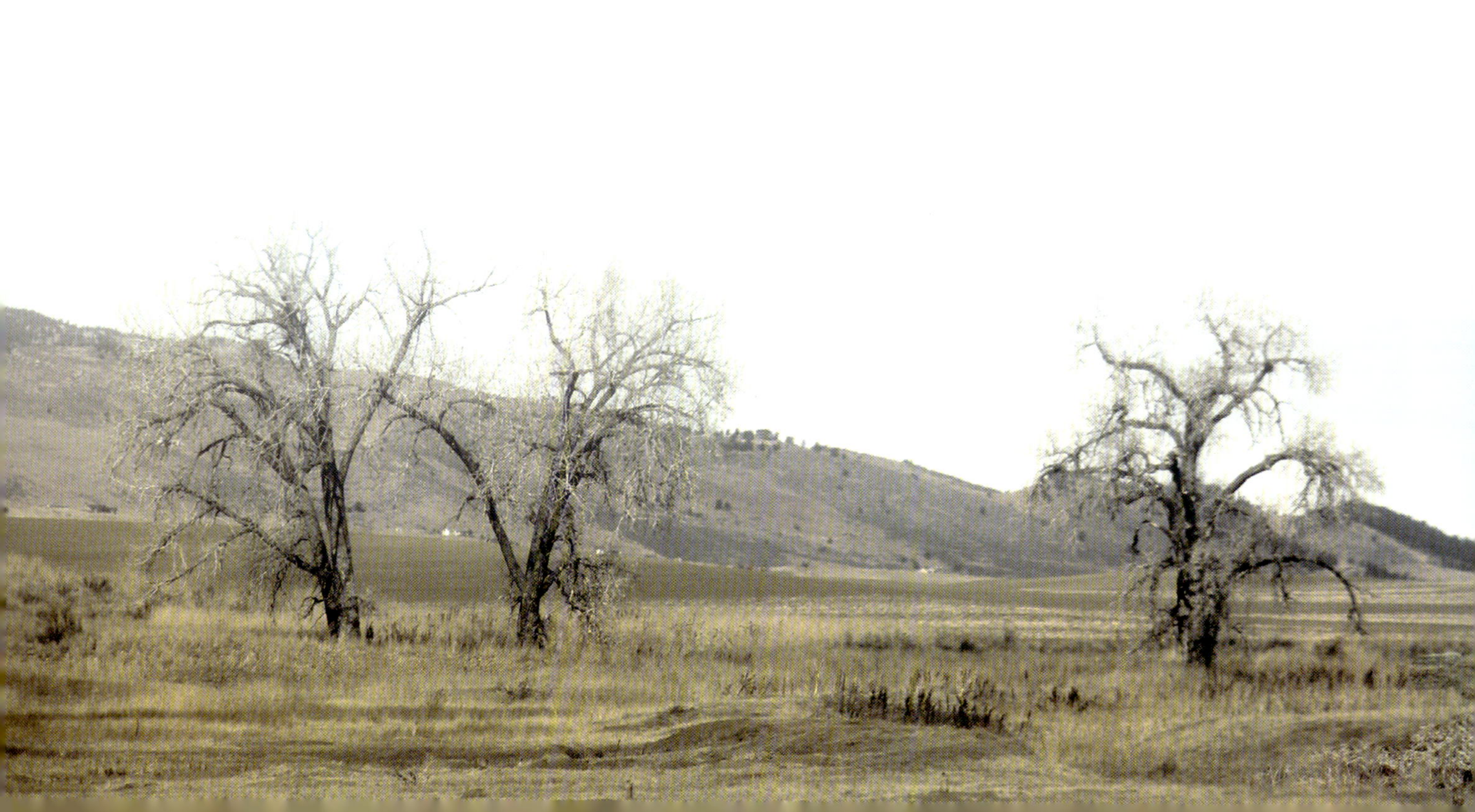

THE GREAT HORNED OWL

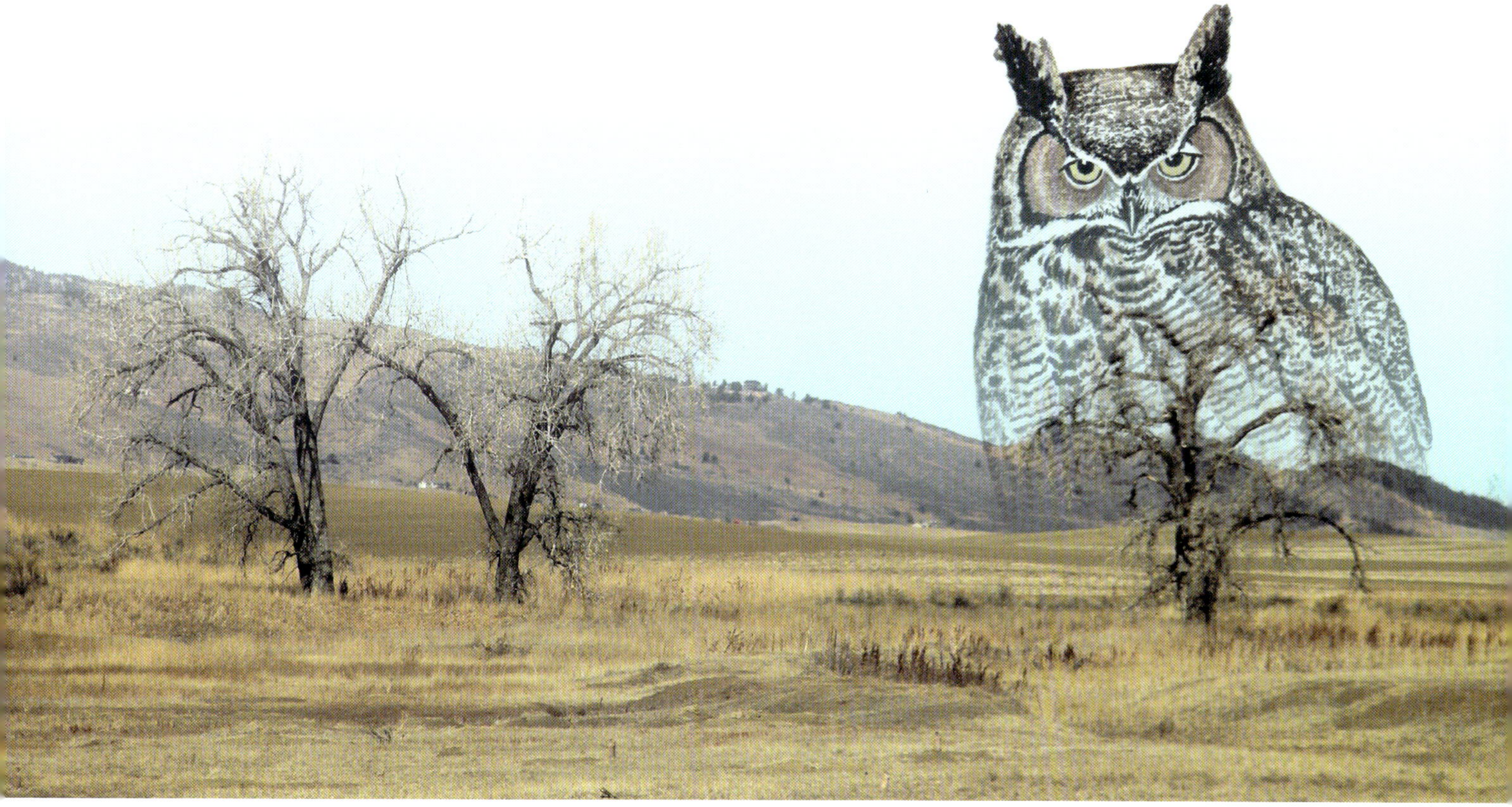

AN IN-DEPTH STUDY

Written and Illustrated by SCOTT RASHID

Foreword by Paul Bannick

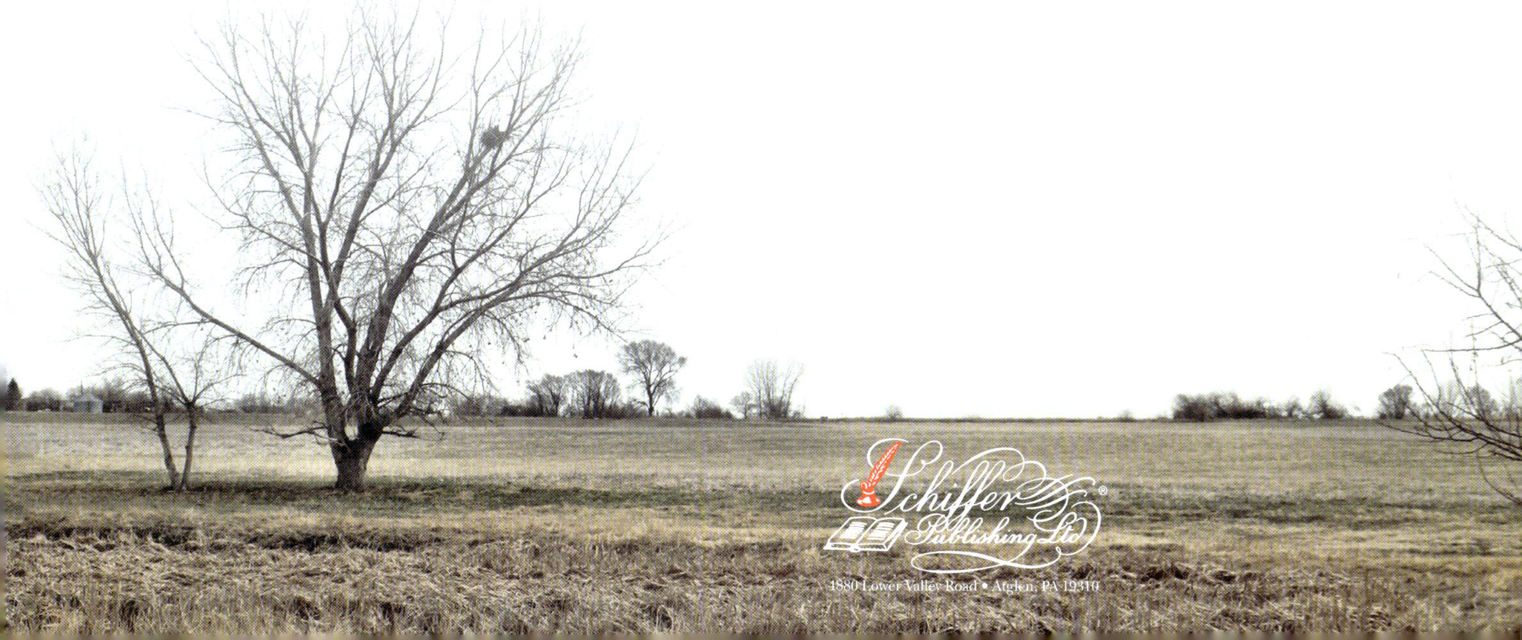

Published by Schiffer Publishing, Ltd.
4880 Lower Valley Road
Atglen, PA 19310
Phone: (610) 593-1777; Fax: (610) 593-2002
E-mail: Info@schifferbooks.com

For our complete selection of fine books on this and related subjects, please visit our website at www.schifferbooks.com. You may also write for a free catalog.

This book may be purchased from the publisher. Please try your bookstore first.

We are always looking for people to write books on new and related subjects. If you have an idea for a book, please contact us at proposals@schifferbooks.com.

Schiffer Publishing's titles are available at special discounts for bulk purchases for sales promotions or premiums. Special editions, including personalized covers, corporate imprints, and excerpts can be created in large quantities for special needs. For more information, contact the publisher.

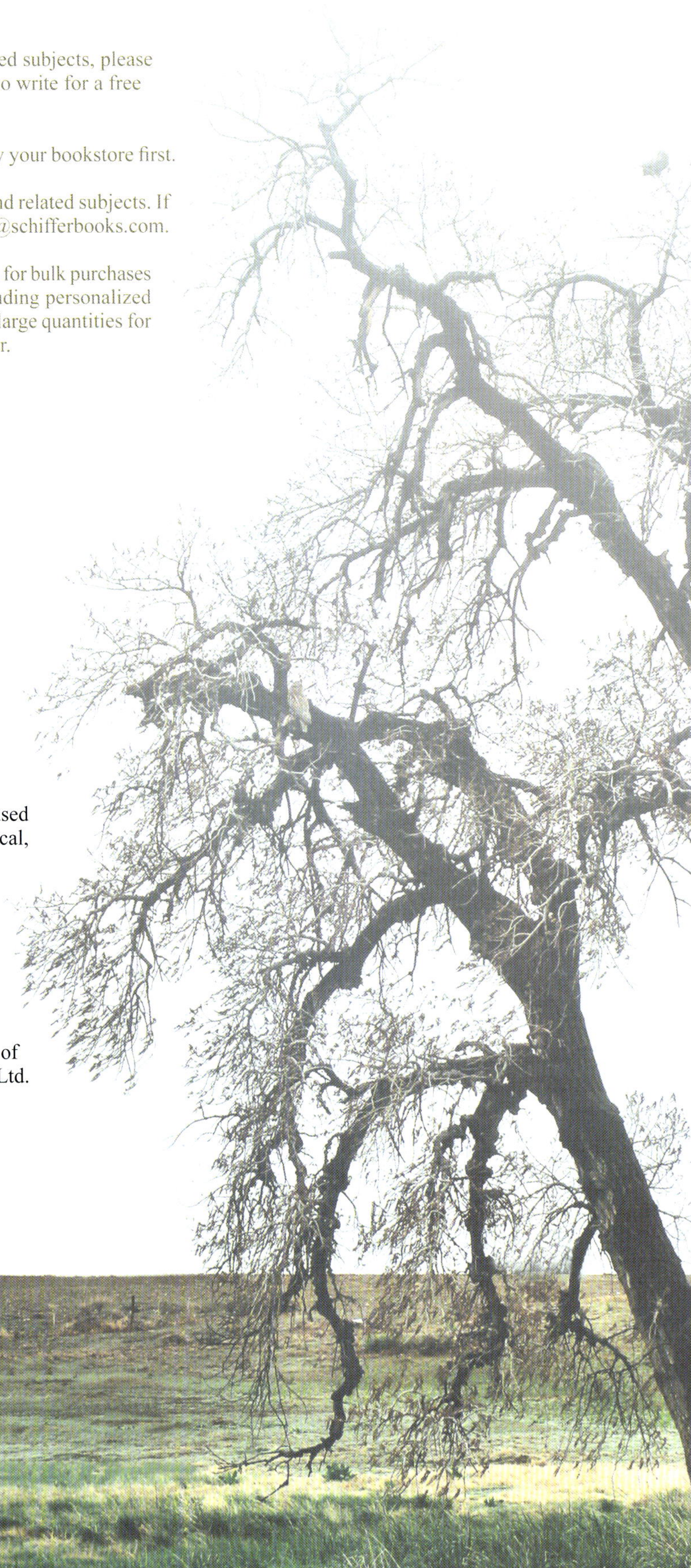

Library of Congress Control Number: 2014954914

Designed by RoS
Type set in Alexon/ZapfEllipt BT

ISBN: 978-0-7643-4766-5
Printed in China

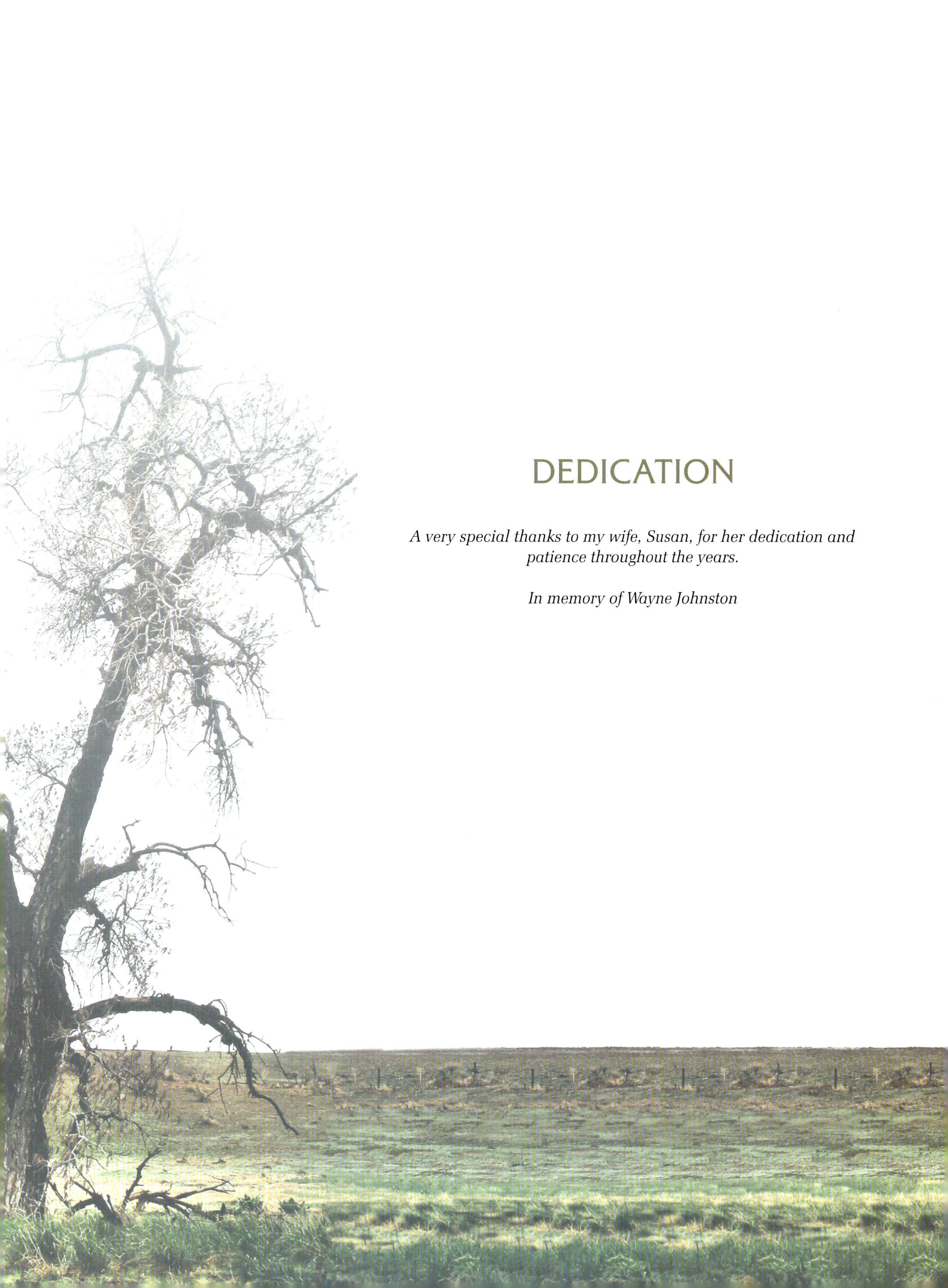

DEDICATION

A very special thanks to my wife, Susan, for her dedication and patience throughout the years.

In memory of Wayne Johnston

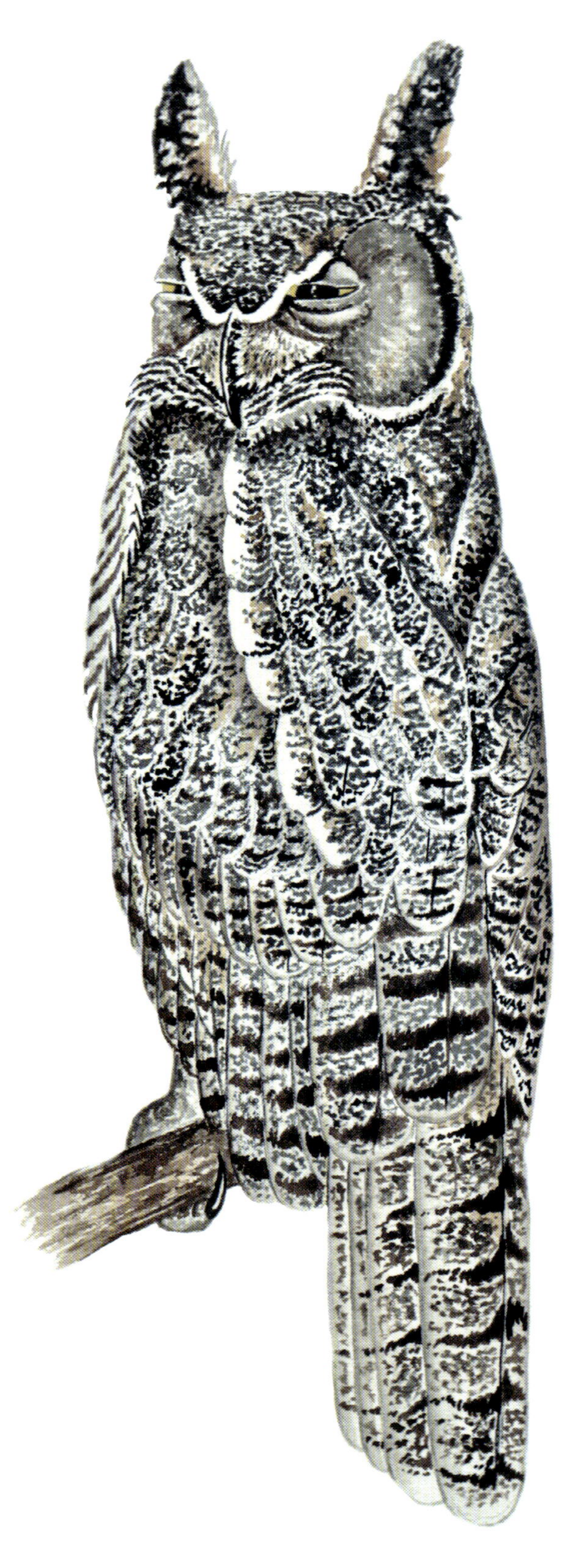

CONTENTS

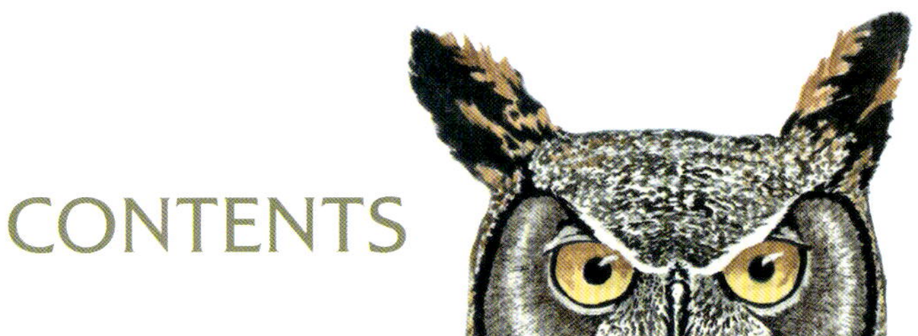

Foreword ___8
Acknowledgments ___9
Introduction ___10

CHAPTER 1: Description / Anatomy ___15
CHAPTER 2: Distribution / Range ___25
CHAPTER 3: Vocalization ___32
CHAPTER 4: Nest Description ___37
CHAPTER 5: Hunting / Food Preferences ___60
CHAPTER 6: Monitoring Nesting / Growth of Young ___71
CHAPTER 7: Public Enemy Number One ___91
CHAPTER 8: Rehabilitation of Great Horned Owls ___97

A Few Final Thoughts ___105
Glossary of Scientific Names ___106
References Cited ___109

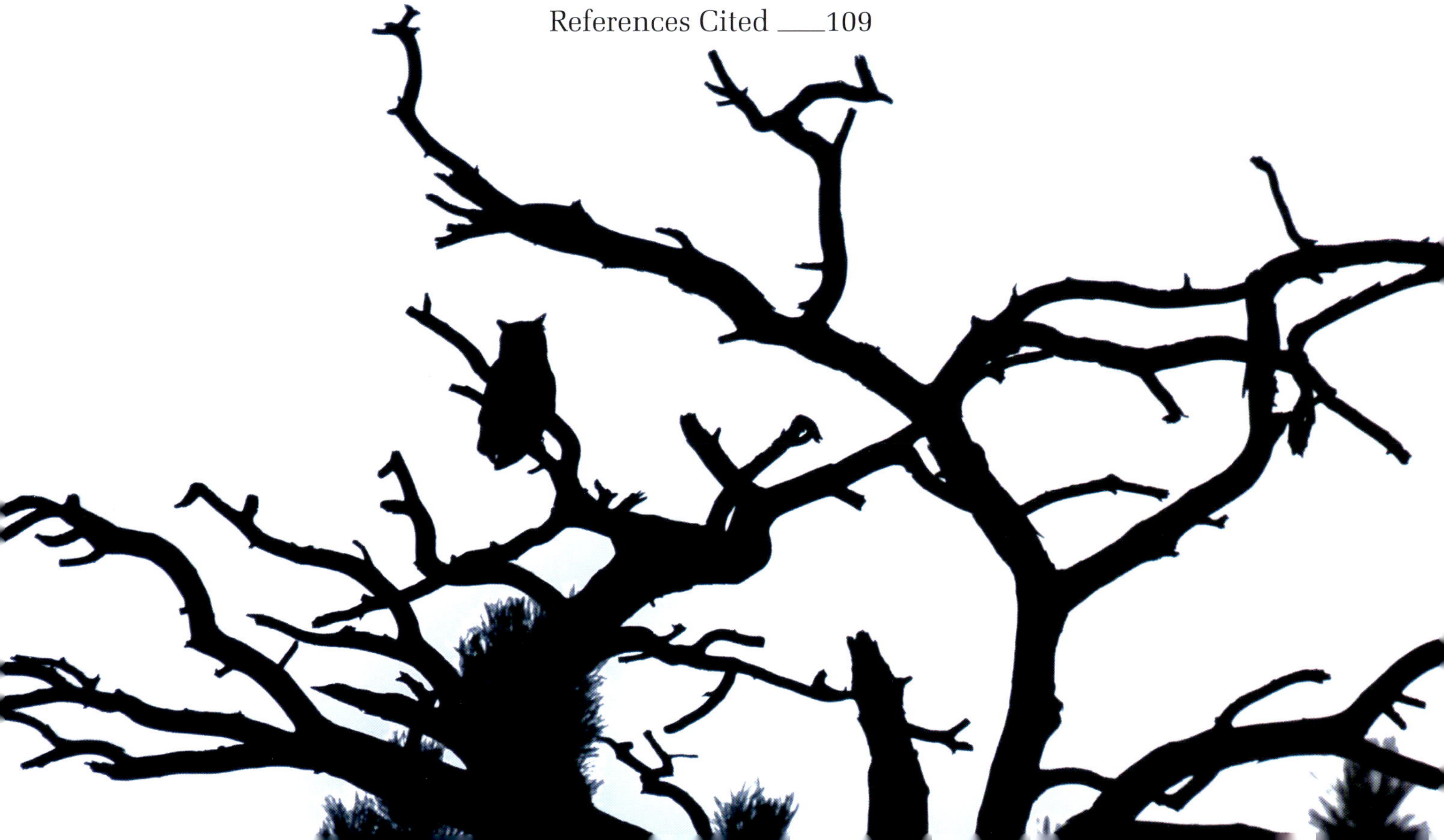

FOREWORD

We marvel at birds. They fascinate, inspire, and even soothe us, yet how much do we really understand them? While some may enjoy them and look for the next target, and others may study a specific element of a particular species's behavior in a certain geography, it is the rare naturalist who sits for days on end observing a species, often without an agenda, in the hopes of learning something new or garnering a better understanding of how it fits into the fabric of its home.

Scott Rashid is not only one of these naturalists, but also a remarkable artist as well, with a keen eye and a sensitive spirit that allow him to notice and record details and behaviors that escape the majority of others. His vast experience in the field allows him to understand first-hand which observations are significant, and his work as rehabilitator gives him an appreciation for the physical attributes of his subjects.

While photographs might come close to capturing the essence of a rare moment, Scott's illustrations bring the apex of the most critical moments and behavior to life in a teachable way that the imperfections of other mediums might miss.

The product, or better yet the gift, of these skills and efforts is a rare personal glimpse into the lives of one of North America's most powerful birds. In this book, we learn in the comfort of our homes what only countless hours of experience, hard work, observation, and artistic skill can accomplish.

Paul Bannick
Award-winning photographer and author
of *The Owl and The Woodpecker*

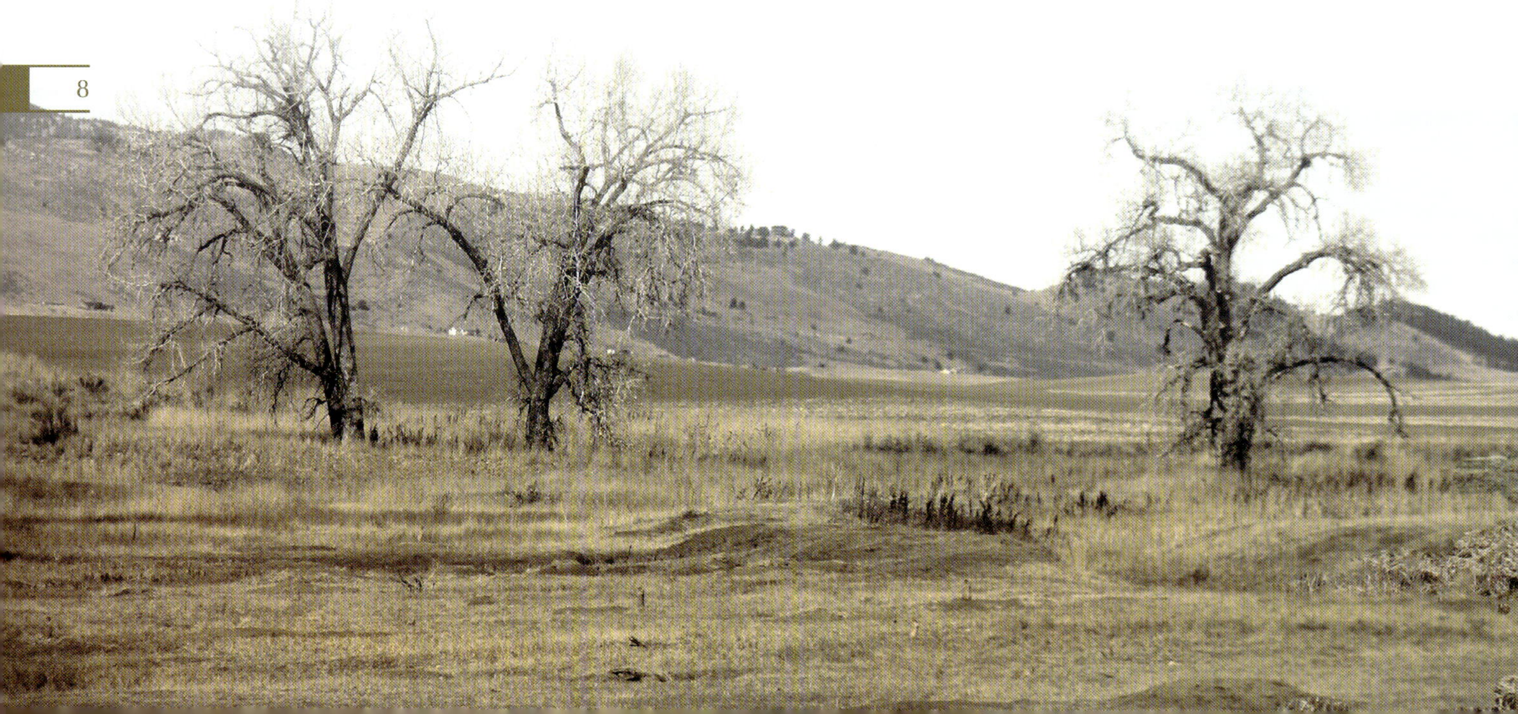

ACKNOWLEDGMENTS

This book would have never happened without the assistance of many individuals. I wish to thank Christian Cold, Wildlife Technician and Educator of the Bureau of Wildlife Management, Wisconsin Department of Natural Resources, who introduced me to the practice of trapping and banding raptors; Dr. Ronald Ryder, Professor emeritus, of Colorado State University, Fort Collins, Colorado, who inspired me to begin researching birds; and Mr. Rick Spowart, of the Colorado Parks and Wildlife.

I would also like to thank Eric Adams, Paul Bannick, Heidi Bucknam, Ryan Carpenter, Jeff Connor, Apryle Craig, Alex Cruz, Jennie Duberstein, Lisa and Matt Dragon, Joe Heyen, Wayne and Diana Johnston, Kay McKeever, Nick Komar, Gary Mathews, Gary C. Miller, Gene Putney, Susan Rashid, Tom Redd, Richard Renyolds, Bill Schmoker, Jim Sedgewick, Will and Shellie Spear, Jeff Stevenson and the Denver Museum of Natural History, Terrie Stewart, Cole Wild, and the National Park Service at RMNP.

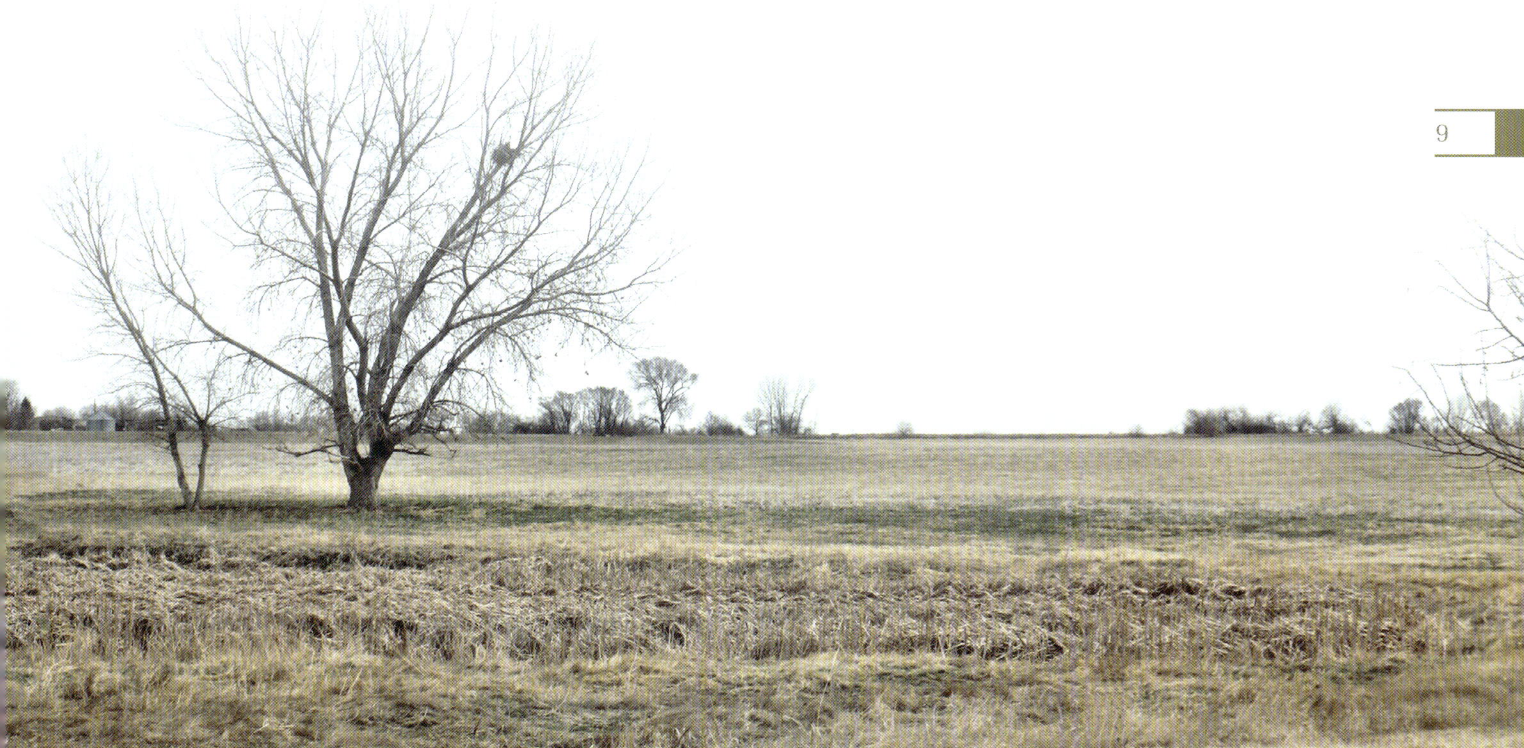

INTRODUCTION

Few species of North American birds have evoked more emotion than Great Horned Owls. They are one of the most controversial birds in the country due to their ability to hunt some of the same species of birds and animals that we as humans raise for food and hunt for sport. Great Horned Owls are quite large, yet they have the ability to remain hidden during the day, making them difficult to observe most times of the year.

The familiar hooting of these owls can be heard in any month of the year, but is most often heard in the spring as the males court the females. As one of the earliest nesting birds in North America, Great Horned Owls pick a nest site before other species even begin searching; the owls do not construct their nests, but rather use abandoned nests of other species. Throughout the range of the Great Horned Owl, they have been documented nesting in unused nests of raptors, such as Red-tailed Hawks, Northern Goshawks, Bald Eagles, and other species.

WHAT'S IN A NAME?

The Great Horned Owl is so named for its large size and significant ear tufts. Its scientific name is *Bubo virginianus* — Bubo from the Latin for "Eagle Owl" and virginianus for Virginia, the location where the first specimen or specimens were collected for scientific study (Terres 1982).

Apart from the name Great Horned Owl, this species has many other names, including Hoot Owl, Big Hoot Owl, Cat Owl, Chicken Owl, Eagle Owl, Flying Tiger, Tiger of the Air, and King Owl. In my opinion, these names were most likely given to the species because of what it looks like, how strong it is, and what it feeds upon.

Due to this species being so widespread, there are at least sixteen recognized subspecies that have also been located throughout its range (Houston et al. 1998). These include:

- THE GREAT HORNED OWL (*Bubo virginianus virginianus*) — found nesting from southern Ontario, southern Quebec, western New Brunswick, and Nova Scotia; south to the Gulf Coast and throughout Florida; and west to Wisconsin, eastern Minnesota, southern South Dakota, eastern Kansas, eastern Oklahoma, and eastern Texas.

- THE WESTERN GREAT HORNED OWL (*Bubo virginianus pallescens*) — found from southeastern California, southern Nevada, southern Utah, northern New Mexico, and north-central Texas and south to the Mojave Desert and lower California into Mexico.

- THE ARCTIC GREAT HORNED OWL (*Bubo virginianus subarcticus*) — found from the treeless limits of northern Canada to Hudson Bay and in northeastern British Columbia to central Alberta, Saskatchewan, Manitoba, and northeastern Ontario.

- THE DUSKY GREAT HORNED OWL (*Bubo virginianus saturatus*) — found in the humid forests of the Pacific northwest, including Washington, Oregon, and north through British Columbia to Alaska.

- THE NORTHWEST GREAT HORNED OWL (*Bubo virginianus lagophonus*) — found from the interior of Alaska and the Yukon, south through central and eastern British Columbia, eastern Washington, northeastern Oregon, and northeastern Idaho to northwestern Montana.

- THE DWARF GREAT HORNED OWL (*Bubo virginianus elachistus*) — found throughout the southern portions of Baja California.

(Source: Austing and Holt 1966)

These subspecies are just a few recognized types of Great Horned Owls found throughout the range of this species; however, there are several species of owl worldwide within the genus Bubo. Some of these include the Snowy Owl, Eurasian Eagle Owl, Pharaoh Eagle Owl, Rock Eagle Owl, Spotted Eagle Owl, Blakiston's Fish Owl, Brown Fish Owl, and the Malay Fish Owl. All of these are large owls with formidable feet and talons, enabling them to prey upon large creatures.

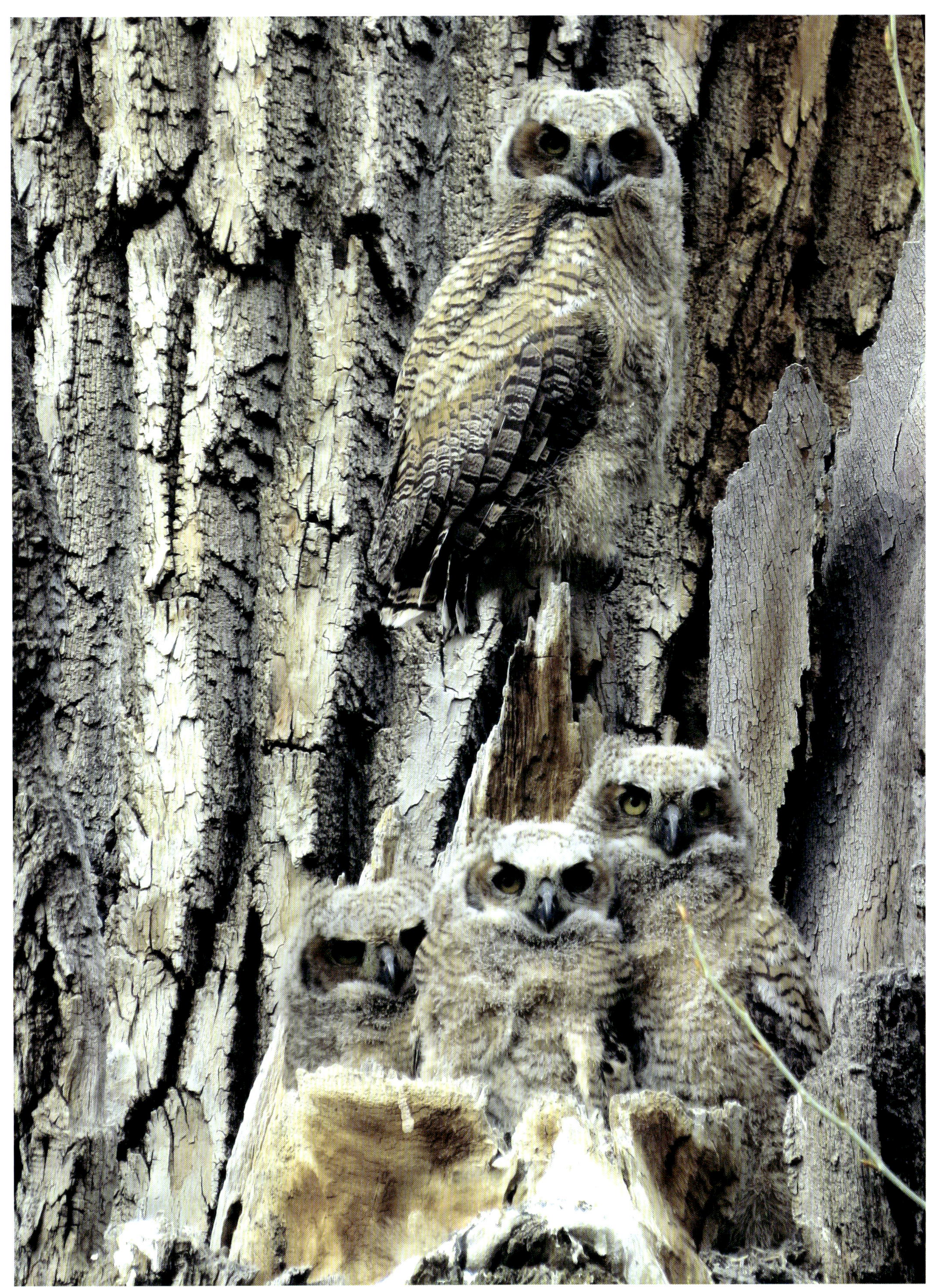

MY FIRST ENCOUNTER

According to the World Owl Trust, there are 217 species of owls worldwide in the order Strigiformes. This order is then split into two families: Tytonidae and Strigidae. Barn Owls and Bay Owls make up the family Tytonidae; the rest make up Strigidae.

Throughout North America these two families comprise nineteen species of nesting owls. Of these species, the most widespread is the Great Horned Owl. It is also the largest of the eared, or "tufted," owls. Due to its large size and the vast numbers seen throughout the continent, when owls are described, often times, the first thing mentioned is whether or not the owl had ear tufts or not — even though there are only seven species of tufted owls in North America. These seven species include Eastern, Whiskered, and Western Screech Owl, Great Horned Owl, Long-eared Owl, Short-eared Owl, and the Flammulated Owl.

With the exception of the Northern Pygmy-Owl and the Ferruginous Pygmy-Owl, the remaining species have no tufts. The two species of pygmy-owls have small tufts that they can raise and lower at will. Unlike the "horned" owls, the tufts of pygmy-owls are actually part of their facial disk versus separate sets of feathers on the tops of their heads.

As its name implies, the Great Horned Owl is most easily identified by its large size: approximately 2 feet (.61m) from head to tail, long ear tufts, which can be 2 inches (5.08cm) or more in length, and a wingspan of more than 3-1/2 feet (1.15m) in length. A few more identifying field marks of the species include its pure white or orange-buff throat patch and the horizontal barring on its breast and belly.

I'll never forget my first encounter with this

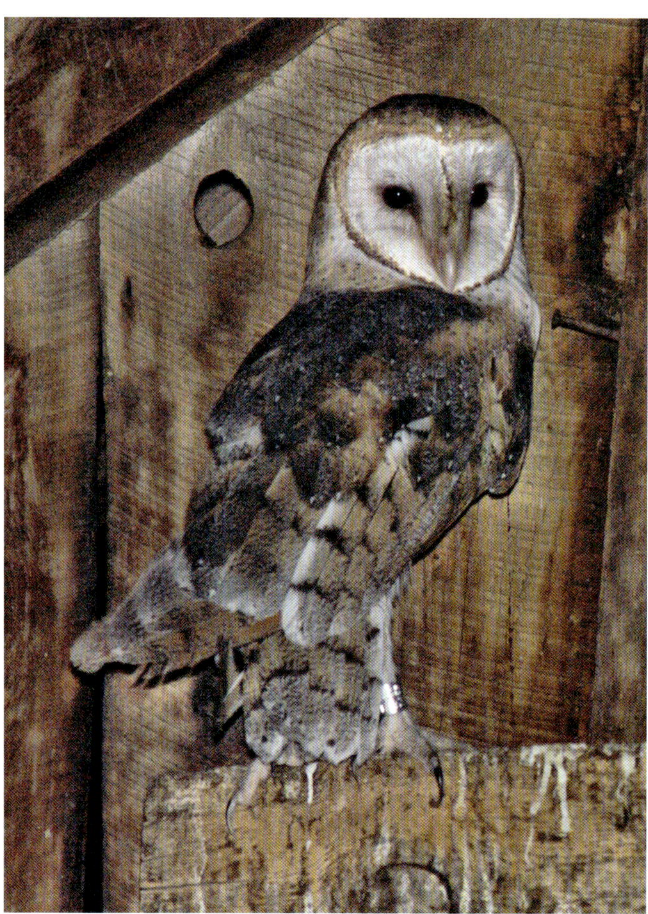

The American Barn Owl is the only North American owl in the family Tytonidae.

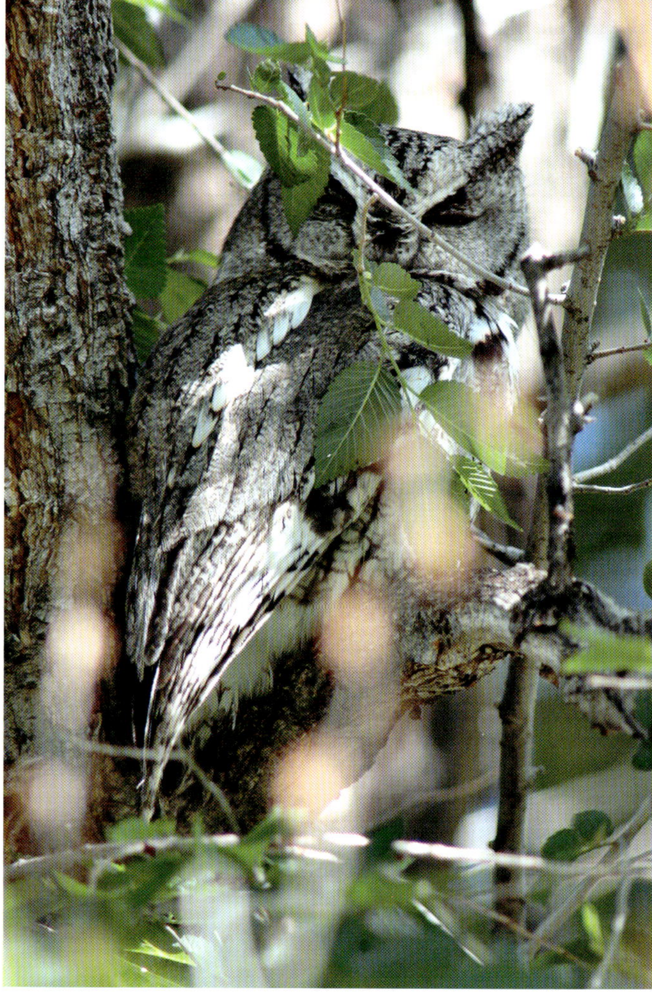

The Eastern Screech Owl is the smallest tufted owl in eastern North America.

magnificent creature. I was sixteen years old and living in North Fond du Lac, Wisconsin, which is roughly 60 miles (96km) north of Milwaukee. The habitat around North Fond du Lac is primarily farm country, and, in fact, my backyard butted up against a farmer's field. Most of the farmers' fields are separated by fences and tree lines and many farmers have a sizable wooded area somewhere on their property, making it is easy to walk from one woods to another by following a line of trees and/or fence rows.

One afternoon in late January, my friend, Todd Jacobson, and I were rabbit hunting near his home. He lived several miles north of town, in farm country as well. On that hunting venture, we had walked about a mile (1.60km) or so when we came upon a medium-sized woodlot that encompassed several acres. We saw a number of rabbit tracks and droppings as we approached the woods. In that part of the country, the woods are primarily oak and maple, with some trees hundreds of years old and 80 feet (24.39m) high or higher.

Todd walked in the woods a few yards while I paralleled him on the edge of the trees. As we moved, I was looking ahead of him in case he scared up a rabbit. About 50 feet (15.24m) ahead of Todd, I noticed a 55-gallon (207.9 liters) drum on its side lying next to a large maple tree. I suggested that he kick the drum in hopes of scaring out any rabbits that might be hiding inside.

Unbeknownst to us, there was a large owl perched in the tree above the drum. As Todd kicked the drum, the owl flew low through the trees into the woods. All we saw was a dark shape through the trees that we agreed was an owl, but which species? We tried to relocate the owl, but couldn't. What was so impressive about the bird was that as it flew through the woods we didn't hear any wing flapping.

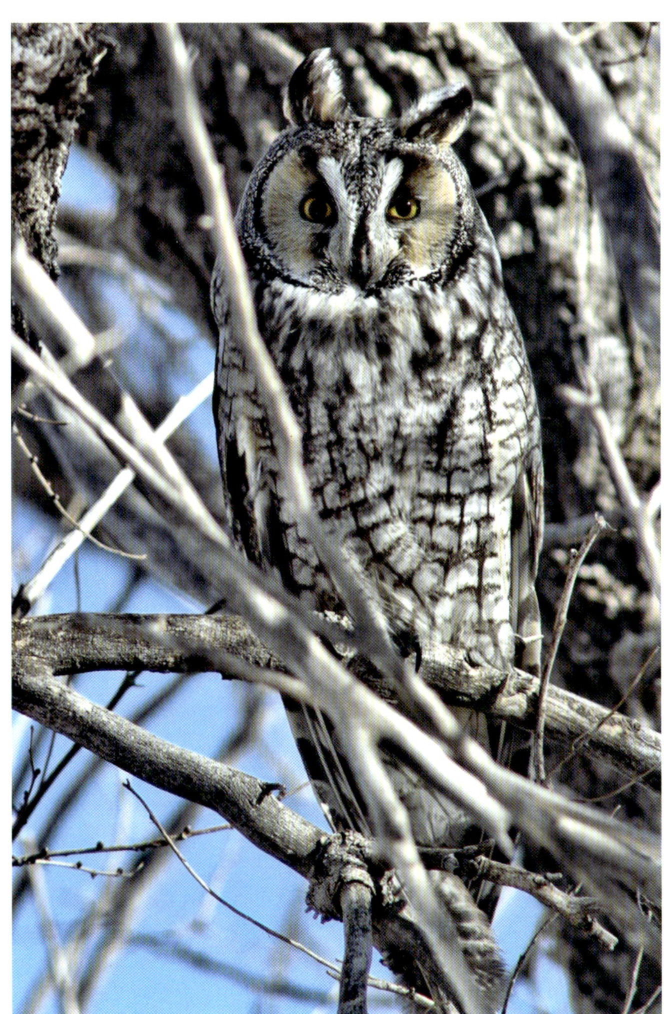

Long-eared Owls can be found in the same habitat as Great Horned Owls.

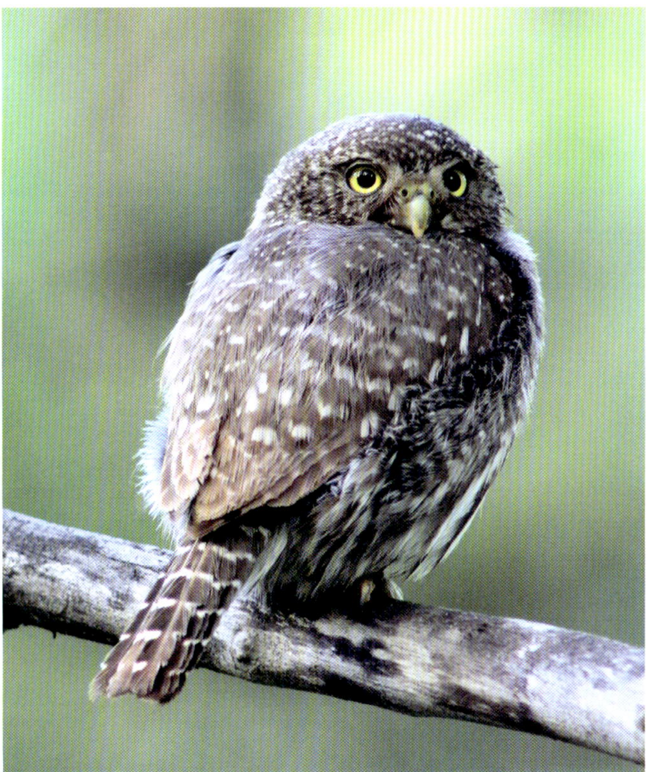

Northern Pygmy-Owls have tufts that are actually part of their facial disk versus sets of tufts on their heads as Great Horned Owls have.

Later that night and in the days following, I looked through my copy of *The Audubon Society Encyclopedia of North American Birds* and determined, by the size and color, that the bird we saw was either a Long-eared Owl or a Great Horned Owl (pages 652-655). I carefully looked at the photographs and read the information about both species, trying to determine which one we would have seen. In one photo, you can see the Long-eared Owls underwing. This was very close, if not identical to what I thought I saw. Not having access to a photo of the underside of a Great Horned Owl's wing, I was leaning toward the smaller, Long-eared Owl. However, after reading about the habitat preferences of the two species, I began changing my mind and was leaning towards it having been a Great Horned Owl.

Two weeks later, I drove back to the woods in hopes of identifying the species in question. While driving along the road on the south side of the woods, I saw a large nest high in an oak tree with something on it. Looking through my binoculars, I saw an adult Great Horned Owl and two owlets in the nest. This was the first time I had seen any owl in the wild — and it was very exciting! I walked a couple hundred yards through the field, to the nest tree, watching the female who was studying me. I walked to within a few yards from the nest into the woods in hopes of locating her mate. After a few minutes, I found him perched about 8 feet (2.44m) off the ground on a horizontal branch of an oak tree. The owl watched me for a few moments before he flew deeper into the woods. Under his perch were several pellets and whitewash. This was obviously his favorite perch.

I returned to the nest once a week until the young had fledged. At one point, after the young had moved into the forest, I arrived at the woods with a brand new, never before used Ricoh 35mm camera. Upon searching the woods, the two fledglings were found perched on a horizontal branch with their mother between them. I began taking what I thought were fantastic photos of the family before the female flew off.

I looked at my camera and discovered that I had taken forty-three photos with a single role of thirty-six exposure film! I was quite impressed that I got so many images on a roll of film. I began rewinding the film to find that I had not advanced the film properly and, subsequently, never took a single photo that day! Since that day in 1981, I have photographed literally hundreds of Great Horned Owls and have yet to get a photo of two owlets perched on either side of an adult. On the plus side, in the summer of 2013, while studying a nesting pair of Northern Pygmy-Owls, I was able to photograph two owlets with their mother perched between them…so I feel that makes up for those original Great Horned Owl photos.

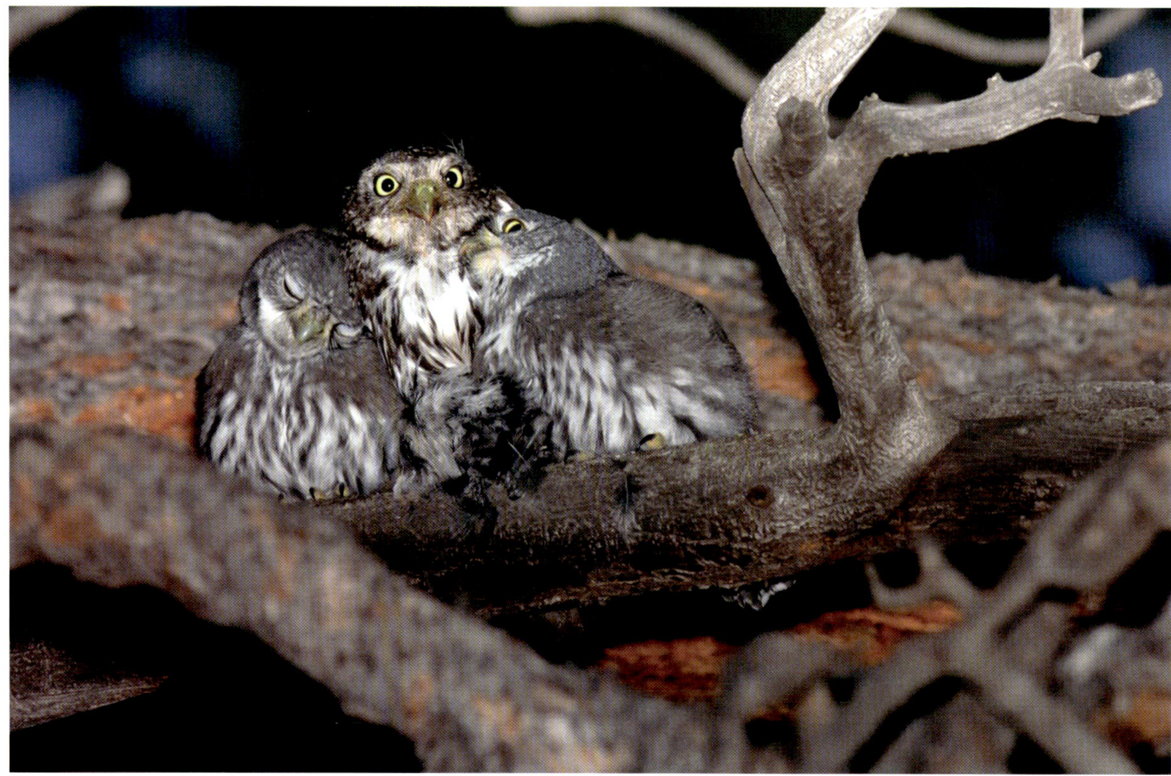

Female Northern Pygmy-Owl feeding two fledglings.

Chapter 1

DESCRIPTION/ANATOMY

The Great Horned Owl is the largest owl found throughout most of North America. They are unmistakable—if you can get a clear view of the adult birds. Great Horned Owls have long, broad wings and relatively long tails. Their long ear tufts and cryptic coloration combine to enable them to remain well hidden during the day, often out of sight of sharp-eyed diurnal raptors and eagle-eyed birders.

The Great Horned Owl is a very impressive and formidable bird. Adult owls are between 18 and 24 inches (46-63cm) from head to tail and have a wing span of more than 4 feet (1.22m). For the most part, females are larger than males, a term known as "reverse sexual dimorphism." This reverse dimorphism enables the smaller male to catch smaller prey that would be more abundant and easier to obtain. It also enables that larger female to catch larger prey as the young get older and need greater caloric intake. Furthermore, the two birds of different sizes won't be competing against each other for food. According to Marti (1974), the most pronounced reverse sexual dimorphism of owls occurs within Great Horned Owls. This may be due to the adult birds being so powerful and the young needing so much food when growing.

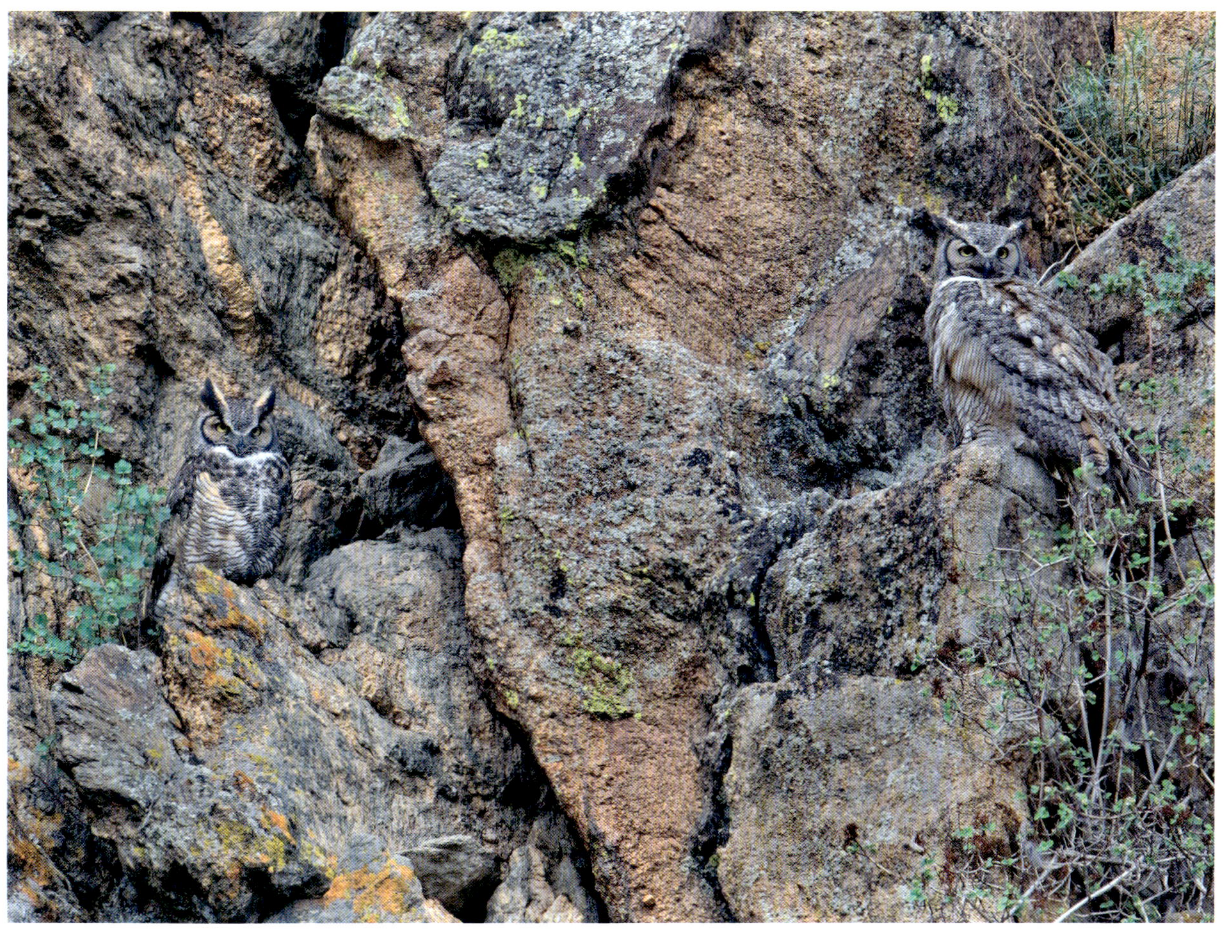

A mated pair of Great Horned Owls. Note how well they blend in with their surroundings. The larger female is on the right. *Photo © Gene Putney.*

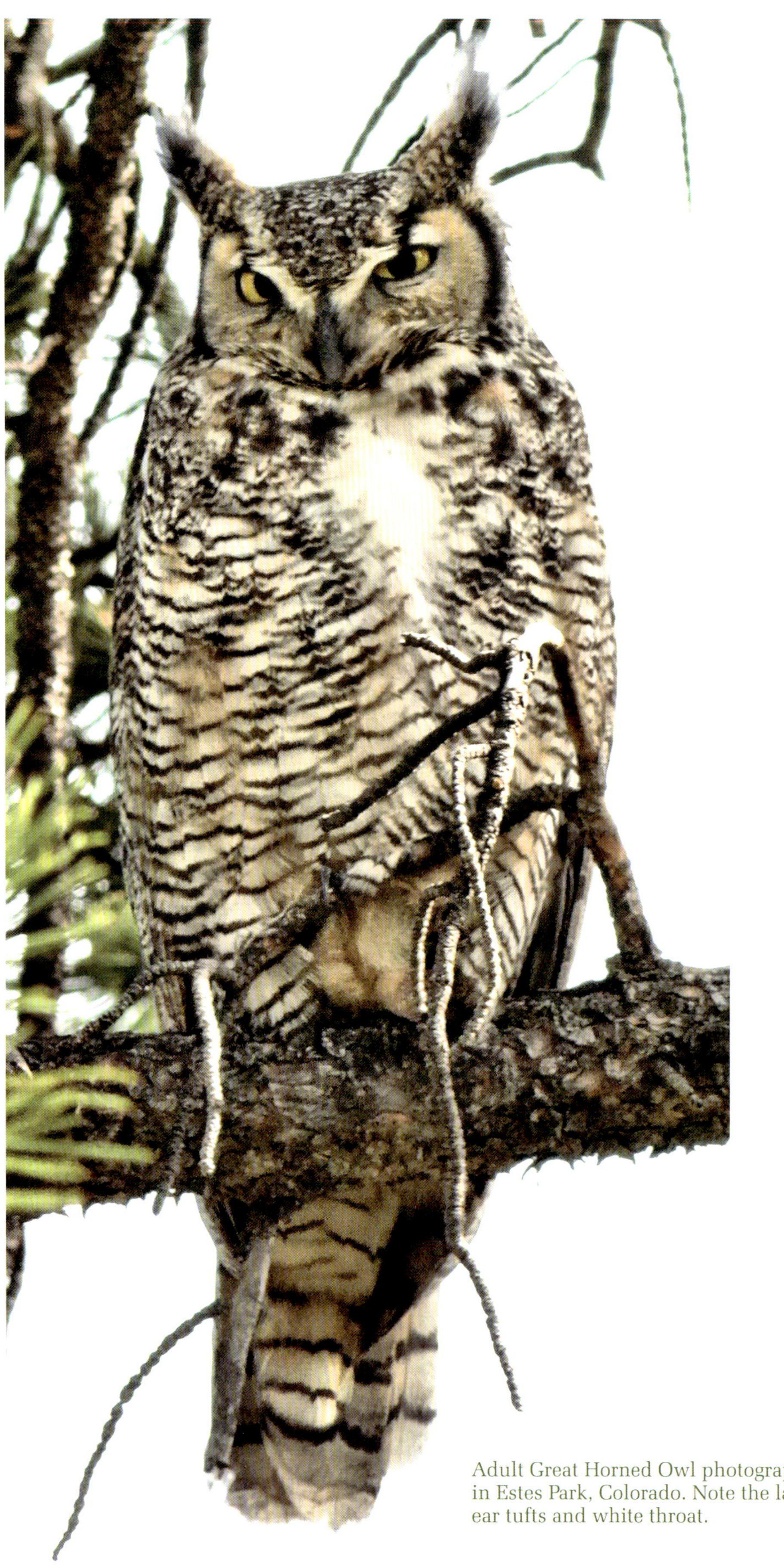

Adult Great Horned Owl photographed in Estes Park, Colorado. Note the large ear tufts and white throat.

A few impressive characteristics of Great Horned Owls are their grand size, white throat, and large ear tufts. The tufts of the Great Horned Owl are the longest and widest of any North American owl species. Seeing their tufts is a great field mark for identification.

Ear tufts are sets of feathers on the top of an owl's head that can be raised and lowered at will. They also aid in camouflaging the birds during the day. When the tufts are raised, they help break up the owl's silhouette and can hopefully deter any potential predator from identifying the owl when it's roosting. Ear tufts may actually make the face of an owl appear to mimic the faces of other mammals, such as foxes or bobcats. When a mammal confronts an eared owl, the owl raises its tufts and the predator may actually believe it is confronting another mammal and, not wanting the confrontation, withdraw from attack (Mysterud and Dunker 1979).

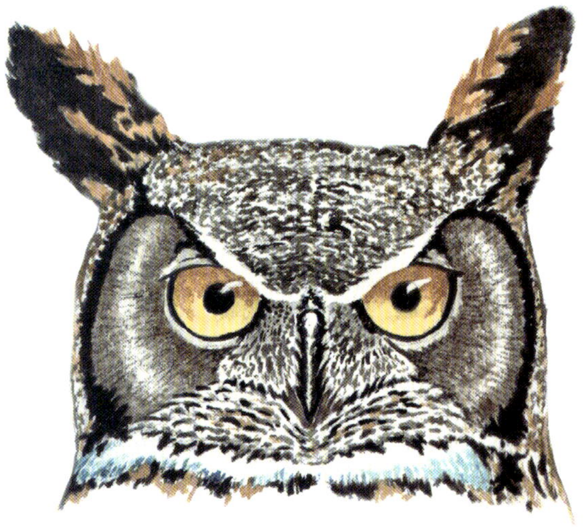

A portrait of a typical Great Horned Owl.

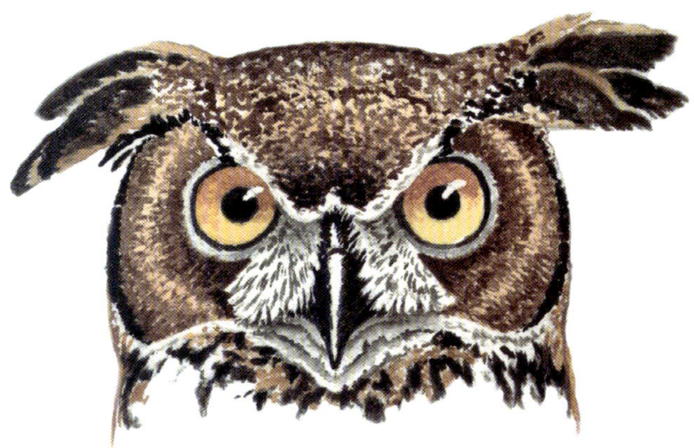

A portrait of a relaxed Great Horned Owl.

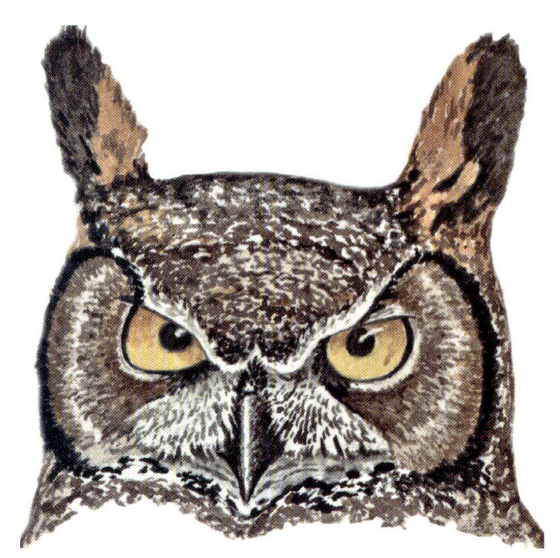

A portrait of a Great Horned Owl that is trying to intimidate its viewer.

Of all the tufted owls, the owls that are most often mistaken for Great Horned Owls are Long-eared Owls and the screech owls. However, all of these owls are much smaller than the Great Horned Owl. The Long-eared Owl is much smaller and thinner, being 13-3/4 – 15-3/4 inches (35-40cm) with a wingspan of only 35-7/16 – 39-3/8 inches (90-100cm) (Cornell Laboratory of Ornithology). The screech owls are even smaller, with Whiskered Screech Owls being only 6-1/2 – 7-1/2 inches (16.5-19cm) from head to tail and a wingspan of 13-7/8 – 16 inches (35.3-40.6cm). The Eastern Screech Owl is slightly larger, being a whopping 8-3/16 – 9-3/16 inches (20.83-23.37cm) from head to tail, with a wingspan of 21 – 22 inches (53.34-55.88cm) (The Owl Pages.com).

Long-eared Owls usually nest in much more dense habitats than the larger Great Horned Owls, often nesting in American Crow or Cooper's Hawk nests (Armstrong 1958). The screech owls, being even smaller, nest in natural cavities and nest boxes (Belthoff and Ritchison 1989).

Long-eared Owls are often confused with Great Horned Owls. Long-eared Owls are much smaller and thinner.

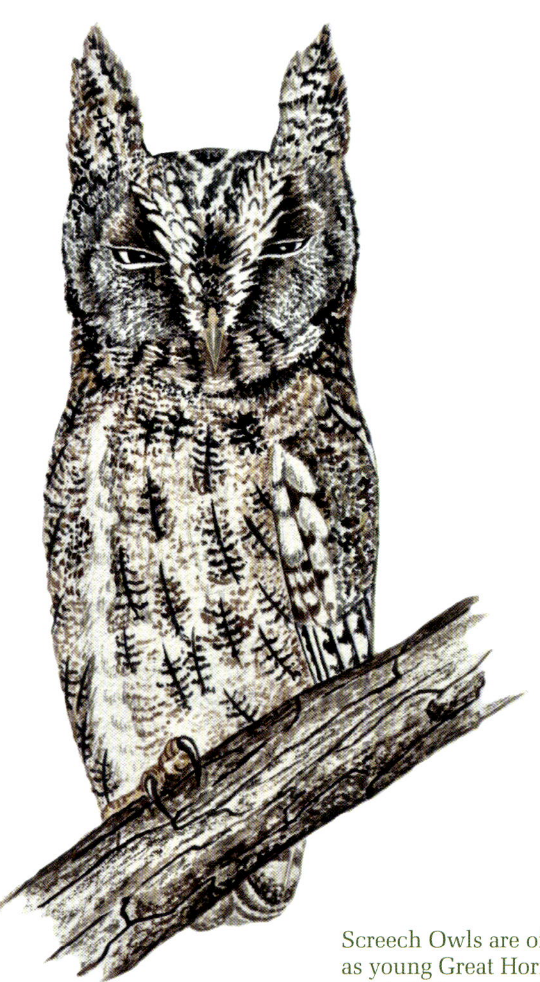

Screech Owls are often thought of as young Great Horned Owls. This one is in its concealment posture.

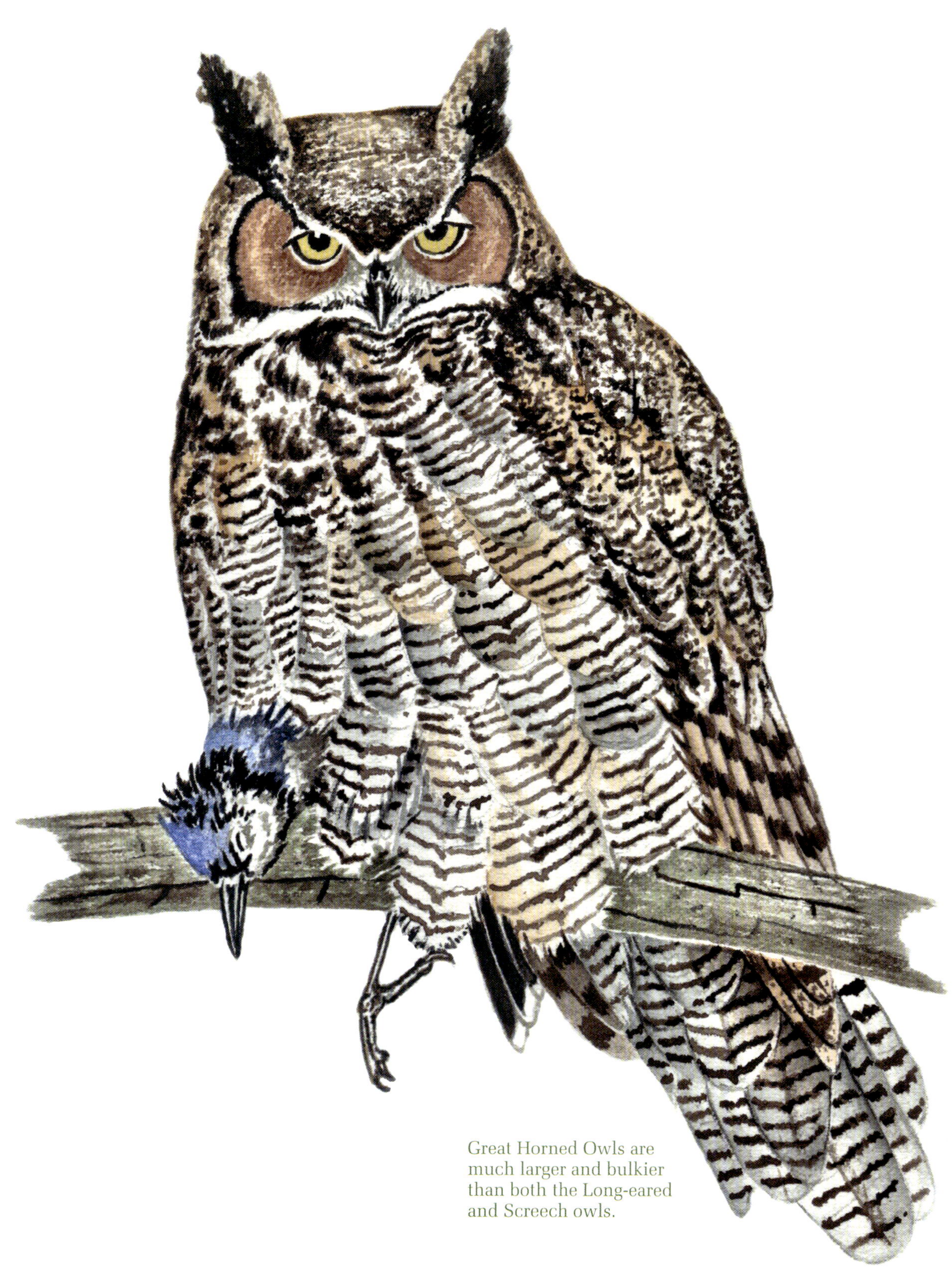

Great Horned Owls are much larger and bulkier than both the Long-eared and Screech owls.

Apart from the Northern Pygmy-Owl, Ferruginous Pygmy-Owl, and Flammulated Owls, the North American owls are silent flying creatures, capable of moving through their respective environments without their potential victims hearing their approach. This silent flight is achieved due to the fringed edges of their flight feathers and soft fluffy contour feathers. These comb-like edges of their flight feathers are most evident when looking at the leading edge of the birds' outer primary flight feathers. This adaptation enables air to flow through the edges of the feathers as opposed to around the edges, as it does with a magpie or grouse, for example.

Like all owls, Great Horned Owls have large, forward-facing eyes with binocular vision, but their eyes are basically immobile in their sockets (Johnsgard 2002). Having binocular vision gives owls a three-dimensional view of their environment, which, as you might imagine, is very important in determining distance. Judging distance quickly and correctly is vital for a predator that hunts living and often moving prey (Austin and Holt 1966). Due to the owl's eyes being fixed in their skull and set wide apart in their heads, their ability to focus on close objects is very limited; as a result, at times the birds may actually have to lean back or even step back to see objects close to them (Austin and Holt 1966). According to Johnsgard (2002), the Great Horned Owl is not able to focus on any object that is closer than 2.78 feet (.85m).

The fringed edges of the primary flight feathers allow air to flow through the edges of the birds' feathers, enabling them to fly silently.

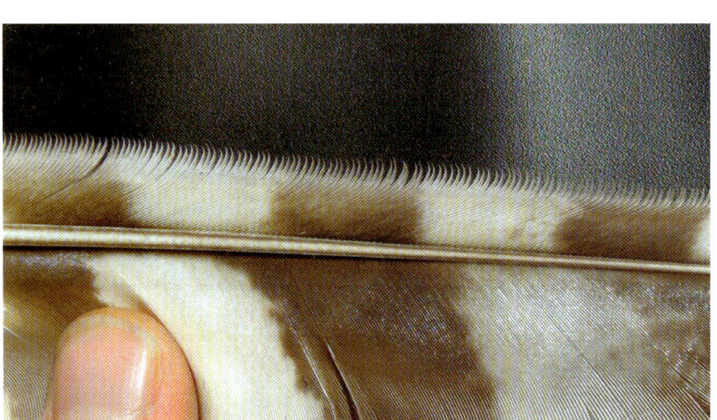

The edge of the wing feather of a Black-billed Magpie.

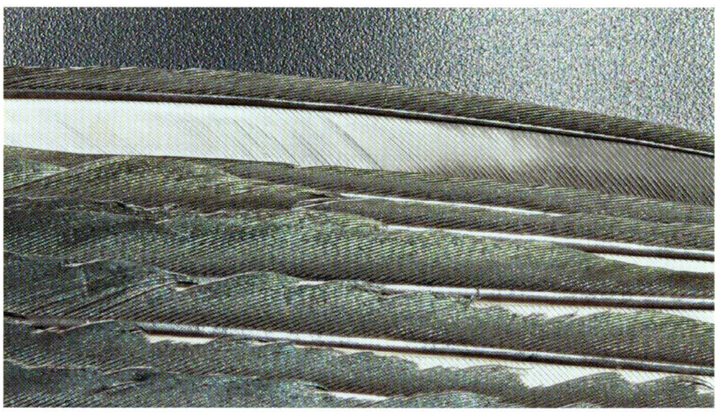

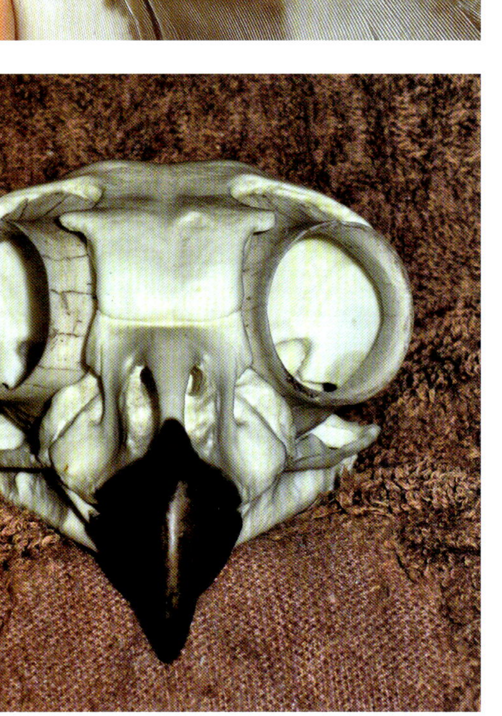

The skull of a Great Horned Owl, showing the symmetrical ear openings.

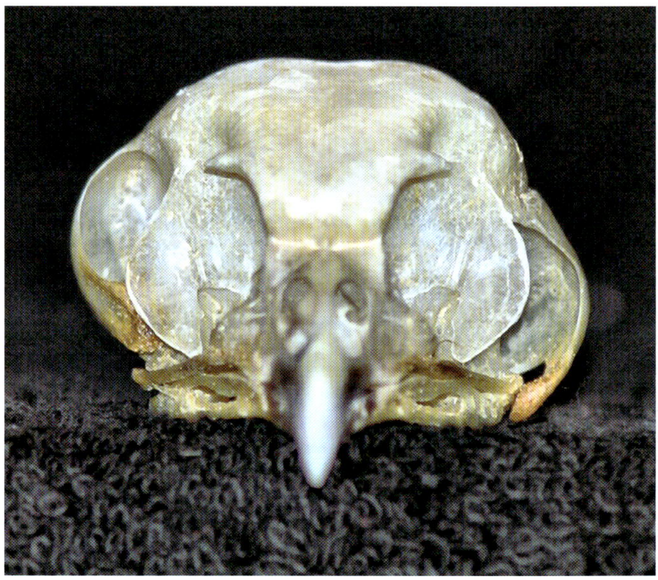

The skull of a Boreal Owl, showing the asymmetrical ear openings.

As a result of having their eyes in the front of their heads, owls have a narrow field of view—only 60-70 percent—whereas humans have a field of view of almost 180 percent, even though our eyes are in the front of our heads, too (Terres 1982). Due to their small field of view, when a perched owl focuses on a subject, such as a mouse or rabbit, it often moves its head side to side and up and down. By moving its head in this manner, the owl is able to focus on a specific object (an object of prey or even a potential predator), versus what is around that object (the ground, branches, etc.). Because its head and eyes are moving but the object in question is not, the owl can determine the exact spot of its subject. As the owl is moving through its environment, it is able to focus instantly on everything in its field of view.

As for the owls' color vision, studies suggest owls see primarily in black and white, but may see a few colors — probably blues, yellows, and greens (Toops 1990).

With the exception of the pygmy-owls, around the owls' eyes are tightly woven feathers that make up the facial disks. These disks seem to amplify and direct sound to the bird's ears. Like pygmy-owls, the ears of Great Horned Owls are symmetrical or nearly symmetrically arranged on the sides of their heads (Smith 2002). Their ears are surrounded by deep, soft feathers that the owls can open to create funnels to each ear opening. The owls have moveable flaps of skin — often called ear flaps — that may serve to focus on sounds from below when they are perched, listening for the movement of potential prey beneath them (Terres 1982).

As sounds emitted by potential prey reach the owls' facial disks, the sounds are directed to their ears, enabling owls to pinpoint where the sounds are coming from. They often bob their heads from side to side or up and down, allowing them to easily identify the location of potential prey and move in for the kill. For example, if a perched owl hears a mouse moving under some leaves, the owl will bob its head up and down and side to side. In doing this, the sound created from the moving or squeaking mouse reaches each of the owl's ears at two slightly different intervals, enabling the owl to identify the exact spot where the mouse is. The owl will then swiftly—and quietly—move in and grasp the mouse before the mouse even knows what has happened. Several species of owls, including Northern Saw-whet and Boreal Owls, have asymmetrical ear openings.

Great Horned Owls are extremely heavy birds, weighing between 2 and 5-1/2 lbs. (.91-2.5kg) (Houston et al 1998). It is the heaviest owl found throughout most of its range. The only exception would be the Snowy Owl, weighing between 3-1/2 and 6-1/2 lbs. (1.6-3kg) (National Geographic.com), which move south into areas where both Snowy and Great Horned Owls can be seen in the winter. However, if measured from head to tail, the Great Gray Owl is, by far, the largest of all North American owls—between 1-1/2 and 3 lbs. (.68-1.35kg)—despite the fact its skeletal structure is actually smaller and weighs less than either the Great Horned or Snowy Owl.

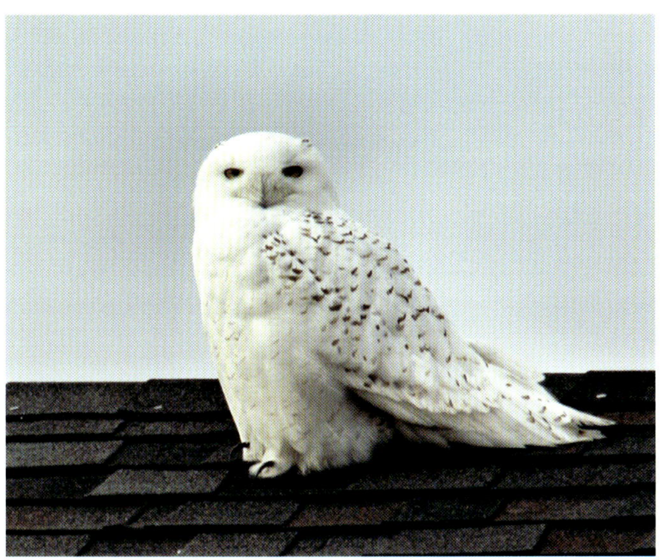

Snowy Owls are the heaviest owls in North America.

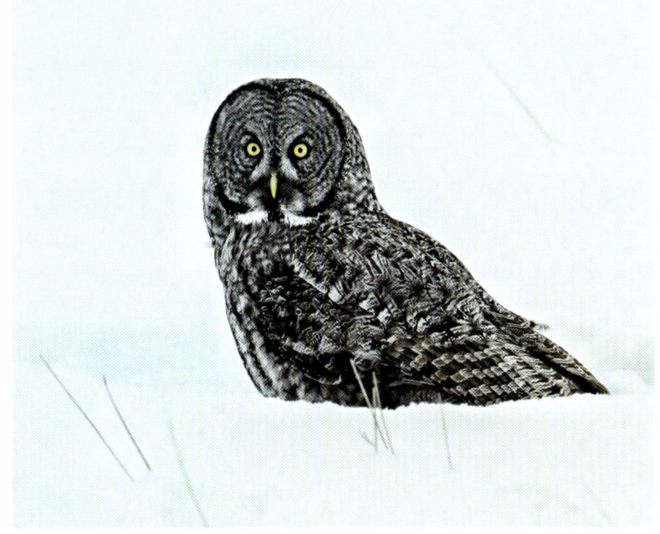

Great Gray Owls are the largest owls in North America—if measured from head to tail—but have a smaller skeleton than either Great Horned Owls or Snowy Owls.

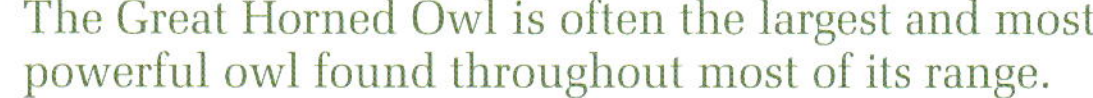

The Great Horned Owl is often the largest and most powerful owl found throughout most of its range.

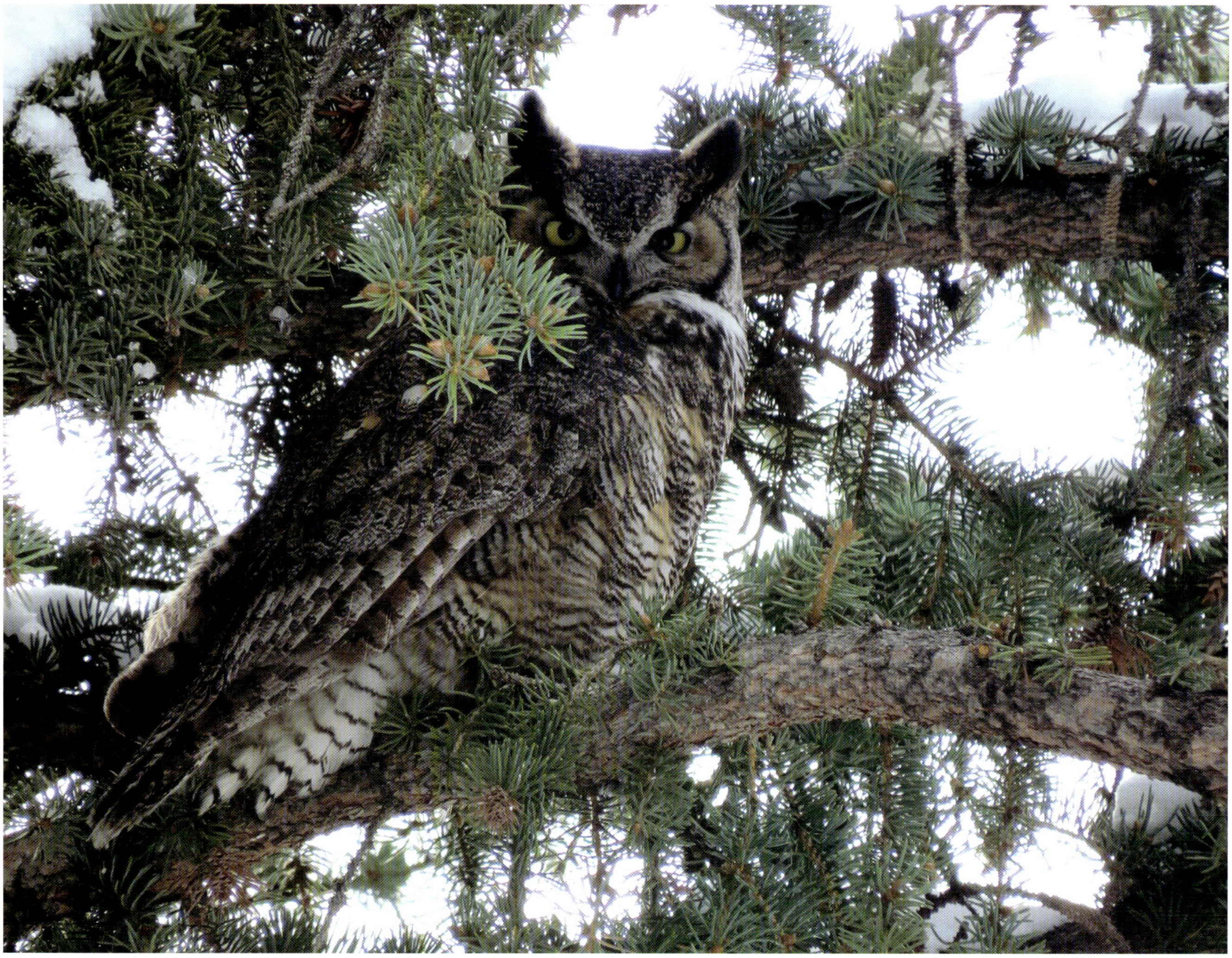

COLOR VARIATIONS

The overall color of Great Horned Owls varies greatly throughout their range. The individuals on the edge of the Arctic tundra can be almost as light as young female Snowy Owls, yet individuals in the far southern portions of its range as well as individuals along the Pacific coast can be very dark, almost black in color. I've seen Great Horned Owls in and around Rocky Mountain National Park (RMNP) so dark that at first glance might make you think they are black, yet I've seen others that are as light as most of the birds seen in the eastern portions of the United States.

One individual that I found in Broomfield, Colorado, was so light brown that it appeared tan and actually blended in perfectly with the color of the cliff where it often perched. That bird was the exact color of the clay and blended in so well that if I hadn't seen it move its head, I would have missed it. Another individual on the Pawnee Grasslands near Nune, Colorado, was so pale gray it appeared almost white, yet its mate was dark brown. Even though these two individuals differed greatly in color, they were still able to keep concealed and out of sight during the day.

Another interesting adaptation that owls, including the Great Horned Owl, have is their ability to rotate their necks roughly 270°, enabling them to look directly over their back. They are able to do this, in part, due to their short necks having only fourteen cervical vertebrae (Johnsgard 2002).

In addition, the outer toe of each foot is reversible, or zygodactyl. This gives owls (as well as ospreys and woodpeckers) more surface area when attacking and grasping prey. This adaptation is most often observed when the owls are perched. When perching, they will often have two toes on the front of the perch and two toes on the back.

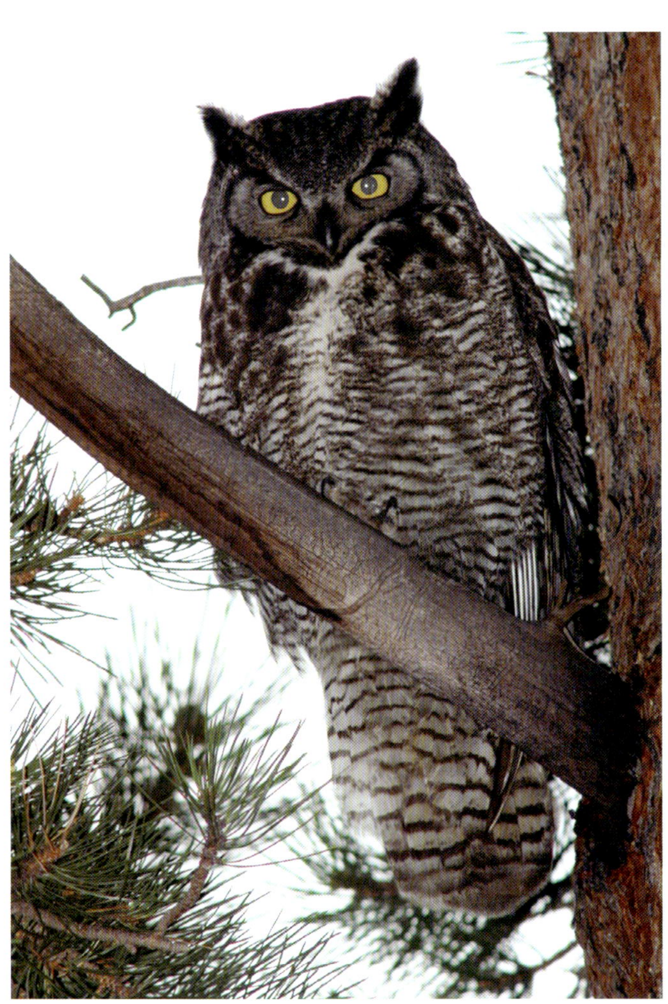

A dark morph Great Horned Owl photographed in Estes Park, Colorado.

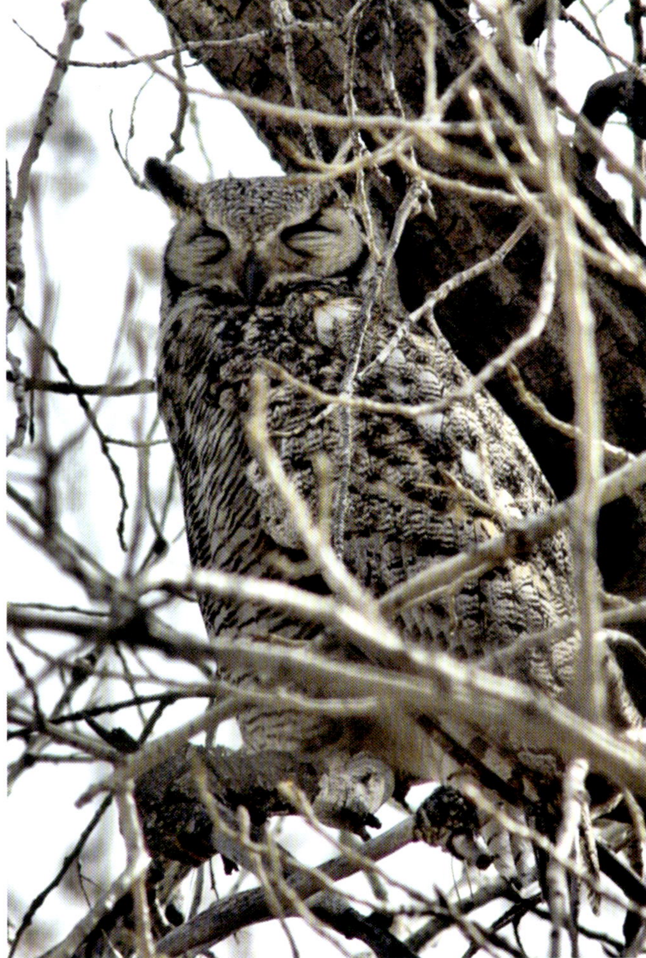

A pale Great Horned Owl photographed on the eastern plains of Colorado.

A light brown Great Horned Owl photographed near Longmont, Colorado.

Chapter 2

DISTRIBUTION/RANGE

There is no other owl species in North America with a larger range than the Great Horned Owl. It breeds from central and western Alaska, central Yukon, Nunavut, northern Manitoba, northern Ontario, northern Quebec, Labrador, and New-Foundland south, through both North and South America, to Tierra del Fuego (Johnsgard 2002).

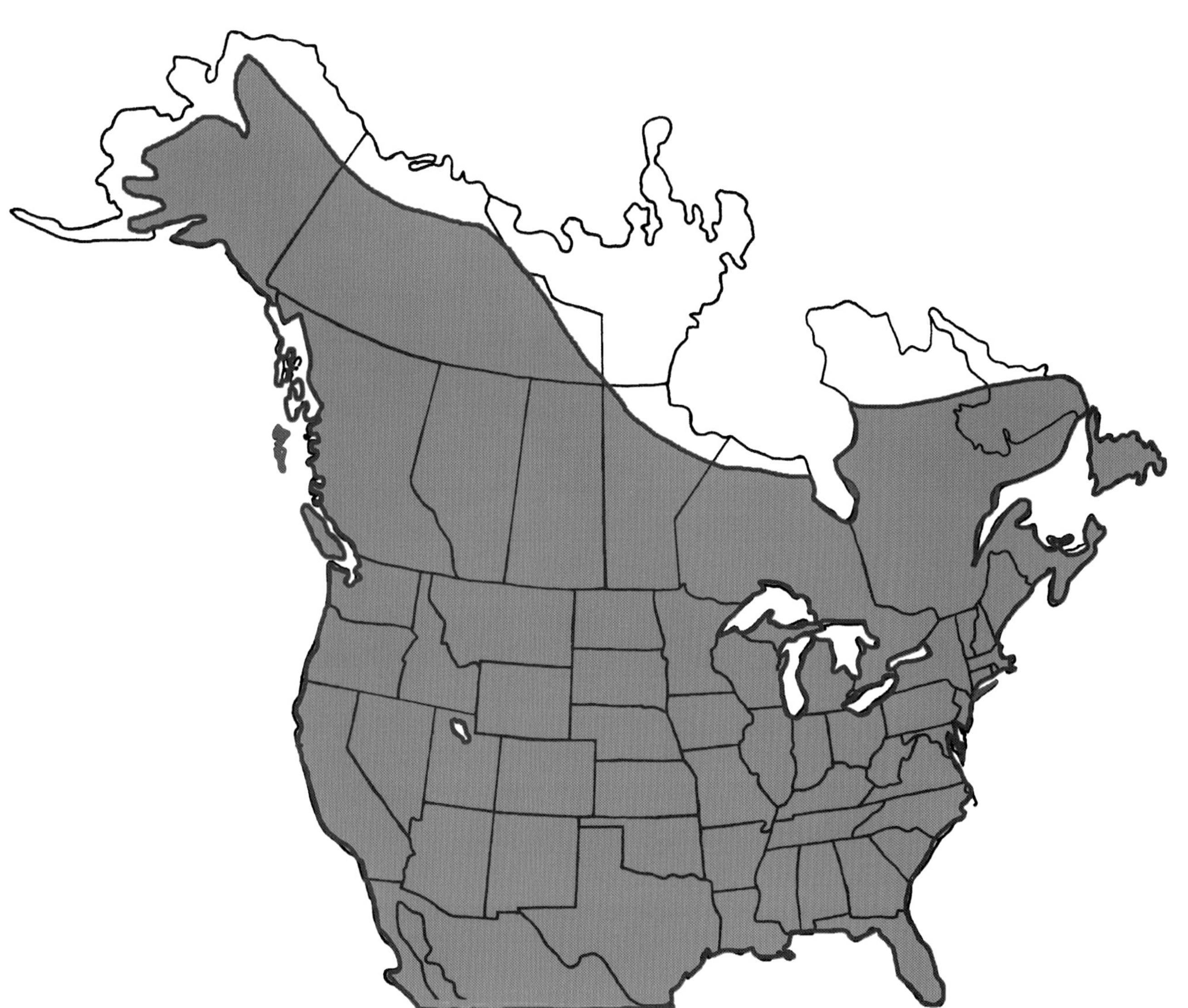

The range map of the Great Horned Owl — the green section is where the species is found year-round.

HABITAT/TERRITORY SIZE

Great Horned Owls are found in every habitat type in North America, with the exception of the higher mountains of the West and the Arctic tundra. The species nests comfortably within deciduous forests, mixed hardwood, coniferous forests, secondary temperate woodlands, swamps, orchards, agricultural areas (Houston et al. 1998), and in many cities throughout their range.

Most researchers and biologists agree that Great Horned Owls tend to live in the same general areas year-round (Dixon 1914, Baumgartner 1939, Austing and Holt 1966), with Baumgartner (1939) being able to locate at least a few males in the same roost regularly throughout the year.

Most Great Horned Owls maintain a permanent home range year-round. A home range is a portion of property that fulfills the biological needs of the species. For Great Horned Owls, this area must have suitable nesting sites for raising their young, areas where the adults can remain concealed during the day, and fairly open areas for hunting (Austing and Holt 1966).

Any Great Horned Owl's home range, or territory, will vary with food supply and nesting sites. According to Austing and Holt (1966), the territory size of Great Horned Owls in the West and Midwest is a square mile or less, due to the large number and variety of available prey. However, in the east, where the owl's food supply is less plentiful, they must hunt over a larger area to sufficiently satisfy their dietary needs. This is why the home range of eastern owls is often larger than that of their Midwestern and Western counterparts.

Great Horned Owls often nest in cemeteries like this one in Fort Collins, Colorado.

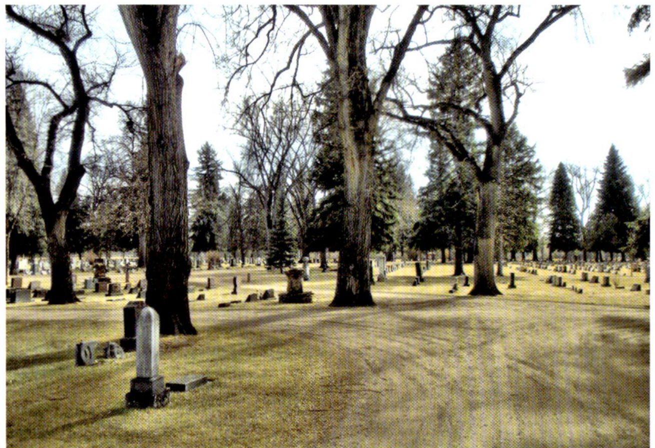

Great Horned Owl habitat, just east of Fort Collins, Colorado.

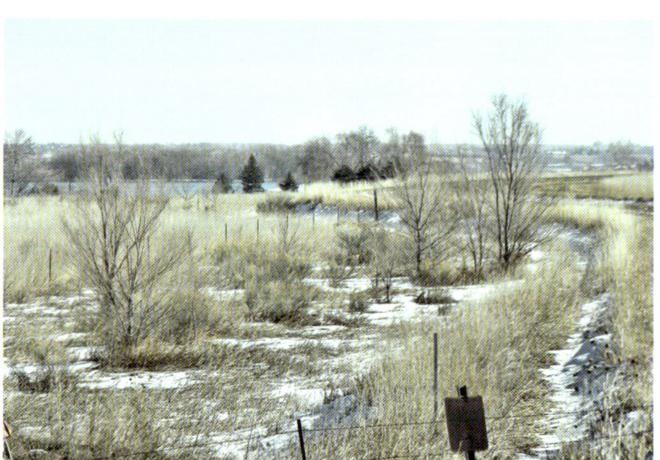

Typical Great Horned Owl habitat in Estes Park, Colorado.

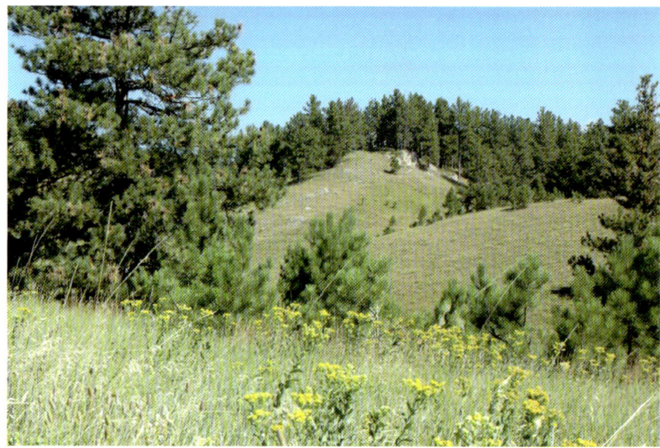

Great Horned Owl habitat in Custer State Park, South Dakota.

The Great Horned Owl requires an area with an ample supply of prey items: nesting sites, which are extremely varied (this will be discussed in detail in Chapter 4); roosting sites, which seem to be chosen to maximize the concealment of the adult birds during the day (Johnsgard 2002); areas with large meadows and/or fields; and an active water source, such as a river, creek, or lake.

Pairs of owls that maintain specific home ranges often have more than one nest site within their territory. They hunt a small section of their territory, often near their nest for a few years, and then, as the prey base decreases, they move to an alternate nest in a different section of their territory. In doing this, they either advertently, or inadvertently, assure that there will be enough food to raise their young. If disturbed too much during the nesting season, the owls may also move to an alternate nest the following season.

In and around Rocky Mountain National Park (RMNP) in Colorado, Great Horned Owls are found on the edge of mature mixed pine, fir, and aspen forests, often with a water source nearby. In the foothills and plains of Colorado, the species can be found in a variety of habitat types, including farmland, city parks, and cemeteries. Within the city of Estes Park, Colorado, and RMNP, there are a pair of owls about every mile and a half or so.

The size of the owl's territory seems to vary depending on prey availability. When prey is abundant, other owl species can be found within the territory of the Great Horned Owl. I saw this myself, just after sundown on the evening of March 19, 2007. I was hiking along a section of the Cub Lake trail inside RMNP, searching for Northern Saw-whet Owls. Since I've been living in Colorado, I have heard six different species of owls within the national park and along the Cub Lake trail, including the Great

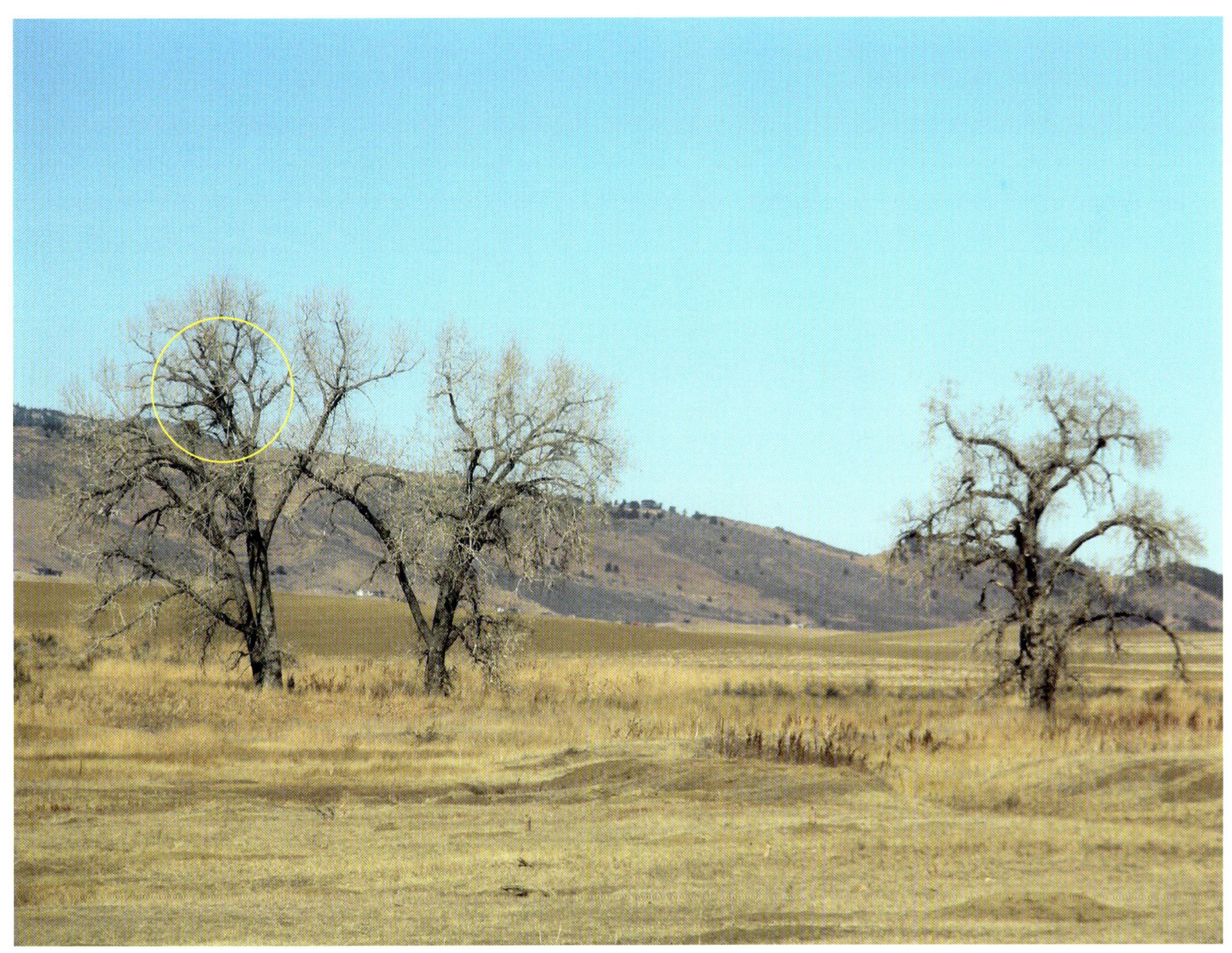

A Great Horned Owl nest tree between Loveland and Fort Collins, Colorado. The owls used an abandoned Red-tailed Hawk nest in the far left tree.

Horned Owl, Northern Pygmy-Owl, and Northern Saw-whet Owl.

Just up the trail from the trailhead, there is a large open meadow to the east. This area is often where the Great Horned Owls can be seen after dark as they scan the open meadow for potential prey. The trail follows south, and a bit farther up, it turns to the west and moves slightly upslope, into ponderosa pines and junipers. At this point, you can see the creek on the south side that flows from west to east. Also, at this corner you will find large ponderosa pines on the north side, river birch and alder along the creek itself, and to the south, you will find spruce, ponderosa, juniper, and aspen. I was hiking along the trail, heading west for several hundred yards, until it began to get dark. At that time, I started making my way back to the car. As I was hiking, a Great Horned Owl began vocalizing a few yards ahead of me, near the corner where the meadow opens. I walked toward the owl and saw it perched atop a live ponderosa pine. It flew from the top of one tree and then another, as it continued to give its distinctive "who-who-who-oooo." Due to the tonality of the call, I identified the bird I was hearing was an adult male owl.

About five minutes after the Great Horned Owl began calling, a tiny Northern Saw-whet Owl began giving its distinctive "toot, toot, toot, toot, toot, toot, toot, toot" south across the creek in a dense stand of spruce and aspen. A short while afterwards, a Long-eared Owl began giving its single hollow "hoot"… "hoot"… "hoot," upslope several yards. For several minutes, I heard all three species calling simultaneously. I listened for a while, but did not see or hear any interaction between the species. I returned the following evening with a friend who was hoping to see a Long-eared Owl in the park, but the only owl

A Great Horned Owl nest near Longmont, Colorado.

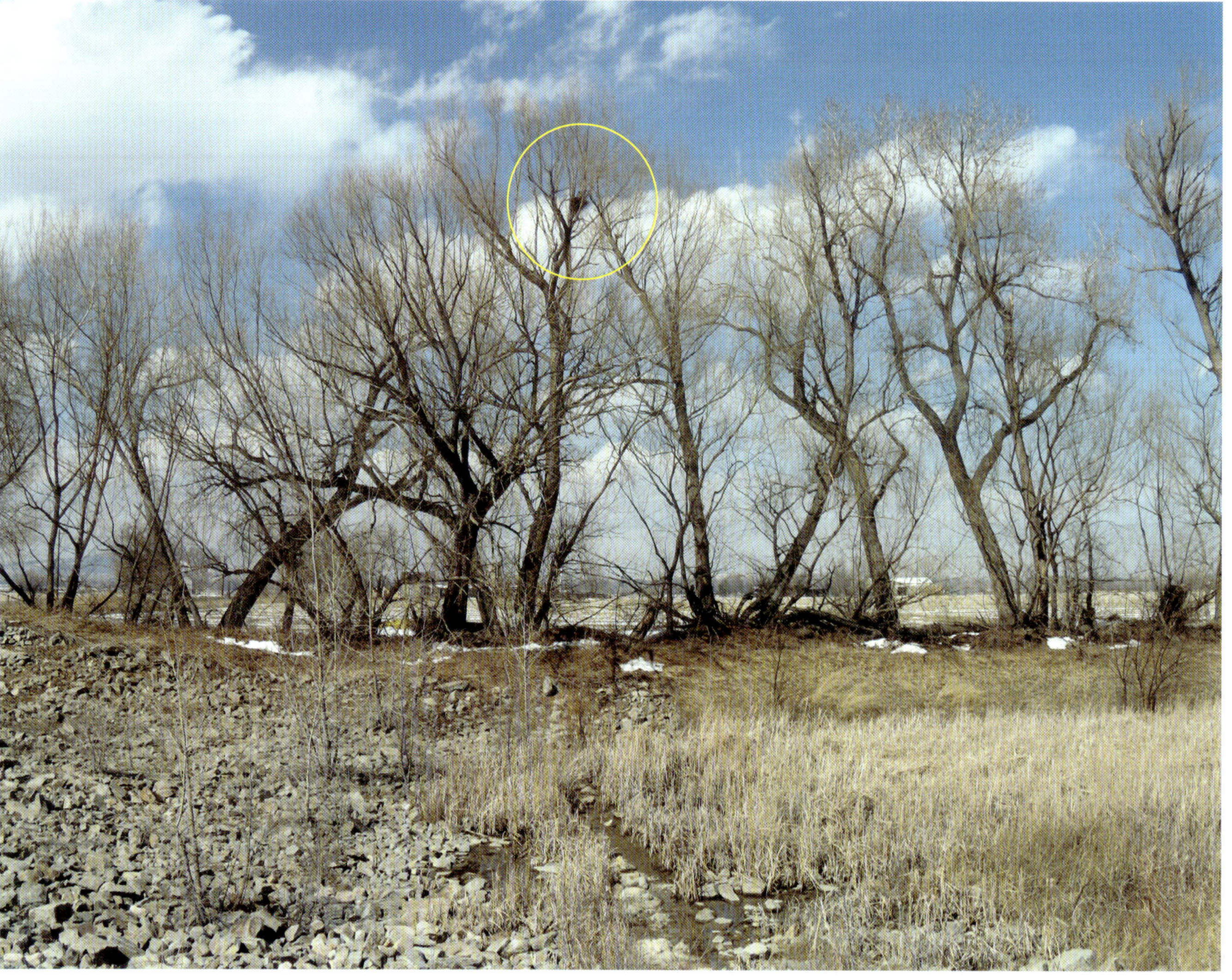

vocalizing was the diminutive Northern Saw-whet Owl. In February and March, as the Great Horned Owls are vocalizing in thc mountains, it is common to hear Boreal Owls, Northern Saw-whet Owls, Long-eared Owls, and Northern Pygmy-Owls vocalizing simultaneously. The smaller owls are well-concealed and often in dense vegetation when near the larger owls.

It's always amazing to me how hard it is to find one of these large owls roosting during the day. Concealment and/or roosting areas can be anything from a cliff ledge, large snag, a dense conifer or thick bush, or even man-made structures, such as barns, abandoned buildings, and overpasses (Houston et al 1998). During the nesting season, the male finds a favorite roost site, under which can be found regurgitated pellets and whitewash or feces, while the female is on or near the nest.

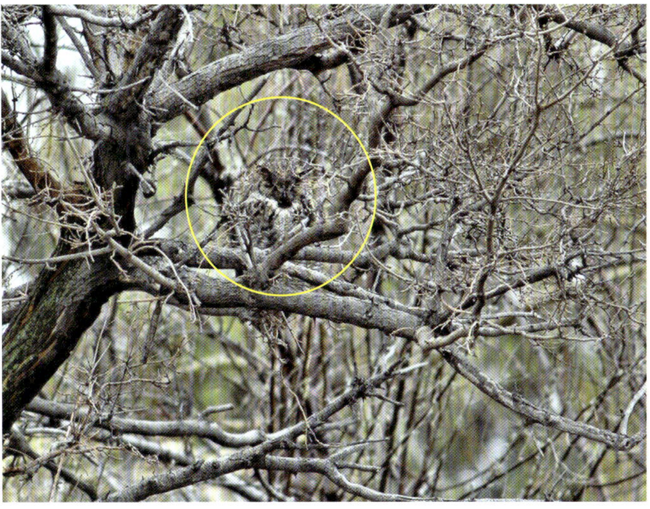

This photo shows how well one of these large owls can remain concealed.

An adult male Great Horned Owl in Estes Park: Note how well the bird's plumage matches the bark of the ponderosa pine.

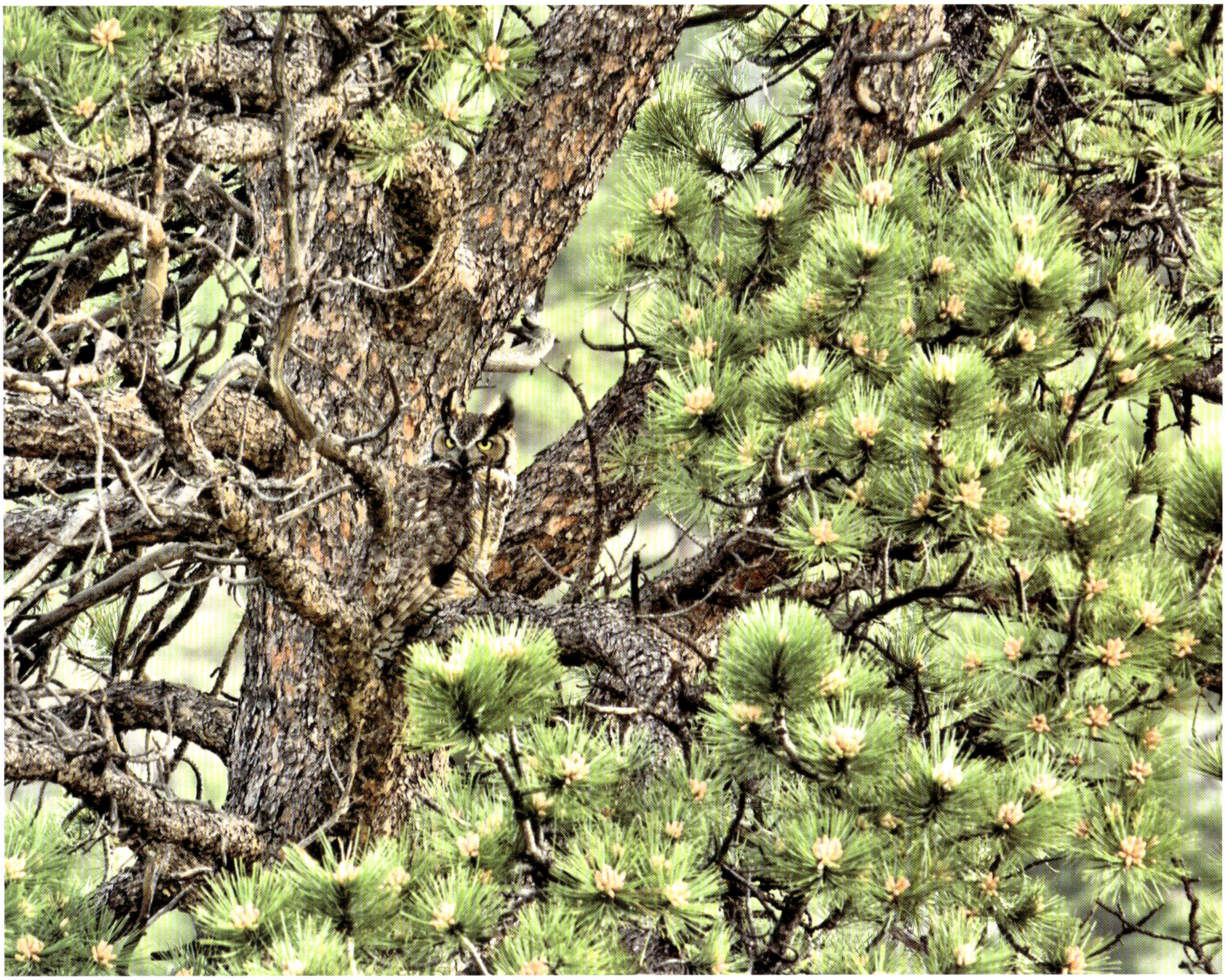

The forests from New England through central Michigan, central Wisconsin, and central Minnesota north are a mixture of conifers and hardwoods. Within these stands of hardwoods, there are often a few pines, spruce, and/or hemlocks interspersed. In northeastern Massachusetts, Austing and Holt (1966) found several Great Horned Owls roosting in specific trees within their territories. One roost site was in a small group of white pines in a red maple swamp, set apart from an extensive hillside stand of pines. Another roost was the largest white pine within a white pine grove and yet another was a lone hemlock tree within a stand of white pines. All of these roosting sites had certain characteristics that distinguished them from the surrounding growth. There seems to be a strong propensity for individual Great Horned Owls to be attracted to a roost tree that is set apart either by location, type, or size.

On January 1st of each year, a group of us participate in a Christmas bird count in Loveland, Colorado. The section that my group counts is on the west side of town, on a private dude ranch. This area of the property is comprised primarily of cottonwoods and various shrubs. However, it has one large spruce near the horse barn, which can be a good place for Great Horned Owls to day-roost. In fact, most years we find a roosting Great Horned Owl in that spruce. The jays and crows often alert us to the roosting owl.

Classic Great Horned Owl habitat in Wisconsin. *Photo © Chris Cold.*

The spruce tree is the roost site of a pair of Great Horned Owls that inhabit that territory.

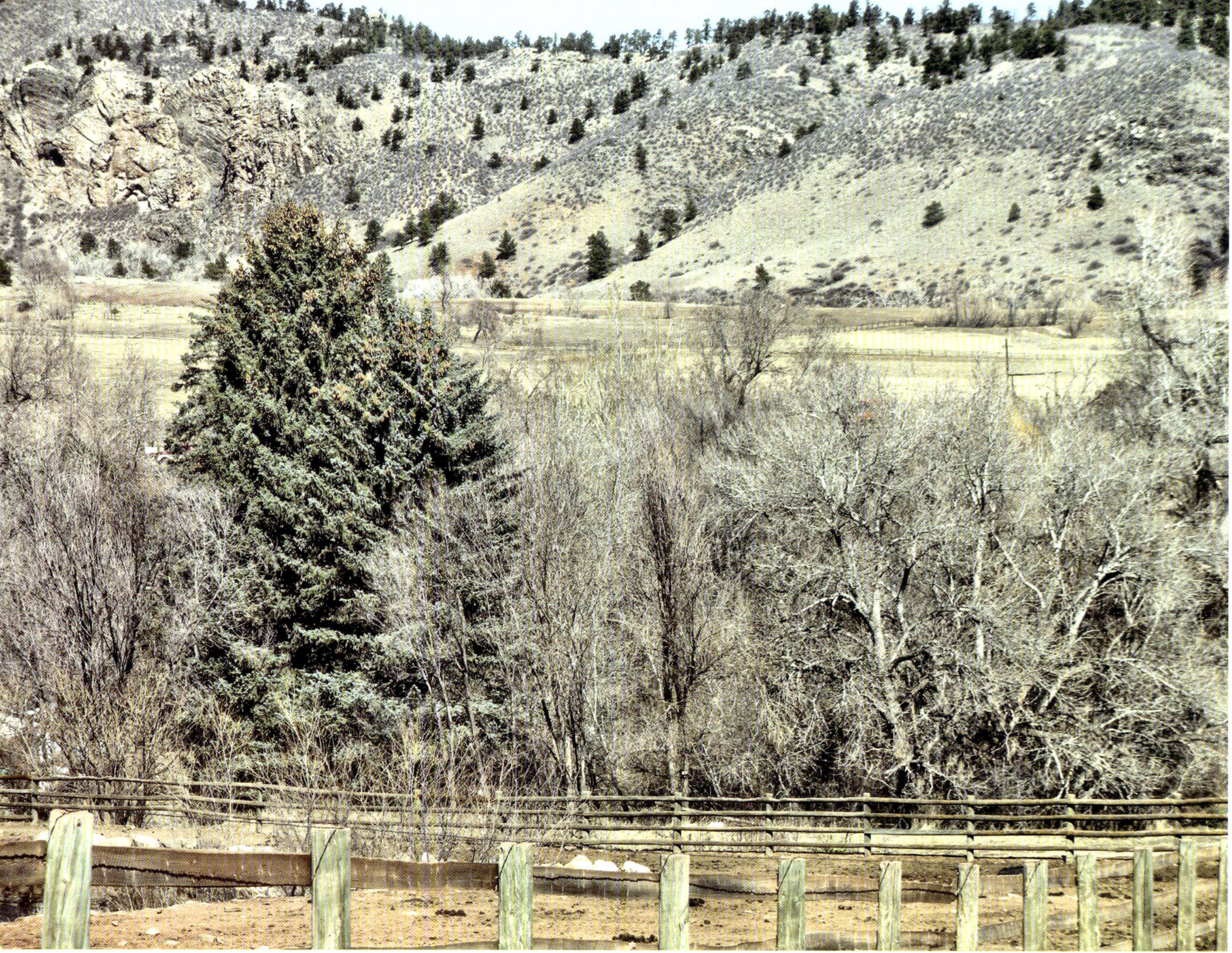

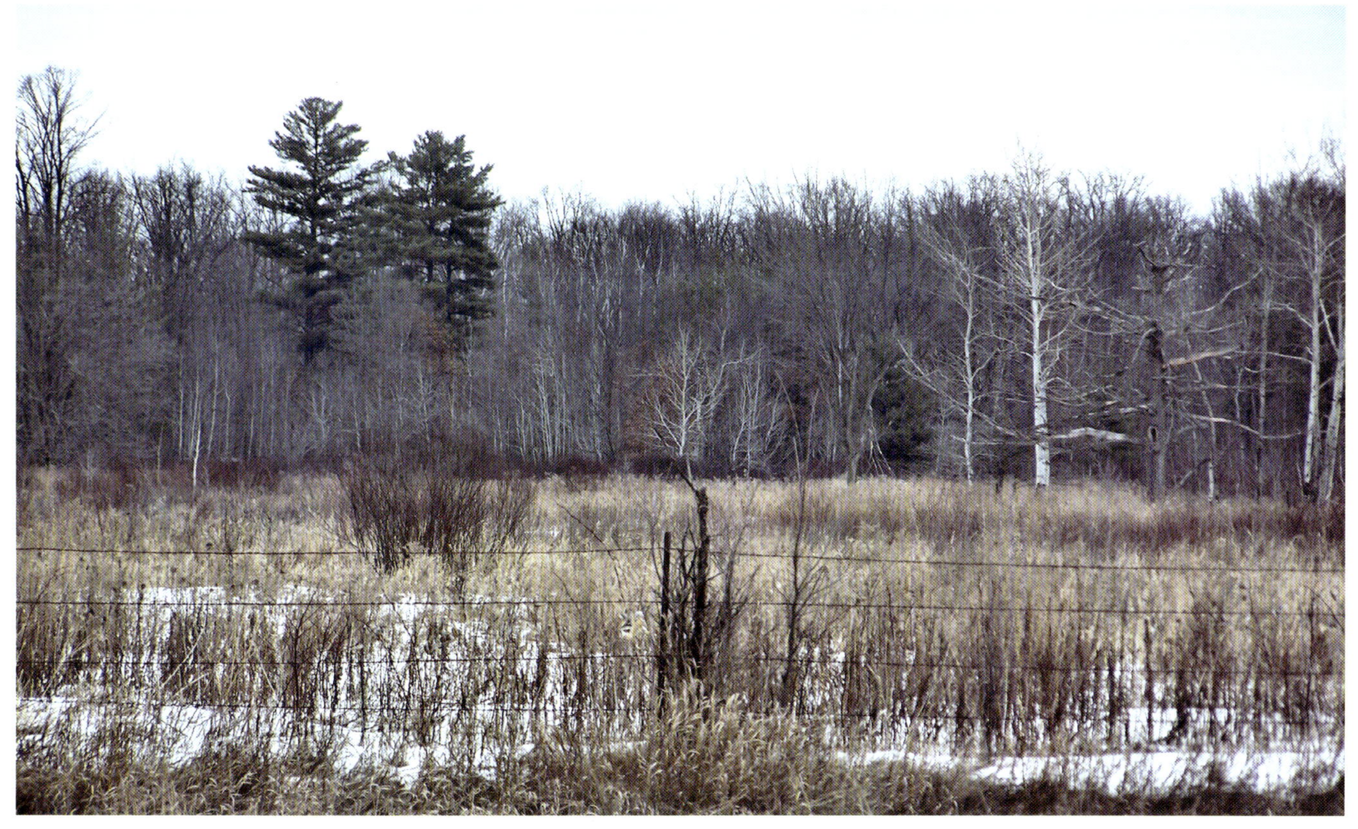

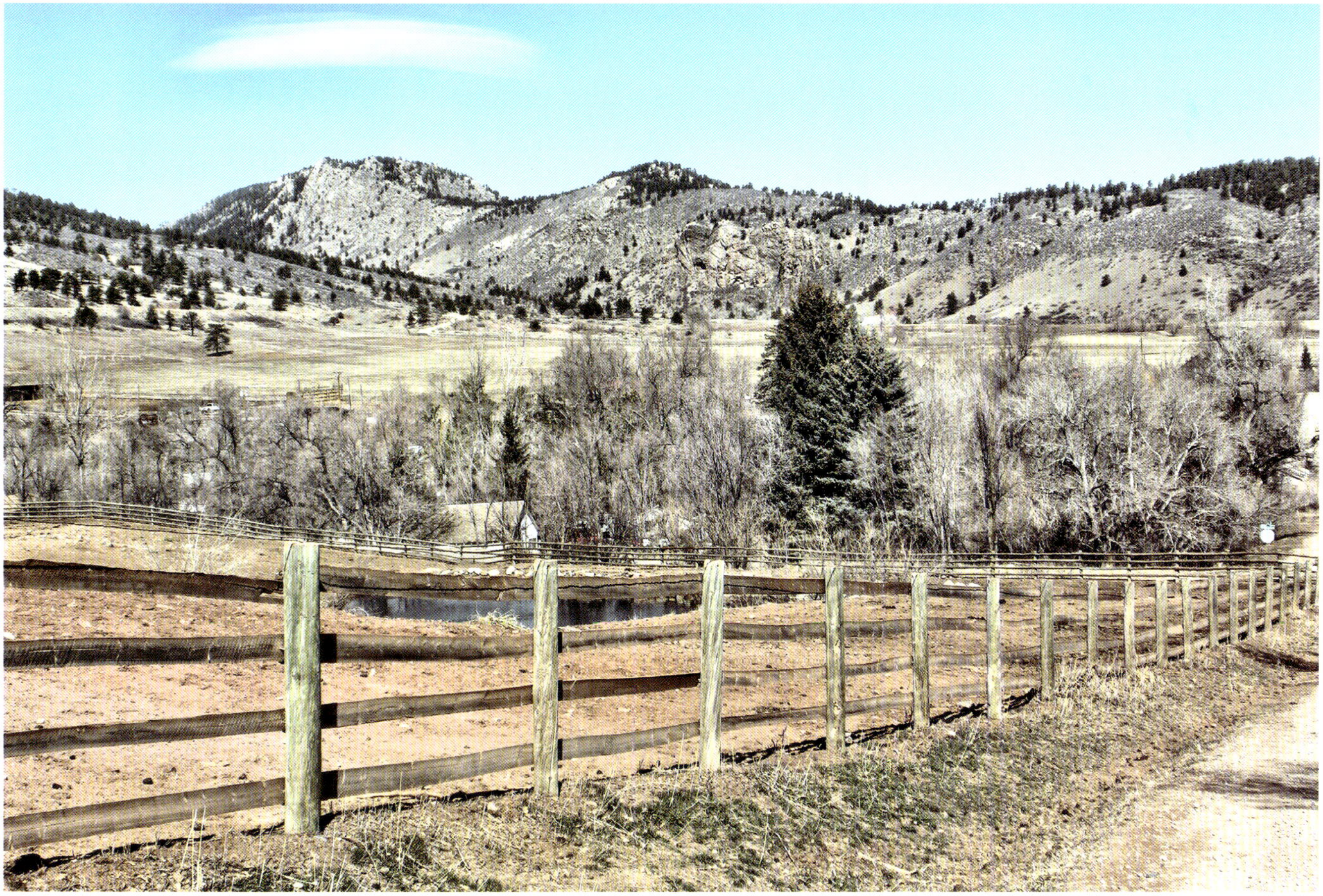

Habitat of Great Horned Owls in the foothills west of Loveland, Colorado.

Chapter 3

VOCALIZATION

Of the nineteen species of owls nesting throughout North America, only six actually "hoot." These six include the Great Horned Owl, Long-eared Owl, Great Gray Owl, Barred and Spotted Owls, and the tiny Flammulated Owl. The hooting of the Great Horned Owl carries over a mile on a windless evening and, in most of North America, it is the most commonly heard owl call. The Great Horned Owl's distinctive hooting is often heard from late summer through early spring as both the young owls practice their calls and the adults rekindle their relationships with their partners.

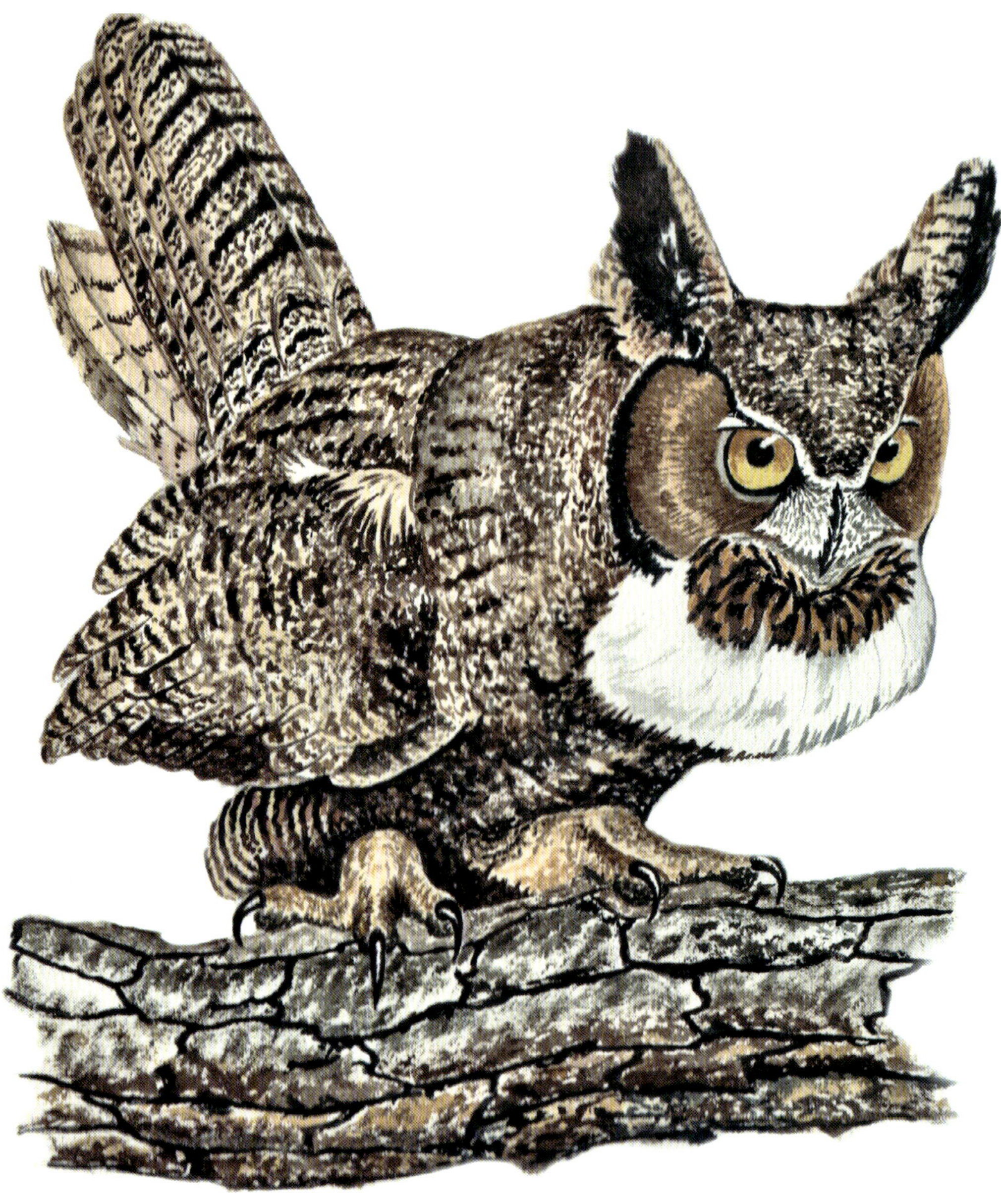

Typical Great Horned Owl vocalizing posture.
Painted from a photograph taken by Paul Bannick.

Within the range of the Great Horned Owl, the most commonly heard call of the adult birds is a series of hoots, often in a series, similar to "Who-Whoo-Who-Whooooo" or "Who-Whooo-Who." Having a pair of these owls near my house year-round, I've heard several variations of these calls. I have also heard "Who-Whoo-Who-oo-Whoo-oo."

On September 4, 2011, at about 5:30 a.m., I heard a Great Horned Owl vocalizing with a "Whooo-Whooo-Who-Who-Whooo"; on September 6, 2011, "Who-Who-Who-Whooooo-Who"; and on September 28, 2011, "Whooo-Whoo-Who." On the morning of September 20, 2013, I heard a female owl give a "Who-Who-Who...Who-Who" call. On the morning of October 9, 2013, an owl outside of my home was making a three-note hoot "Who... Who-Who... Who...Who-Who," etc. I presumed this bird was a young owl from the past spring who was learning his call.

Throughout much of the range of the Great Horned Owl, the Barred Owl can be heard as well. However, the call of the two species differs in tonal quality, pitch, and cadence. The call of the Barred Owl is the familiar "whoo-whoo-to-whoooow-hoow-hoo-to-whoooooo," often described as "who cooks for you, who cooks for y'alllll." This call is in a higher key with less bass than the Great Horned Owl. The call of the Great Horned Owl is then conversely in a lower key, deeper bass, and a softer tone than the Barred Owl (Austing and Holt 1966).

In parts of the American West, the hooting of the Spotted Owl can be heard and at times may be confused with the Great Horned Owl as well. As with the Barred Owl, the tonal quality of the Spotted Owl is in a higher key and has less bass, with the rhythm being "hoo-hoo------hooooooo." Frank Stephens (1892, in Bent 1938) writes: "The ordinary notes heard were a succession of three syllables, alike in tone and volume, the first followed quickly by the second and then a pause of considerable length before the third."

The call of the Long-eared Owl, also a hoot, differs from the Great Horned Owl by being a single hollow hoot often described as air-blowing over a bottle. Grinnell and Storer (1924) in Bent (1938) say that "the hoot of the adult bird is a low mellow, and long-drawn-out, and bears a resemblance to the note of the Band-tailed Pigeon."

The call of the Great Gray Owl is a deep, booming "Who-oo-oo-oo" (Bent 1938). It is often considered to be a very soft, low-pitched hooting series of "whooo-ooo-ooo-ooo," with the notes given slowly over a six- to eight-second period. Calls are repeated every fifteen to thirty seconds. Under good conditions, I have heard this territorial call carry up to a half-mile away.

The smallest of the "hooting" owls, the Flammulated Owl, utters a series of very quiet hoots that seldom carry more than a few yards. The male utters a two-note, low-pitched hoot; more often than not, you will only hear the second of the two notes when you are almost on top of the tiny owl. The female Flammulated Owl, on the other hand, gives a high-pitched, single note hoot.

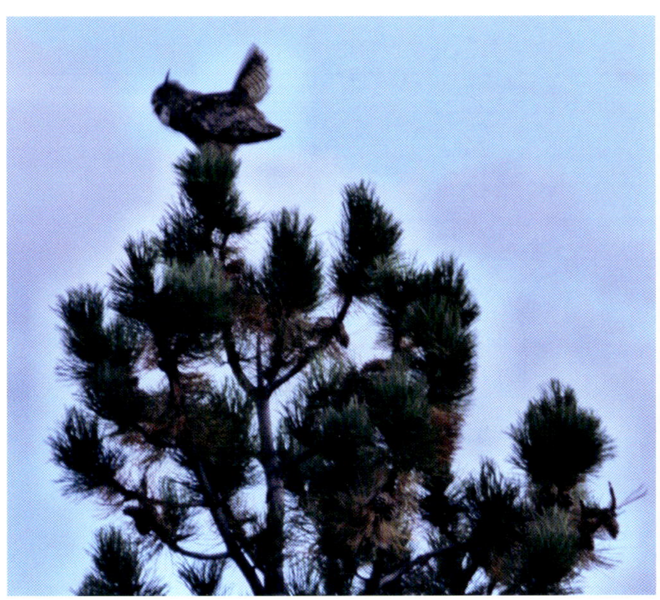

Typical Great Horned Owl vocalizing posture.

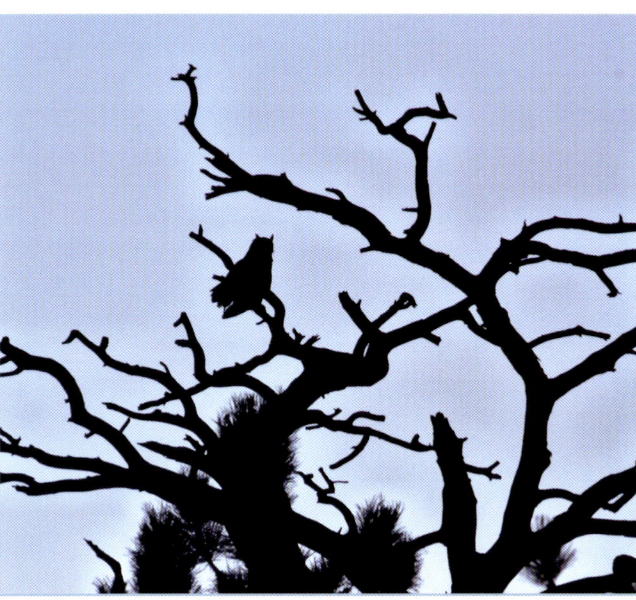

A silhouetted Great Horned Owl showing its ear tufts.

Hooting of the male owl has a three-fold effect (Baumgartner 1938):

1. It's an expression of physical vigor and vitality.

2. It's a challenge to other males, letting them know that a particular territory is taken and they should stay away.

3. It's used to attract a mate—and this is often its most important function. On March 5, 1935, Baumgartner (1938) heard a "Quack, quack, Waugh! Hoo-oo! quack, quack, quack, quack" given by a male of a pair of Great Horned Owls after the male had arrived at the nest to take over the incubation duties.

On February 1, 2010, I heard a male hooting from my front yard. That evening it was snowing lightly and the temperature was -12° Fahrenheit (10.4°C), showing that the cold temperature doesn't seem to hinder the owls from vocalizing.

COURTSHIP/MATING

Due to the nocturnal courtship activities, eyewitness accounts of the activity are few in numbers. One of the earlier accounts was described by Floyd Bralliar in 1922 (Bent 1938):

> So [sic] he [male owl] began bowing his head, riffling his feathers, raising his wings, and spreading his wings in a curious manner. ... Aside from watching his antics, she took no notice of his presence. Growing more earnest, he began hopping from branch to branch, continuing his maneuvers and snapping his bill fiercely, as if to show that even tho [sic] he was not large as she, what he lacked in size he made up in bravery.
>
> Finally, he attempted to approach and caress her, but she ruffled her feathers and rebuked him sharply. He took flight, sailing up and down, around and around, eventually doing all the stunts of the race, now and again punctuating his efforts by snapping his bill. After a few moments, he alighted again and began his bowing and dancing all over again.
>
> A rabbit came running down the bank and its white flag caught his eye. Rising in noiseless flight, sailed downward without the flap of a wing, caught his prey from the ground, glided back into the tree, and presented his offering to his lady love. Apparently, she was convinced of his sincerity. Together, they devoured the rabbit, and when he again began his love dance she joined in with as much enthusiasm as he.

A similar account was described by Austing and Holt (1966):

> The courtship display itself is a weird and ludicrous sight, with the male solemnly approaching his mate, bowing his head, ruffling his feathers, and performing other curious antics. Then moving into position beside her, he suddenly pitches his head forward, droops his wings, and at the same time thrusts his short tail skyward; from this peculiar stance he swells his white bib in frog-like fashion and gives a drawn out "whoo-whoo-whoo-hoo-whoooo-whoooo," after which he pops back into the upright position again. Now the female takes her turn, addressing the male in much the same manner and with a similar call, though noticeably higher in key and faster in rhythm; the two then continue to call and answer each other for varying lengths of time. Often throughout the ceremony they face one another and rub bills together, much as though kissing; usually the whole performance is emphatically punctuated by a staccato snapping of their bills, similar to the sound of a typewriter, injected at moments between the calling and caressing. These overtures to the nesting season are loud and elaborate, given with deeply expressive tones and gestures, as if the happy couple were announcing their intentions for the entire world to hear.

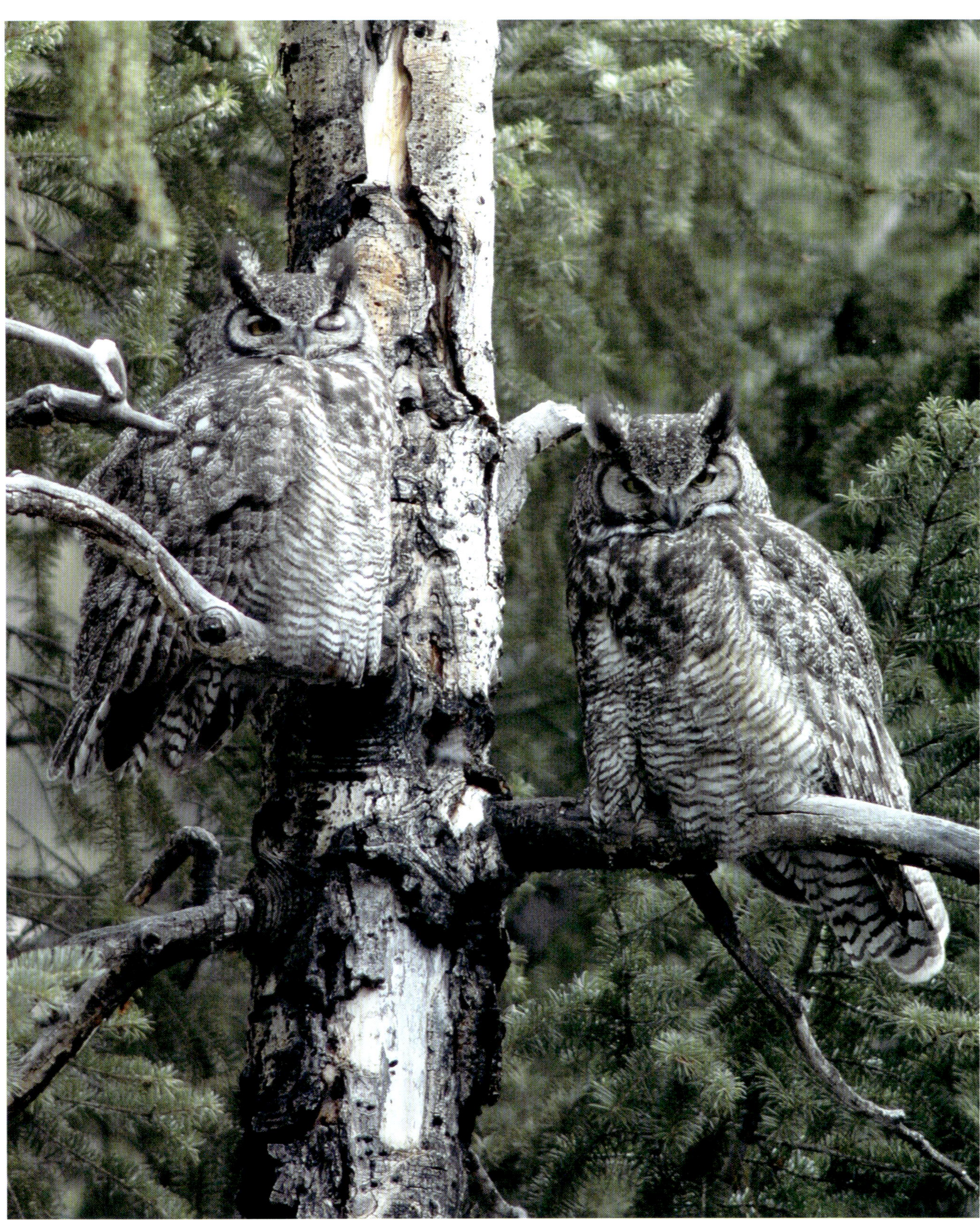

A Great Horned Owl pair inside Rocky Mountain National Park.
The larger female is on the right.

The length of courtship for Great Horned Owls is difficult to determine due to the males vocalizing most months of the year. According to Baumgartner (1938), male owls vigorously hoot for a month to six weeks, whereas the females only seem to vocalize for a week or two towards the end of the six-week period. In Kansas, this vocalizing period begins in late November and lasts until about the first of January.

The act of mating was witnessed by Mr. Fred Hastie of Lawrence, Kansas, in 1938. The nodding and bowing of the birds became quite violent for a period and then they quieted down and went through many repetitions of the billing and cooing performance. Finally, the female crouched down on the limb and the male mounted her back in the fashion of a barnyard fowl.

According to Craighead and Craighead (1969), there were a pair of Great Horned Owls in Wyoming that were observed until 1953 that had continuously occupied the same territory for eight years, where a second pair had occupied the same territory for seven years. Also, Rohner and Doyle (1992) found that four radio-tagged male owls regularly roosted within 90 feet (27.43m) of the incubating female, and after checking nineteen nests, they found that ten males roosted closer than that, with the average distance being 345 feet (105.15m).

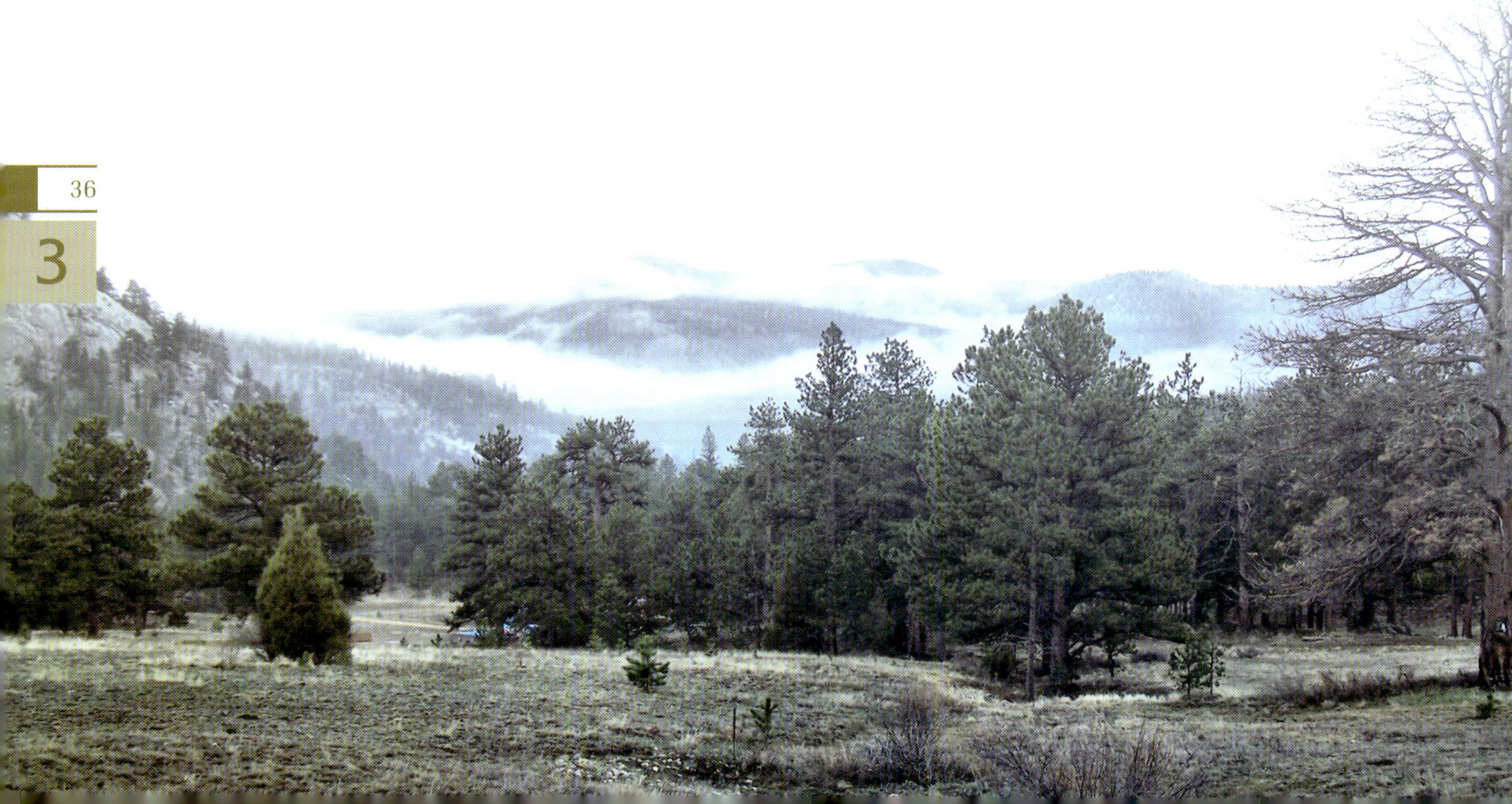

Chapter 4

NEST DESCRIPTION

I've been watching Great Horned Owls since 1981 in Wisconsin, Colorado, and Arizona and have never seen anything that would make me think that the species constructs its own nest. However, Cameron (1907) and Baumgartner (1938) both describe owls that apparently rebuilt their nests over several years. Also Mr. G. Lang of Indian Head, Saskatchewan, apparently found several nests that Great Horned Owls had constructed entirely. One pair built a nest in a spruce tree that Mr. Lang was positive the owls had constructed exclusively.

The Great Horned Owl nests that I've found are usually lined with a variety of materials, including shreds of bark, leaves, pine, spruce, or fir needles — all of which I believe were placed in the nest by the original contractor, not the Great Horned Owls. After the owls have been in the nest for a while, other debris is often identified, which includes down and molted feathers from the female owl, as well as prey remains. As the young hatch from the egg and subsequently grow, the nests have crushed pellets and prey remains, including fur, hair, feathers, and bones in them. When the birds' nest is on a cliff ledge, there is virtually nothing on the ledge prior to the first nesting, but if the nest is reused for years, there may be some debris from the previous season(s).

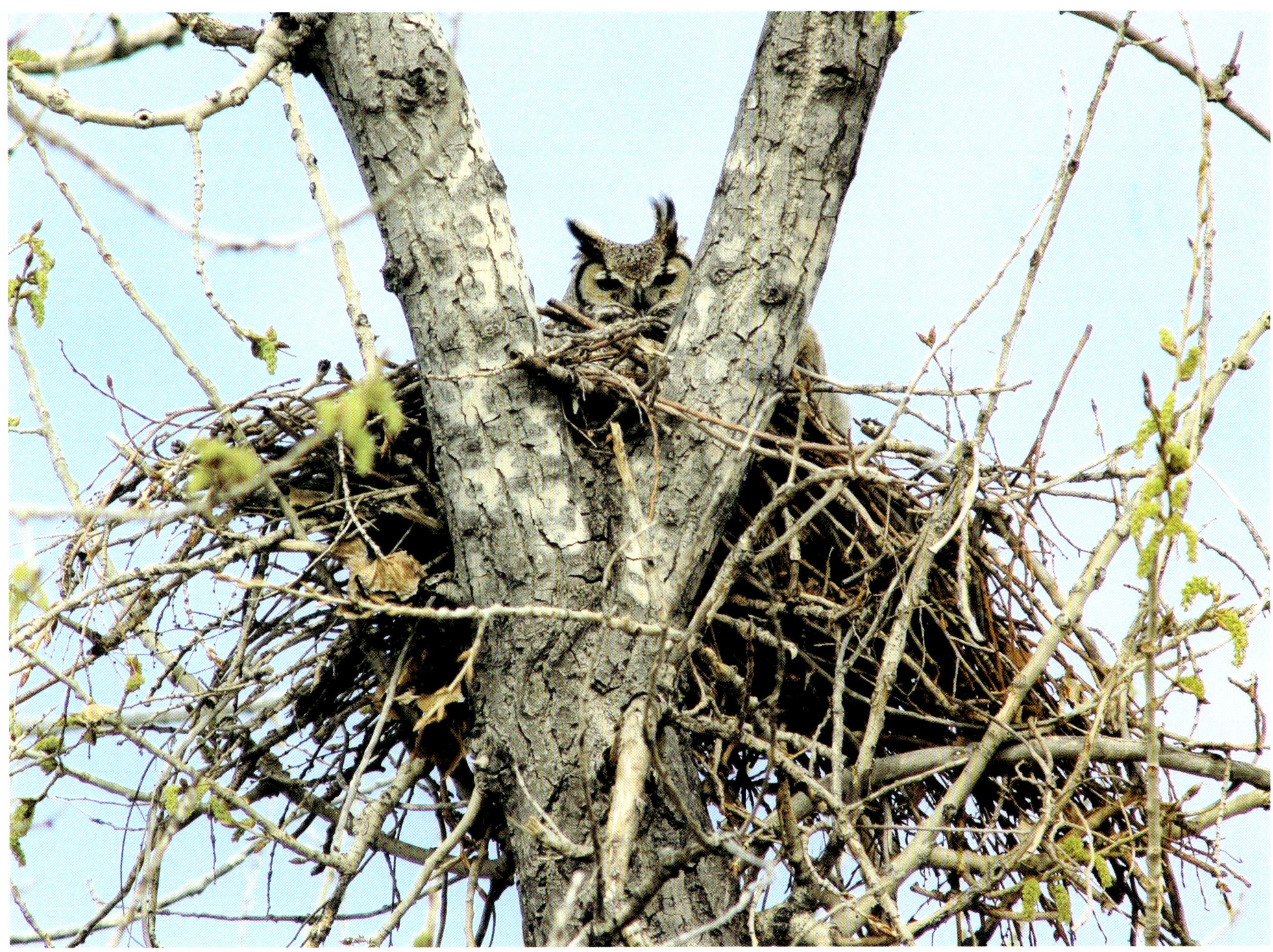

Close-up of a Great Horned Owl in an abandoned Red-tailed Hawk nest.

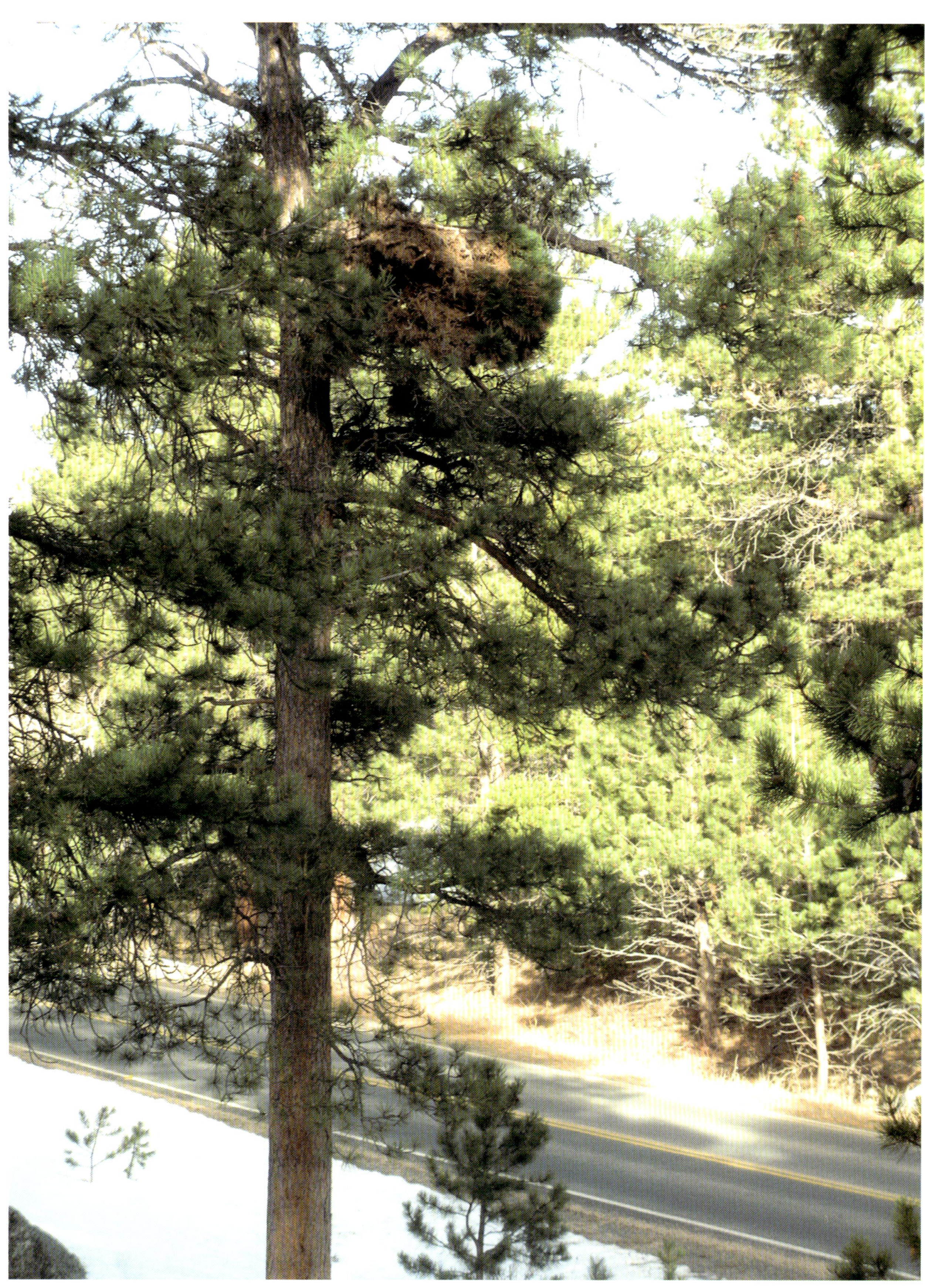

Broad and close-up views of a Great Horned Owl nest in a witches' broom inside Rocky Mountain National Park.

Throughout the Great Horned Owl's range, the species has been found nesting on the ground, as well as in a variety of structures. One structure that the owls seem to favor above all others appears to be the abandoned nests of Red-tailed Hawks (Rohner and Doyle 1992, Austing and Holt 1966, Bent 1938). I routinely find several Great Horned Owls raising their families in these nests.

Many ornithologists consider the Great Horned Owl and Red-tailed Hawk to be complementary species, one hunting during the day and the other hunting at night (Bent 1938). Minor et al. (1993) believes that in central New York, Great Horned Owls are able to use the nests of Red-tailed Hawks because the owls nest about a month earlier than the hawks. They also found that at times the hawks and owls nested approximately 61 feet (18.6m) apart during that same year. They also found Red-tailed Hawks nested successfully in nests that Great Horned Owls had been unsuccessful using that same year. In 2010, I found a Great Horned Owl that was incubating eggs in her nest. She was about 450 feet (137m) from the nest that a pair of Red-tailed Hawks were refurbishing. Unfortunately after three weeks, the owls were not seen again. The hawks did fledge two young.

Over the past twenty-five years, I have seen Great Horned Owls nesting in a number of different situations, including artificial nest structures, abandoned crow, raven, and magpie nests, abandoned heron nests, abandoned hawk nests, cliff nests, and "witches' brooms." Witches' brooms are fungus-induced clumps of dense foliage on the branches on a tree. Rohner and Doyle (1992) also found these owls nesting in witches' brooms. Their owls used "brooms" in white spruce trees at Kluane Lake in the southwestern Yukon. In and around RMNP, Great Horned Owls often use witches' brooms in ponderosa pine trees as a platform for nesting as well.

One such nest is on the south side of the Fall River Road, just inside the park's entrance. This well-known witches' broom has been used by Great Horned Owls on and off for many years. This nest is within a few feet of the road and is easily visible by passers-by. This particular

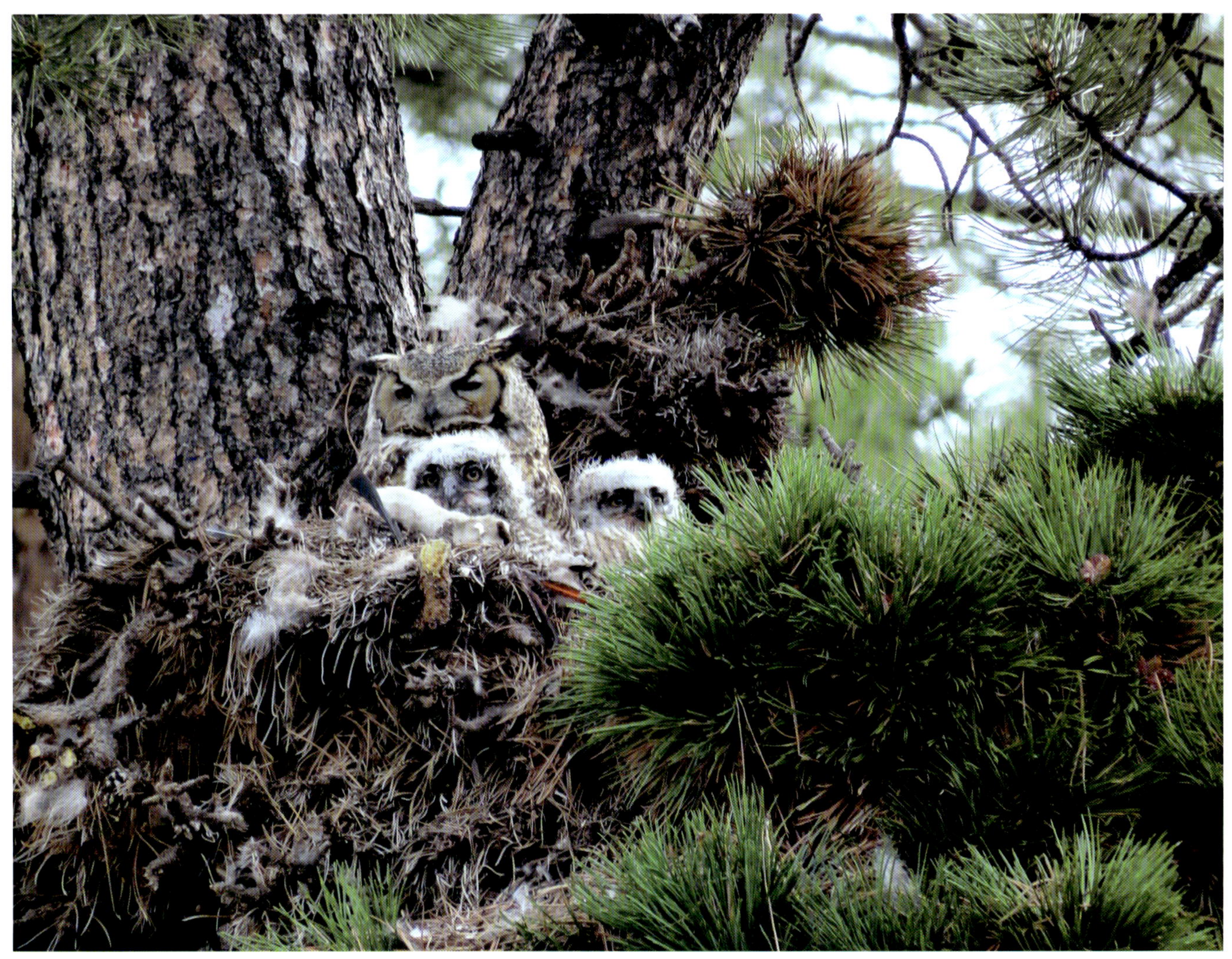

Man-made structures like the dentist sign make good places for Great Horned Owls to nest. *Photo © Terri Stewart.*

A close-up of the owls nesting behind the dentist sign. *Photo © Terri Stewart.*

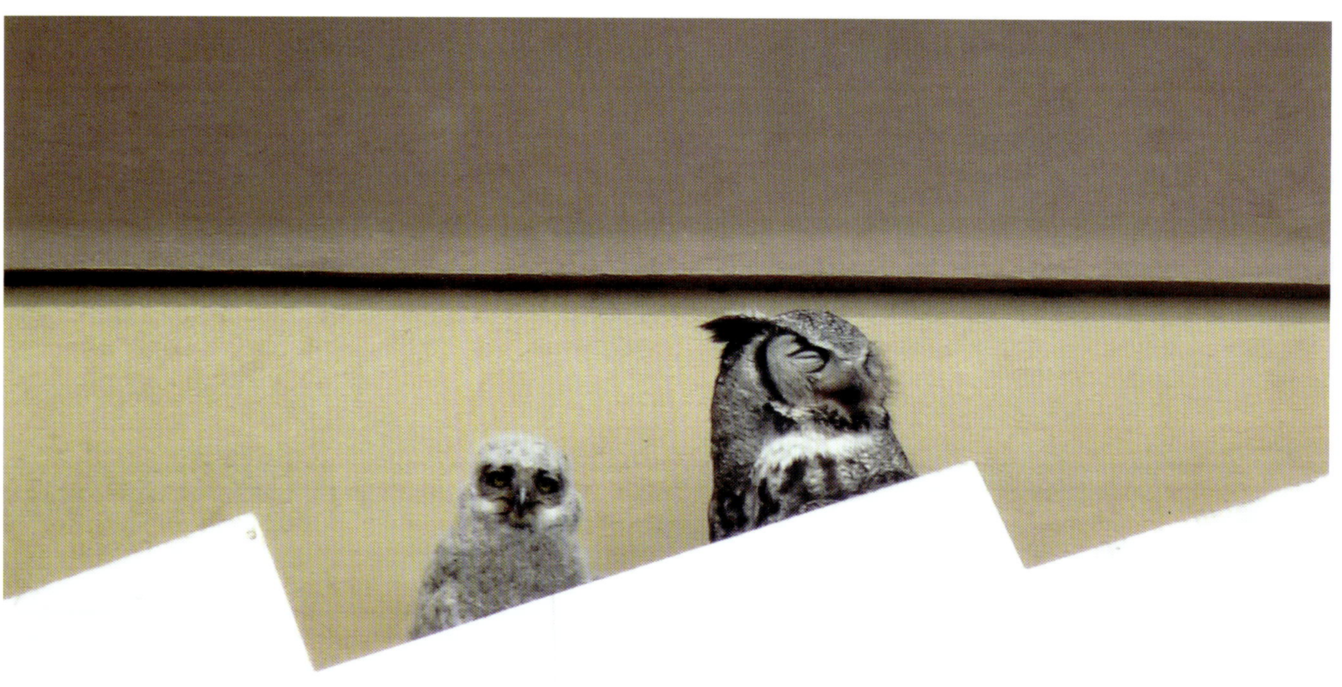

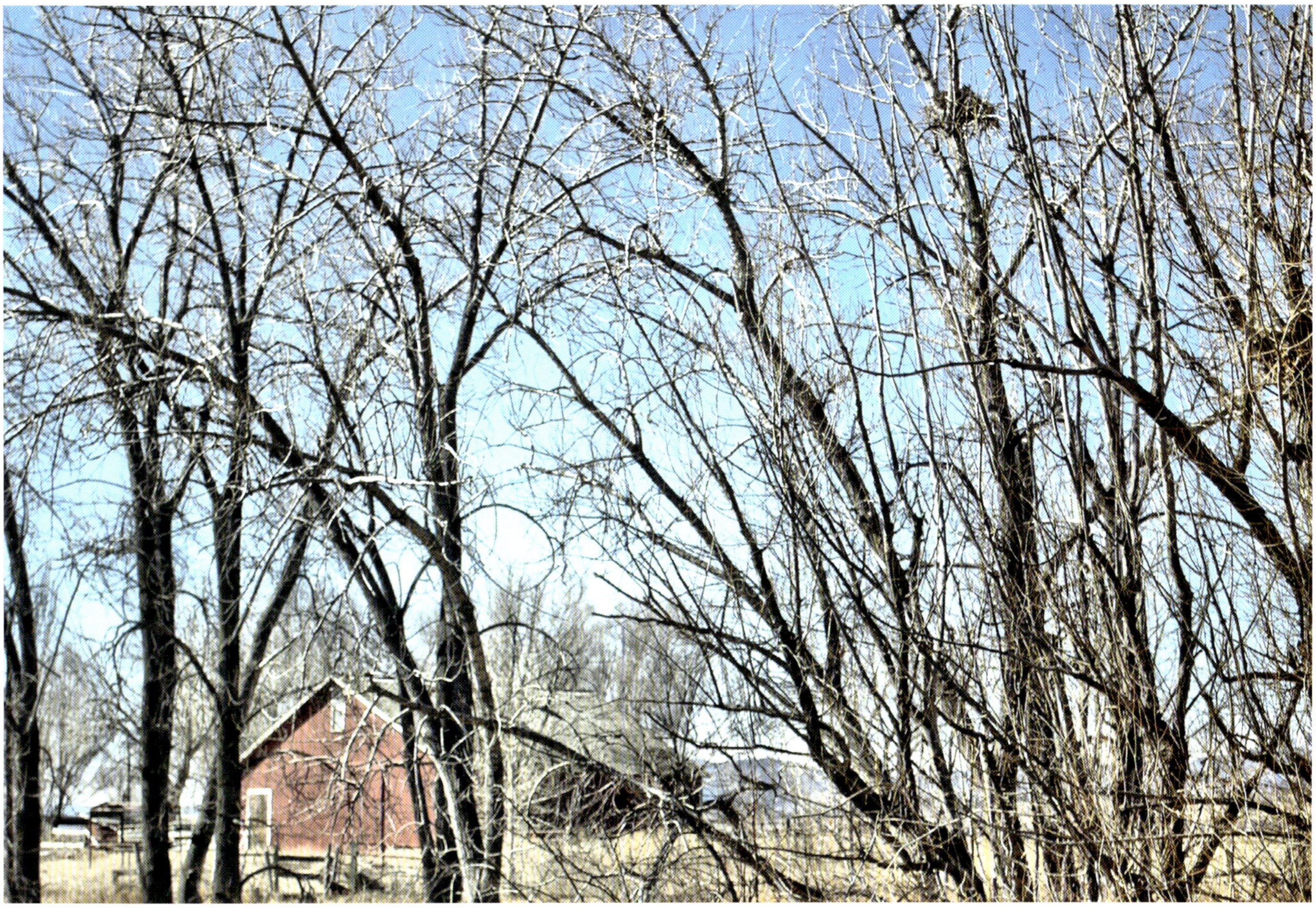

Great Horned Owl nest site in Loveland, Colorado.

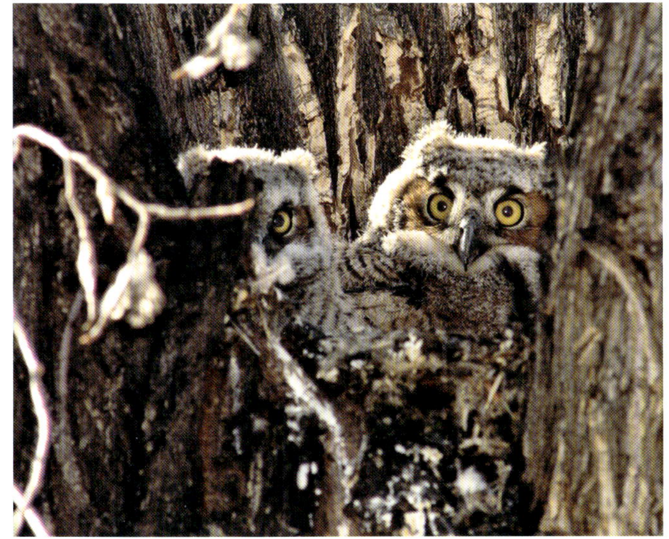

Two owlets sitting comfortably in their nest in the crotch of a tree in a cemetery in Fort Collins (northern Colorado).

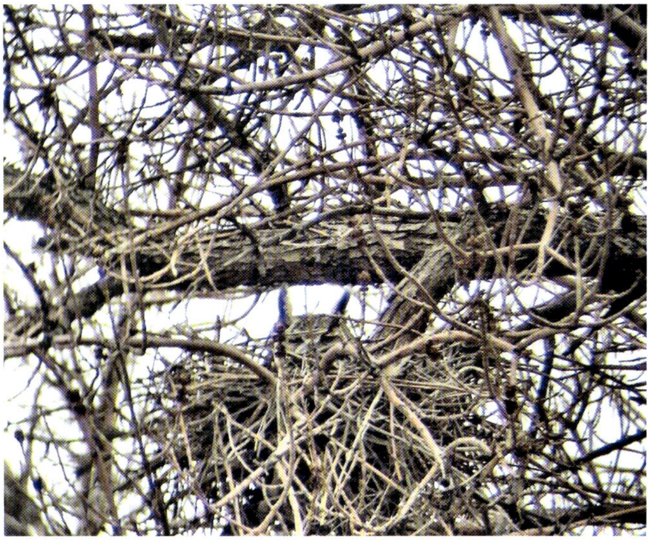

A Great Horned Owl nesting in an abandoned Black-billed Magpie nest near Longmont, Colorado.

witches' broom is not used every year due to the accessibility of the nest to the public. When the owls use this nest, they are inundated with onlookers and photographers. This obviously bothers the female each year and is the reason that she only uses the nest occasionally. The stress of all the onlookers seems to be too much for her to handle. These witches' brooms are common in the mountains, and the owls seem to prefer them when available.

Apart from Red-tailed Hawk nests, Great Horned Owls have been documented in a variety of hawk nests, including Northern Goshawks, Cooper's Hawks, Swainson's Hawks, and Red-shouldered Hawks. Bent (1938) and Wiley (1975) found Great Horned Owls nesting in the old nests of a Red-shouldered Hawk and a squirrel. A pair of Red-shouldered Hawks had built a nest in an old beech in southeastern Massachusetts: "In April 1909, we were surprised to find that a pair of Great Horned Owls had invaded this territory and taken possession of this nest; this was the first and only time that I have known this owl to usurp a nest of this hawk." In 1973, in Orange County, California, Wiley (1975) located an active Great Horned Owl nest in the same tree with an active Red-shouldered Hawk nest. Both nests were in a 62-foot (19m) California sycamore. The hawk nest was 58 feet (17.8m) from the ground while the owl's nest was only 39 feet (12m) from the ground. Both owls and hawks fledged young from those nests. The squirrel nest that the owls were found nesting in was 52 feet (15.8m) from the ground in the top of a white pine. It measured only 18 x 16 inches (45.72 x 40.64cm) and was only 8 inches (20.32cm) deep (Bent 1938). Franks and Warnock (1969) also found a pair of owls nesting in a fox squirrel nest 38 feet (11.59m) from the ground in a European larch. Wiley (1975) also found a pair of Great Horned Owls nesting in an abandoned Cooper's Hawk nest that was 22 feet (6.7m) up in a live oak. Reynolds et al. (1994) and Erdman (per. com) have documented Great Horned Owls nesting in abandoned Northern Goshawk nests as well.

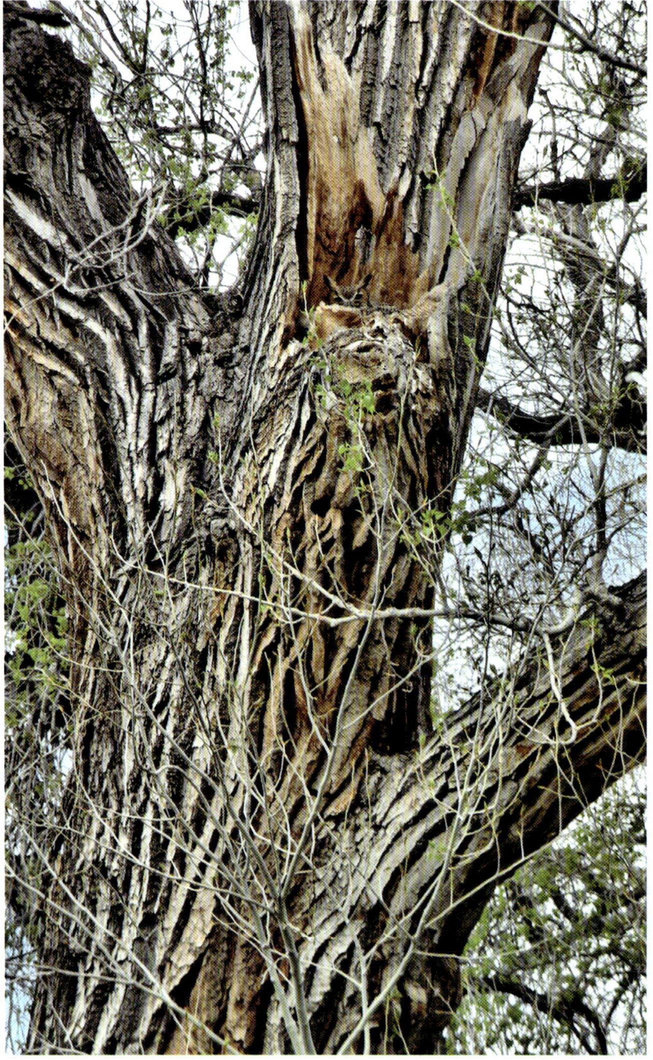

For years a pair of Great Horned Owls nested in a broken off stump of this tree.

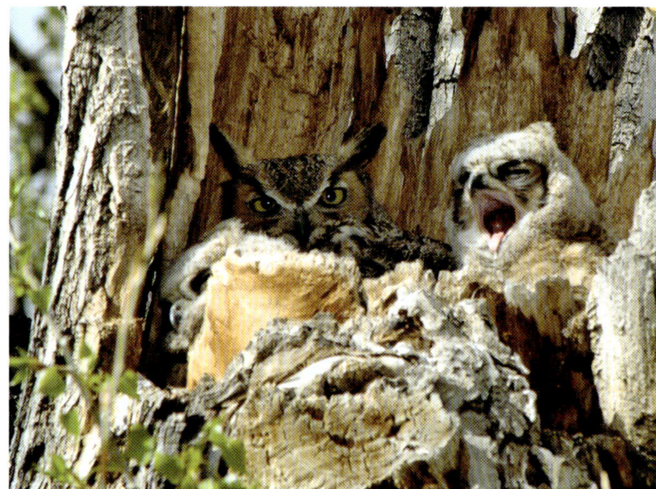

Female Great Horned Owl in the nest with her two young. One is a bit tired.

A Great Horned Owl at its nest in a broken snag. *Photo © Wayne Johnston.*

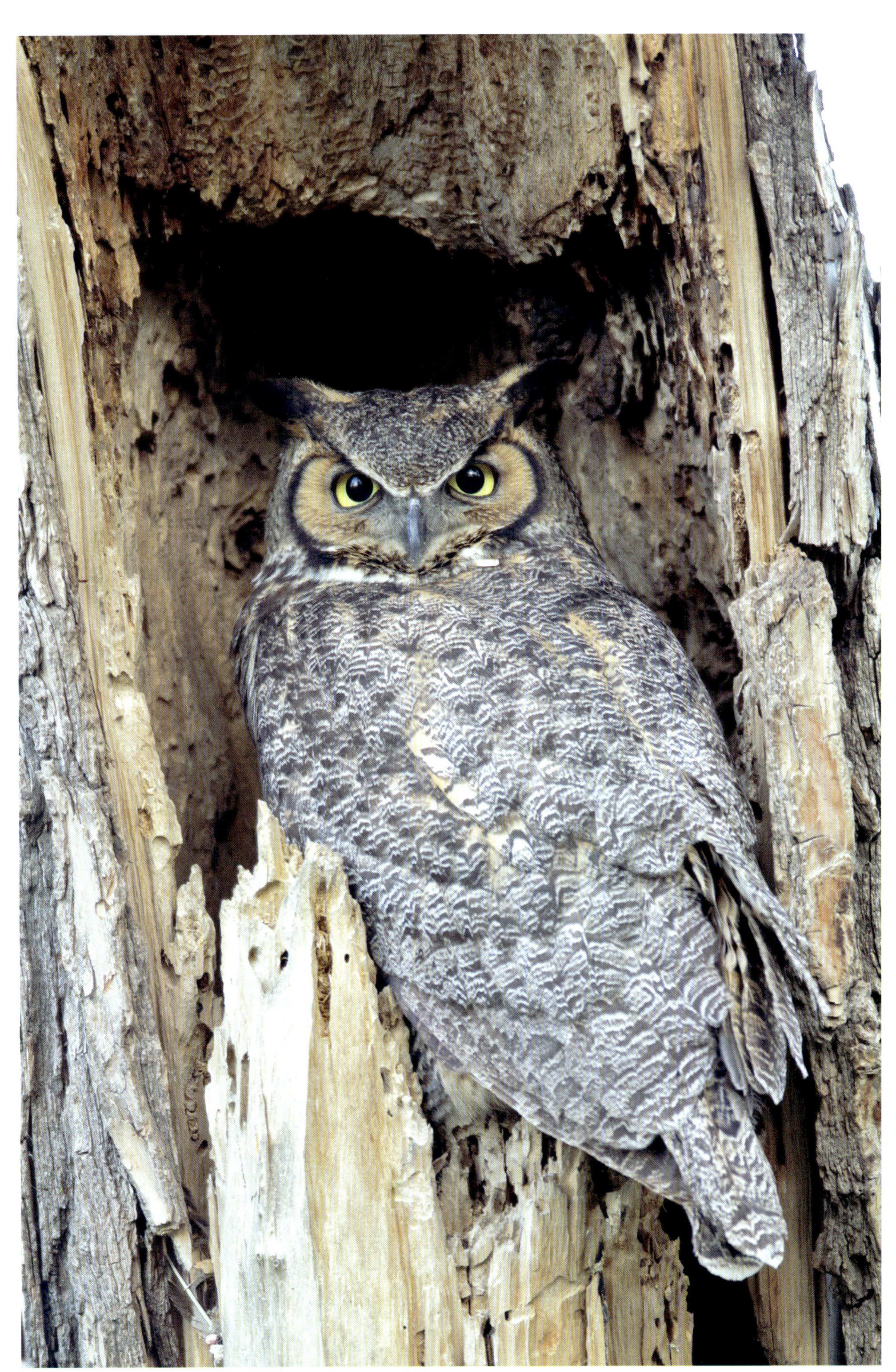

On May 27, 1998, I was assisting Dr. Ron Ryder, professor emeritus from Colorado State University in Fort Collins, checking raptor nests on the Meadow Springs Ranch north of Fort Collins, Colorado, and found a pair of Great Horned Owls nesting in an unused Ferruginous Hawk nest. This nest was a few hundred yards from an active Ferruginous Hawk nest.

In 1986, during ornithology class in college, we went to a Great Blue Heron rookery at the Mead Wildlife Refuge in central Wisconsin and observed a Great Horned Owl nesting in the center of the heronry. According to the wildlife manager, most evenings he could hear the herons making a short-lived ruckus. I remember him saying that he assumed the commotion was most likely due to the owl taking a heron for dinner.

Burkholder and Smith (1988) found Great Horned Owls nesting in a heronry at Knox Lake, Knox County, Ohio, from 1981 to 1984. The owls nested in Great Blue Heron nests each year. All of the nests that the owls had used were in the interior of the heronry, with the minimum distance between an active heron nest and the owl's nest about 6-1/2 feet (2m). As a side note, they also found Long-eared Owls nesting within a heronry along Utah Lake in 1969 and 1982.

On the afternoon of March 1, 2012, while driving back from Longmont, Colorado, I checked a Great Blue Heron Rookery just outside of Hygene, Colorado. This rookery is on the north edge of a large pond. The large trees around the ponds are mostly cottonwoods. Along the north edge of the pond the large cottonwoods house about a dozen nests and to the west of the pond are several large, open fields that are perfect hunting grounds for the owls. That afternoon there were four Great Blue Herons perched on four different nests. Just a few feet east of one the herons there was a lump on the top of one of the nests. I peered through my binoculars to find a Great Horned Owl, most likely keeping some very young owls warm.

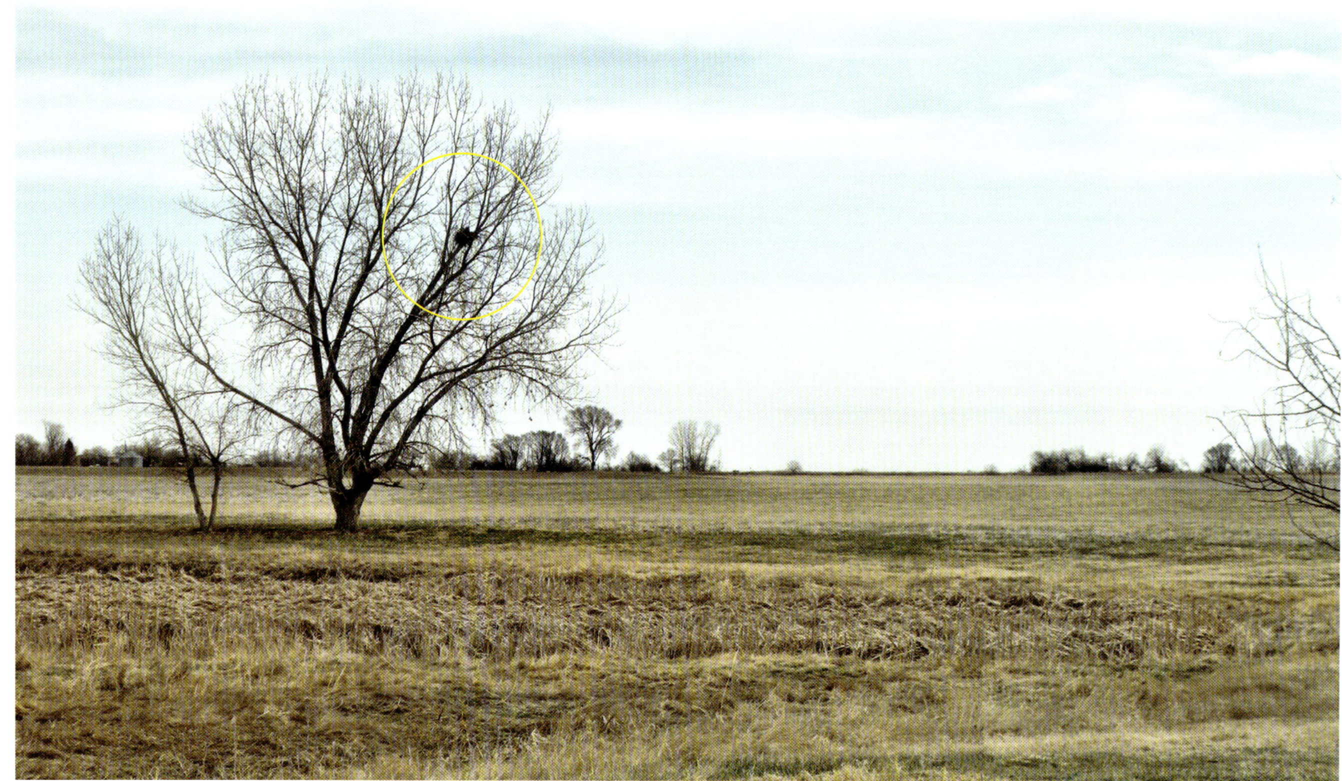

A Great Horned Owl in an old Red-tailed Hawk nest on the eastern plains of Colorado.

At the Birds of Prey Foundation in Broomfield, Colorado, a pair of wild Great Horned Owls had nested in a variety of both natural and artificial nest sites for years. In April 1999, they nested in a broken off limb of a cottonwood tree. Several miles north, in Fort Collins, another pair of owls nested in a broken limb of a cottonwood tree as well. These owls (or at least a pair of owls) have nested in that particular nest for several years; it is just about 450 feet (137m) south of a community college. There are several parking lots within view of the nest, as well as a sidewalk that is just a few feet from the nest tree, and just below the nest is a creek that has running water during most years. This nest is high enough that even though people watch the nest every year, the female still nests there year after year.

Another pair of Great Horned Owls nested in a cemetery in north Fort Collins and for years the female laid her eggs in the triple fork of a maple tree. This nest tree is in the center of the cemetery at a fork in the road. As with most cemeteries, there is a variety of tree and vegetation types around the nest tree. Those owls have added absolutely no nesting material to that nest. To illustrate this even further, after the nest was discovered some years ago, a biology professor, hoping to make the nest even more appealing to the owls, placed some sticks in the crotch of that tree, trying to assist the owl in nest construction. Interestingly enough, the owls abandoned that nest site for several years until all of the sticks had fallen away; after the sticks had fallen away, they returned to that nest site (David Leatherman per.com).

Judge John N. Clark of Saybrook, Connecticut, writes in Bent (1939) that he located "a pair of these owls nesting in a quadruple fork of a chestnut tree some 25 feet (7.62m) from the ground, the eggs lying on bare wood, without any loose material around them whatever, not even a single leaf."

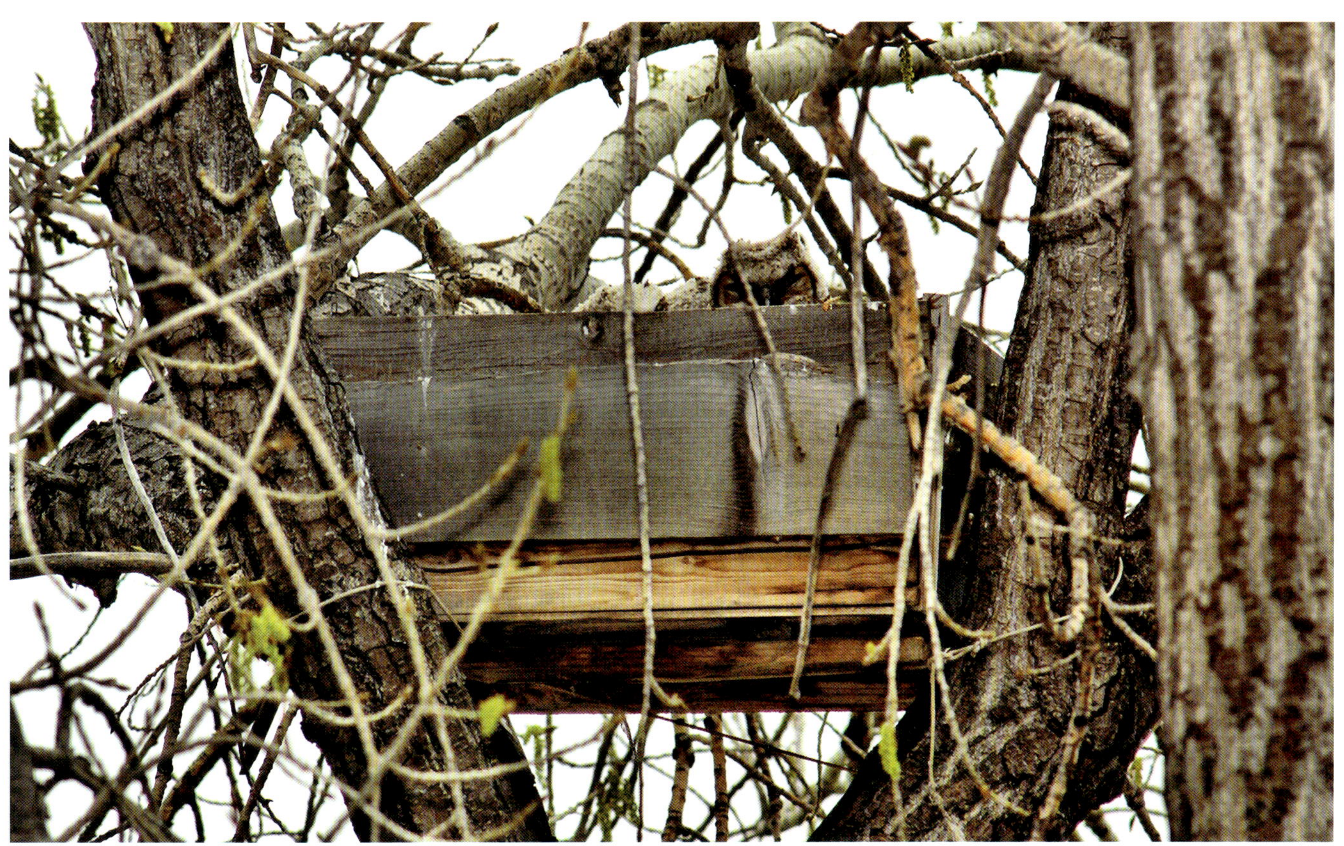

Great Horned Owls will readily nest in artificial structures like this one near Longmont, Colorado.

Throughout the West, where Black-billed Magpies and Great Horned Owls share the same habitat, the larger owl often uses the smaller corvid's nests to raise its family. Over the years, I've found several different Great Horned Owls nesting in magpie nests. Holt and Drasen (2001) also documented Great Horned Owls nesting in Black-billed Magpie nests. Magpies build their nests with two sides and a roof, so if you were to look at the nest from the proper angle, it would look like the shape of a tire. I believe the magpies build their nests in this way so the incubating female can sit on the nest with her head looking out one end and her long tail can protrude from the other without fraying the end of her tail. As a side note, the long tail of a magpie is so important to them that when they land on the ground, they quickly lift their tail so it doesn't hit the ground and fray.

In May of 2011, a Great Horned Owl was found incubating her eggs in a magpie nest at the Birds of Prey Foundation. The pair chose to nest in a Black-billed Magpie nest, which at first doesn't appear to be a big deal. However, this nest was only 6 feet (1.83m) from the ground in a ponderosa pine and about 12 feet (3.66m) from a large flight cage that has several rehabilitating peregrine and Prairie Falcons flying within. That pair successfully raised two young owls, even though during the nesting cycle the foundation ran a one-day Open House that brought several hundred onlookers to see the owls.

Shoemaker (1897) located a nesting Great Horned Owl in an abandoned American Crow's nest 24 feet (7.32m) from the ground. Within that nest were three eggs, sixteen field mice, and the wing of a Downy Woodpecker. Sharp (1942) also found a pair of these owls nesting in an abandoned American Crow's nest; that nest was in a low cottonwood tree on the Valentine National Wildlife Refuge in Nebraska and was used by Great Horned Owls from 1937 to 1939. The nest was virtually "completely worn out" by 1939, forcing the young owls to spend most of their time perched on adjacent branches. In 1940, an artificial nest structure was constructed using 3/8-inch (1cm) hardware cloth and the old material from the crow

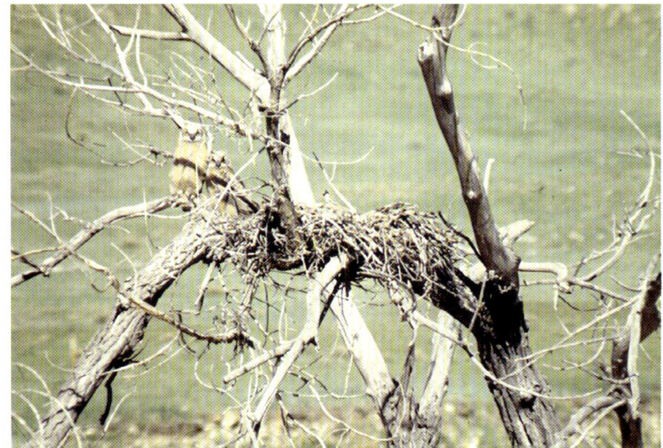

Left: Nestling Great Horned Owls in the abandoned nest of a Ferruginous Hawk in eastern Colorado. Below: Close-up of those two nestlings.

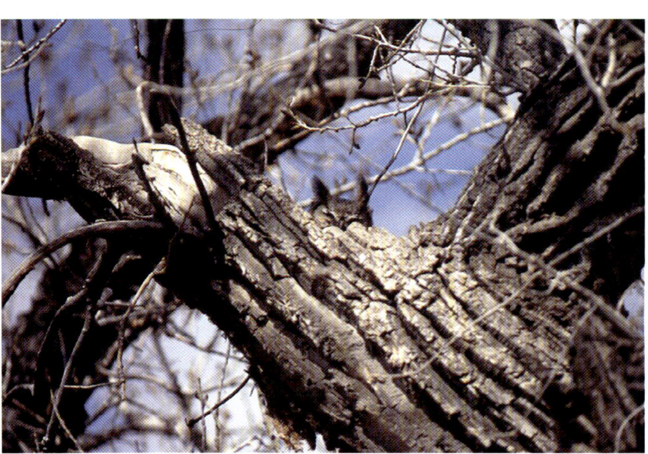

A Great Horned Owl nesting in a broken stump in Broomfield, Colorado.

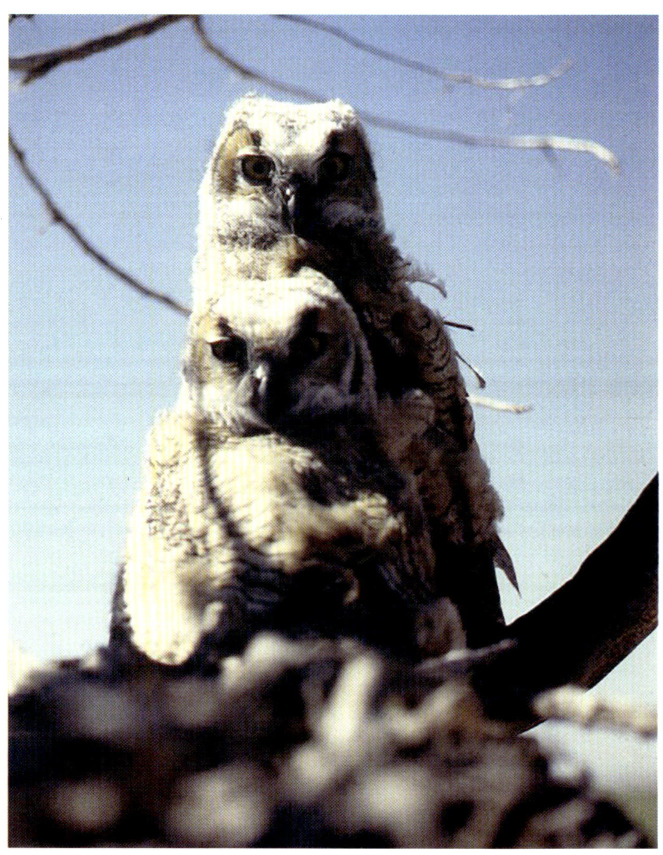

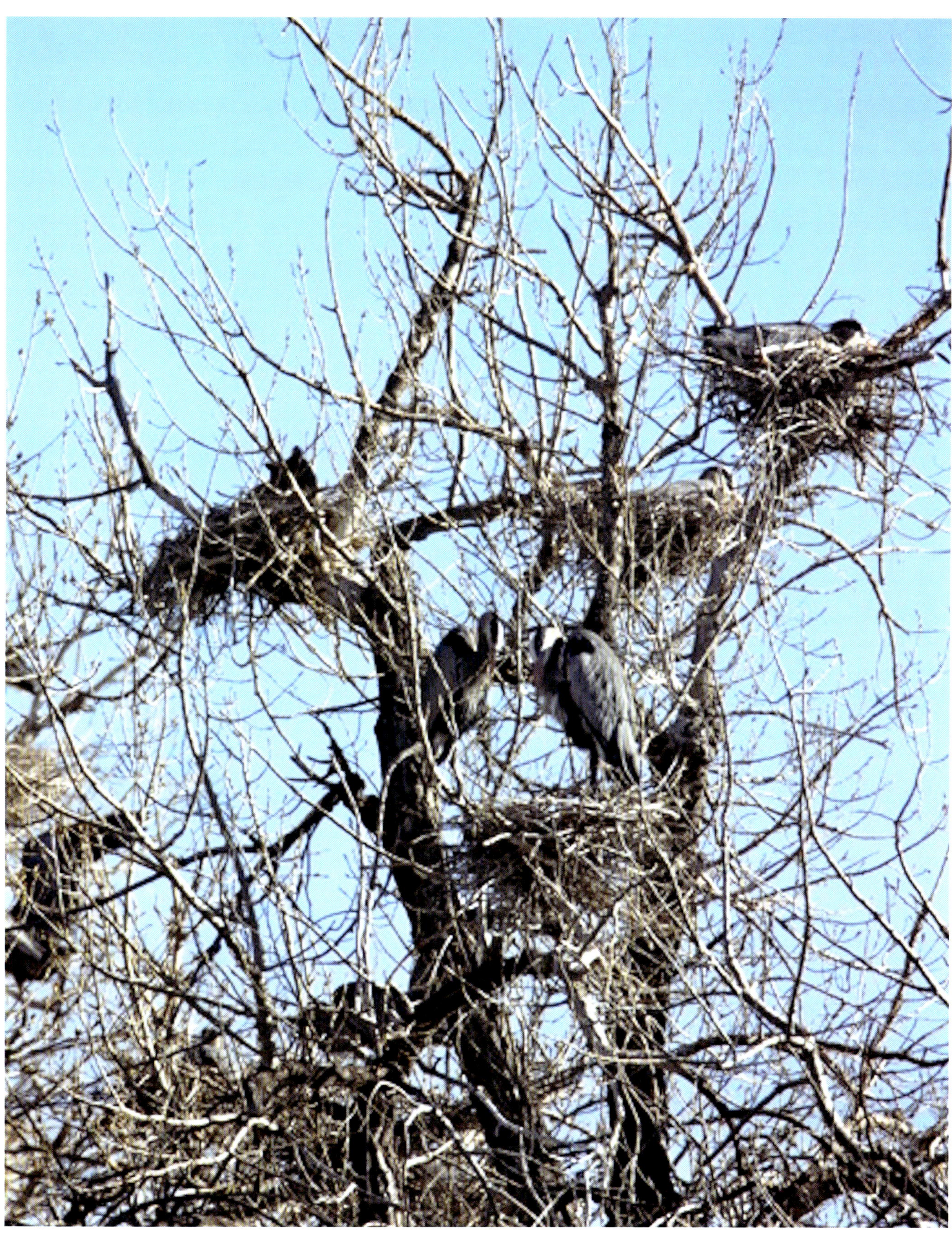

Great Horned Owls often nest in abandoned heron nests right next to the herons.
This photo was taken near Hygene, Colorado. *Photo © Wayne Johnston.*

nest, but, unfortunately, no owls used that structure. Fortunately, in 1941, that nest structure was used by a pair of owls that hatched and raised two young.

In Bridgeport, Connecticut, Devine and Smith (1992) reported a pair of Great Horned Owls that had nested atop an active Monk Parakeet nest that was about 6 feet (1.8m) in length, almost 2 feet (.6m) wide, and almost 3 feet (.9m) deep. It housed seven pairs of Monk Parakeets, which entered the nest from below. A single nestling fledged around May 17th.

In Southern Arizona, Mader (1973) located fifteen Great Horned Owl nests, all in or on saguaro cacti. He suggests that the reason these birds used the cactus was due in large part to the absence of tree nests in the desert. Three nests were built by Harris's Hawks and two were built by Red-tailed Hawks; the remaining nests were constructed by undetermined species, but were most likely built by hawks. The average height of these stick nests was 18 feet (5.5m), with a single nest in a broken arm of the saguaro, which was 15 feet (4.6m) from the ground.

For many years now, a pair of Great Horned Owls has used a ledge of a church in Green Valley, Arizona, for nesting. The male perches a few yards from the nest. He seems to prefer a perch on an "I" beam just under the eve of the roof. Often before and after mass, the birds are watched from inside the church. One morning, during mass, the female hooted and the congregation watched as the male flew towards the nest to see what the female was upset about. Apparently, a Greater Roadrunner approached too close to the nest for the female's liking and she alerted the male. As the roadrunner passed, the family relaxed and the male returned to his perch.

Dr. William L. Ralph writes in Bent (1939) of these owls nesting in Bald Eagle nests in Florida. "In this region these owls always deposit their eggs in the nests of Bald Eagles, and while I think that these are usually, if not always, first deserted by the original owners, the natives say the owls drive the eagles from and appropriate them for their own use. These nests are originally constructed of large sticks and limbs, lined with dead

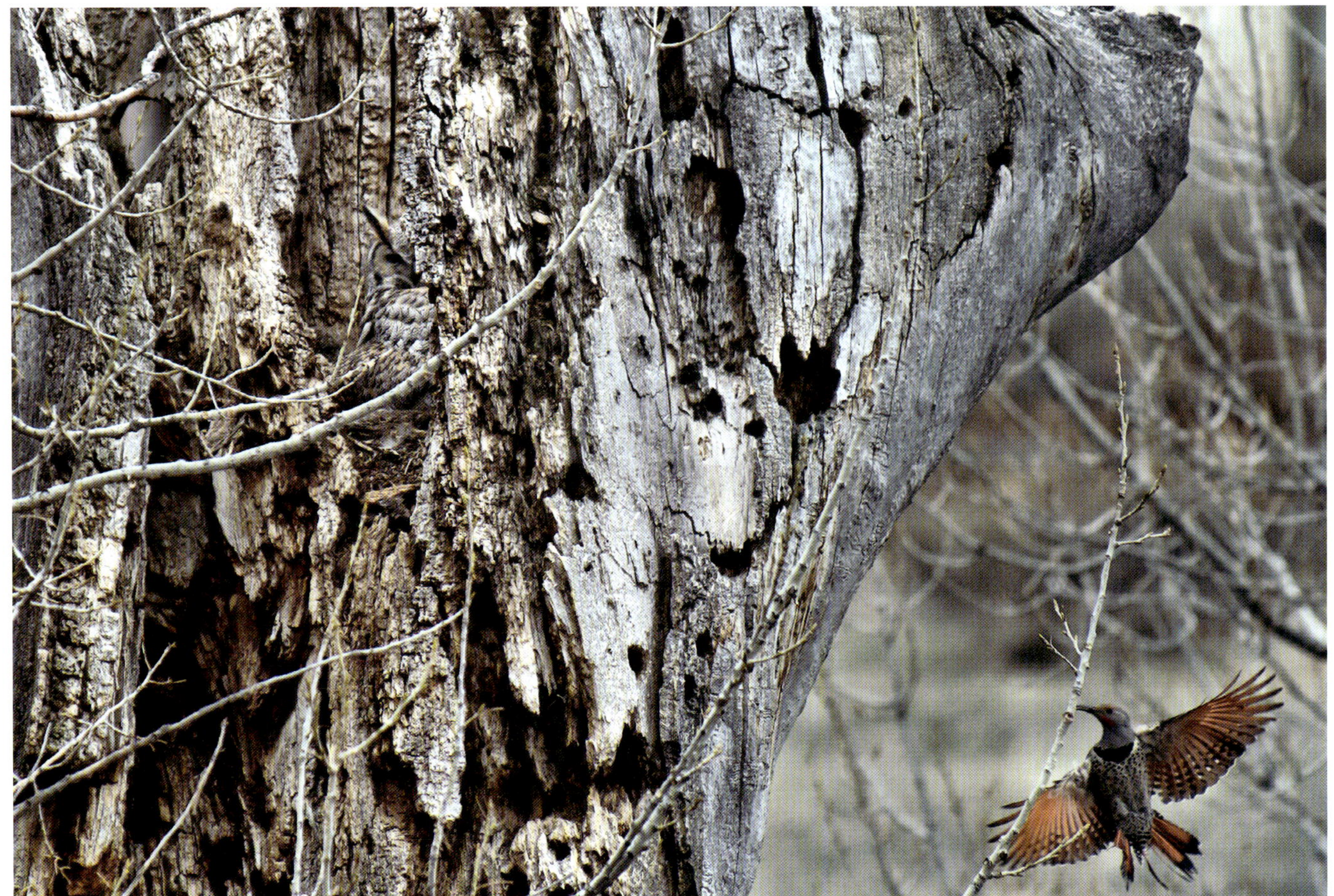

Possibly the best photo of a Great Horned Owl nest that I have ever seen. *Photo © Tom Redd.*

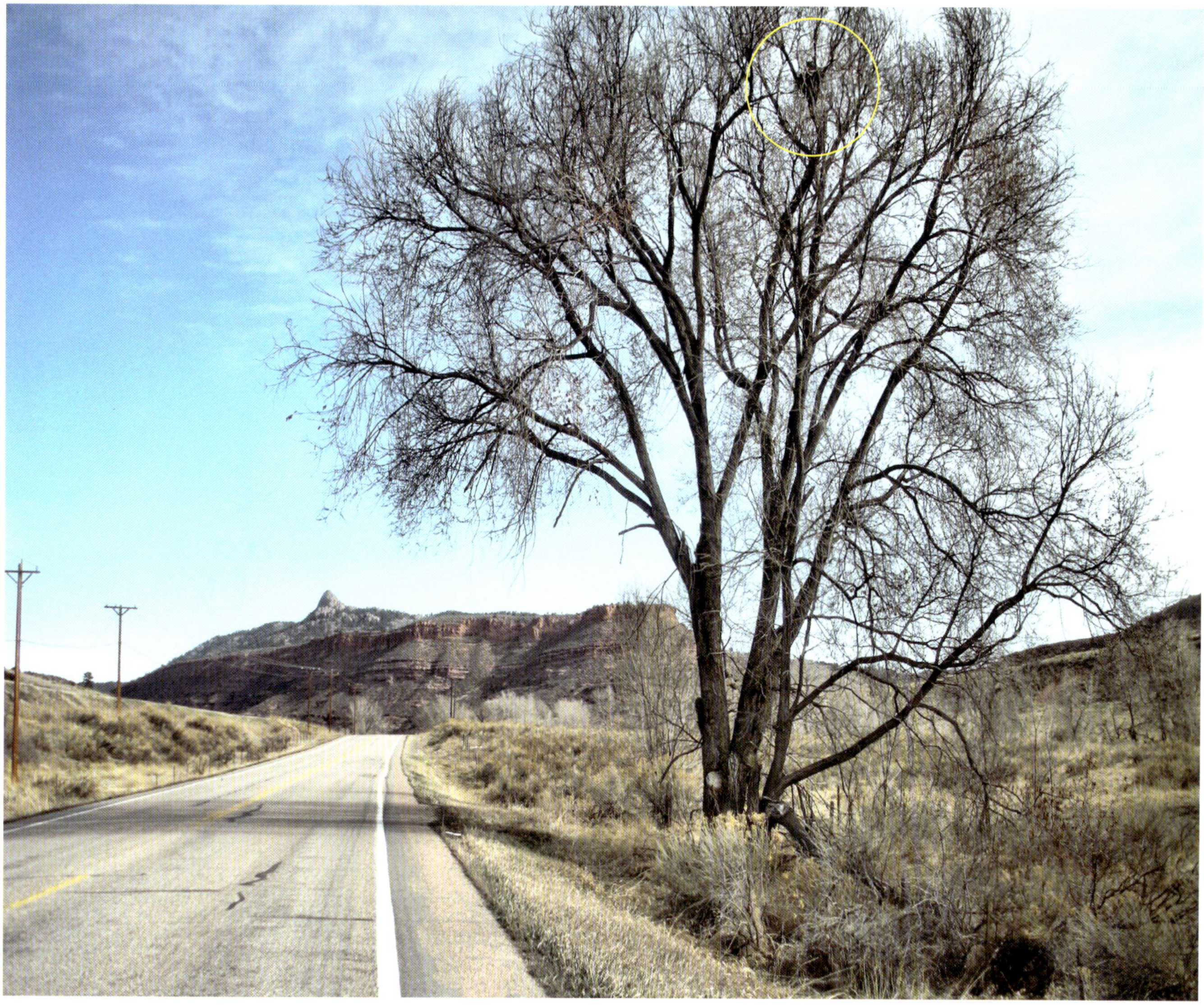

Great Horned Owls are not picky about their nest sites and will often nest over roads if nothing else is available.

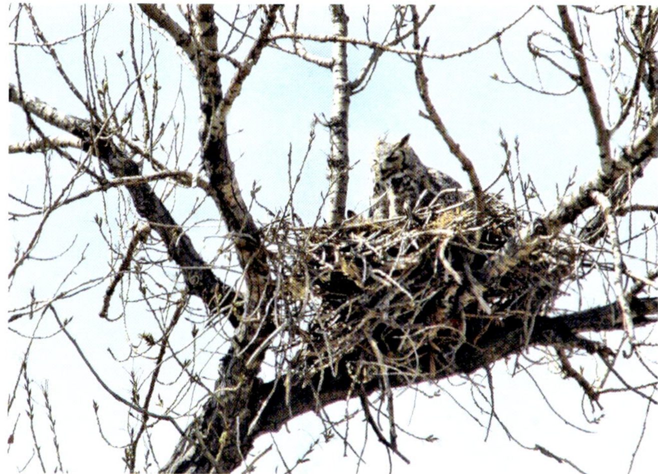

Unlike hawks, Great Horned Owls don't add any material to their nest.

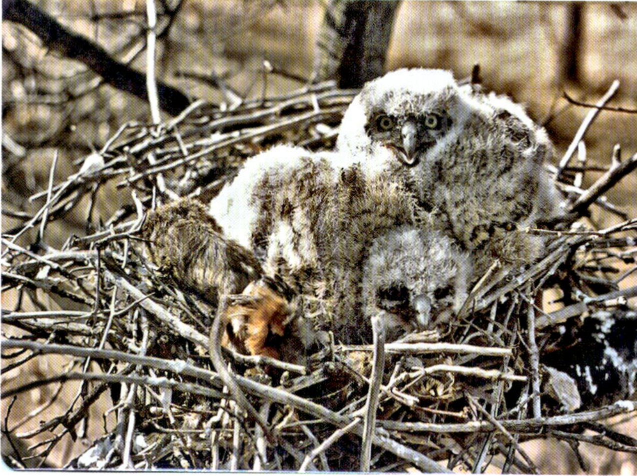

Great Horned Owlets on an old crow's nest in northern Illinois. *Photo © Chris Cold.*

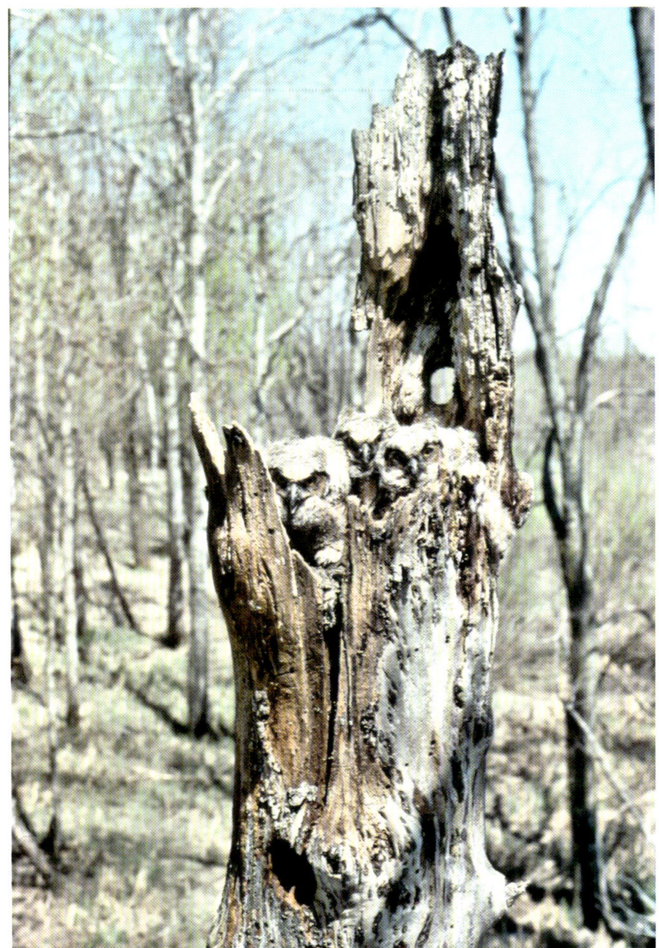

Great Horned Owlets in a broken off tree stump in Wisconsin. *Photo © Chris Cold.*

When nests are in short supply, Great Horned Owls will nest close to people if not bothered. This nest at the Birds of Prey Foundation is slightly above eye level.

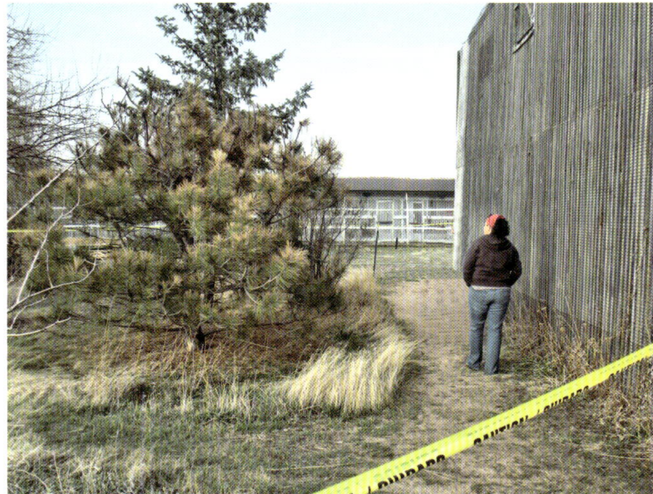

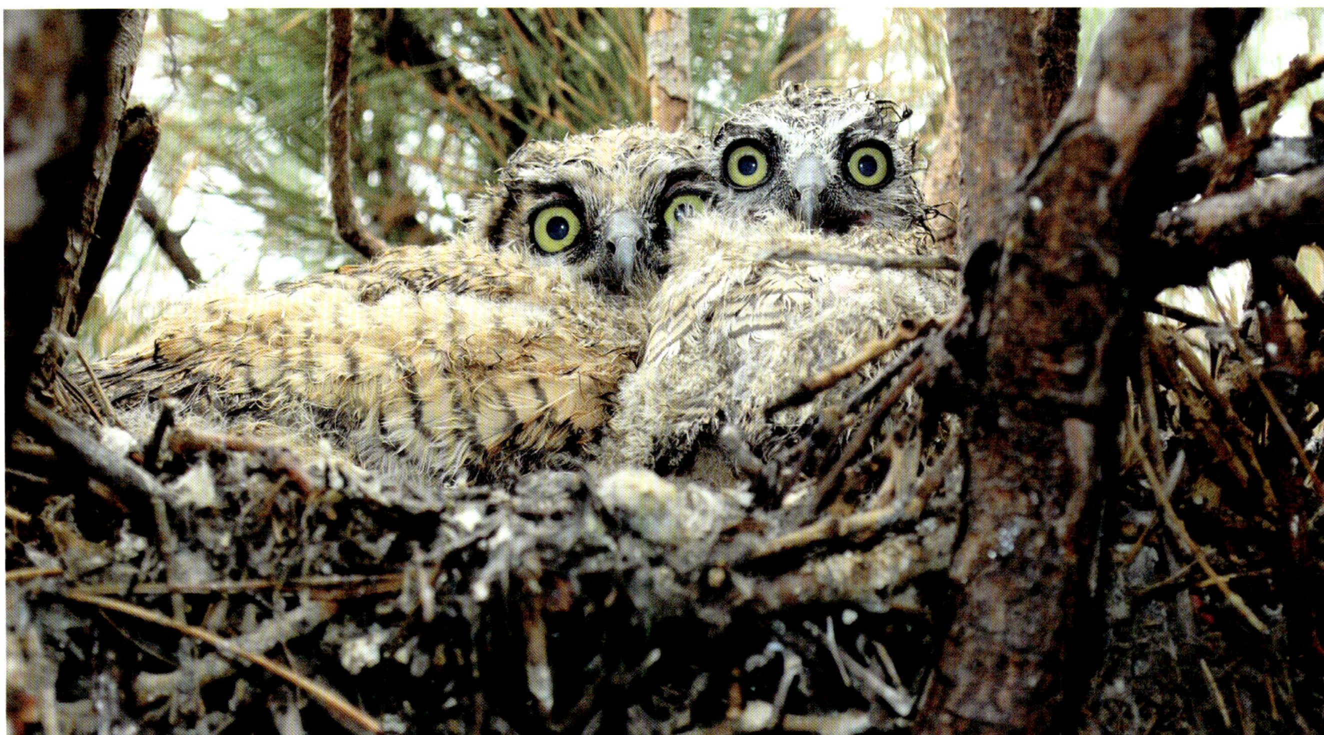

Close-up of the owlets in their nest at the Birds of Prey Foundation.

grasses, palmetto leaves, flags, and weeds, usually with swamp grasses alone; after being taken by the owls [the nests] are always further thickly lined with scales of pine bark, a material I have never found in any quantity in the nests occupied by the eagles."

Mr. George E. Beyer, of New Orleans, Louisiana, wrote to Arthur Bent, date unknown (Bent 1938): "He found a nest of this species (Great Horned Owls) containing three young, in a hollow pine log on the ground." R. C. Hallman in Bent (1939) writes of another Great Horned Owl that nested on the ground in Florida: "The nest, which could hardly be called one, was placed on the ground, and was composed of a few parts of dry palmetto fans, grass stems and small sticks."

Along with Bald Eagle nests, the nests of Ospreys have ended up as housing for Great Horned Owls. Austing and Holt (1966) flushed a juvenile Great Horned Owl from an Osprey nest on Great Island, near Old Lyme, Connecticut. The nest was about 20 feet (6.1m) from the ground in an isolated oak tree surrounded by marsh.

Throughout the West, Great Horned Owls commonly use openings in cliffs for nesting. It is most likely the best place to raise a family due to the inaccessibility from predators and the many surfaces for the young to take short flight to as they master flight. Furthermore, the young owls are often very well camouflaged on these cliffs, as their coloration matches that of the rocks where they perch. To illustrate this, a pair of Great Horned Owls had nested in a cliff in the middle of the town of Estes Park, Colorado. They have nested on this ledge for at least five years and have been undetected by virtually anyone. Even after the young fledge each year and are moving about the cliff, they remain undetected.

A large rock formation south of Estes Park, with an opening on its east side, housed a pair of these owls for many years. The owls nested on an east-facing opening on a large rock outcropping. Below the nest was a large open meadow and to the west of the nest was a large lake that had several species of fish within. Birds, such as gulls, cormorants, and several duck species, along with

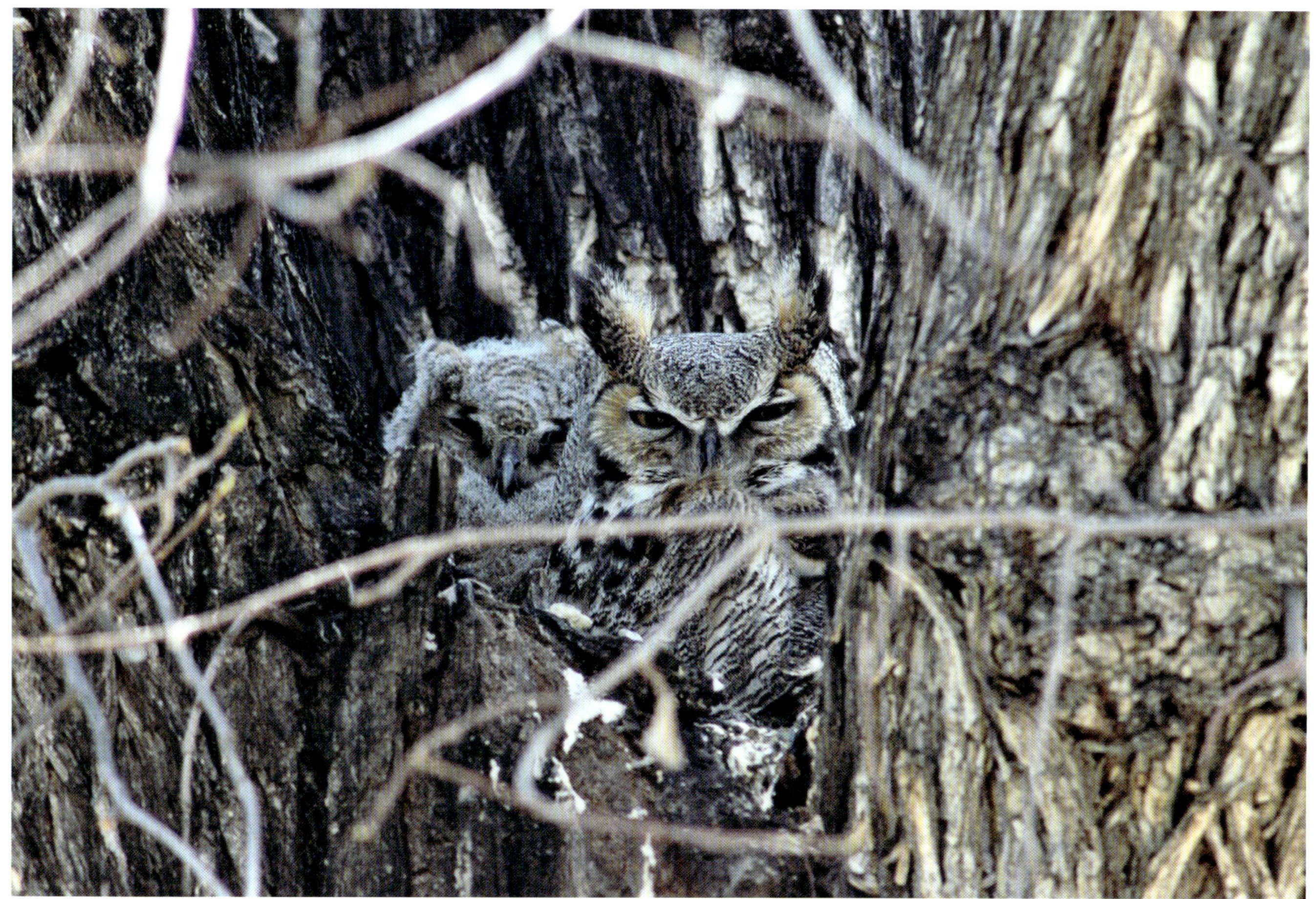

Mom and one of her owlets in a crotch of a tree in the cemetery in Fort Collins, Colorado.

the occasional goose and swan, were found on the lake most years. The rock that the owls nested in was also used by rock-climbing instructors teach people to climb and repel. For several years, the owls used the nest with great success until one year I checked the nest and found the female laying dead at the nest's entrance.

Major Bendire (1892) in Bent (1939) wrote about a Great Horned Owl nest that was on the ground on a tussock of grass in the center of a pond. That nest was previously occupied by a pair of geese. Furthermore, on April 1, 1922, J.R. Whitaker (Bent 1939) had also found a nest of these owls that was on the ground under the exposed roots of a large pine tree. "I looked under the stump, and there on the frozen ground, surrounded by snow, lay the eggs. There was no nest, only about a half a dozen owl feathers." After a thaw that spring, the nest was flooded and the owls moved about 900 feet (274.3m) and laid a second clutch of eggs also on the ground."

In the treeless areas of the owl's range, such as the prairie provinces of Canada, Great Horned Owls have been documented nesting underground in coyote and badger dens (Baumgartner 1938).

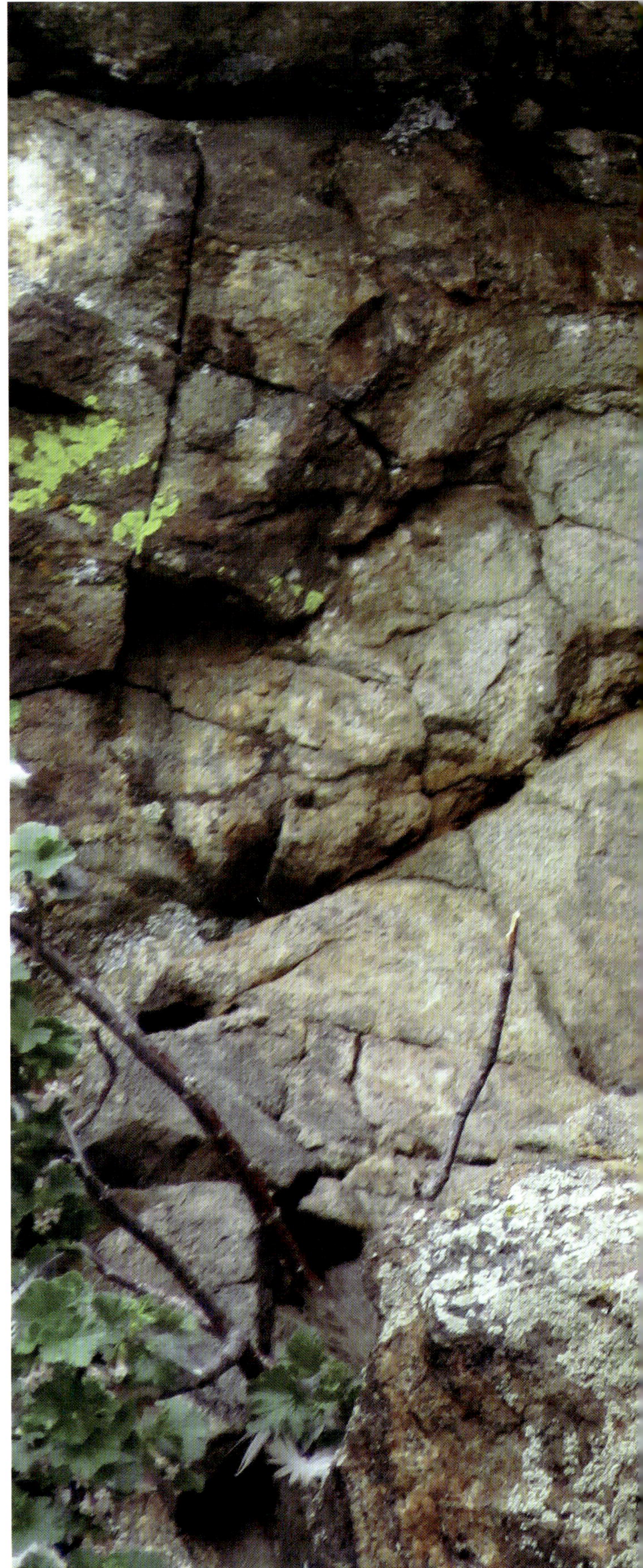

Female Great Horned Owl perched at her nest entrance, always vigil.

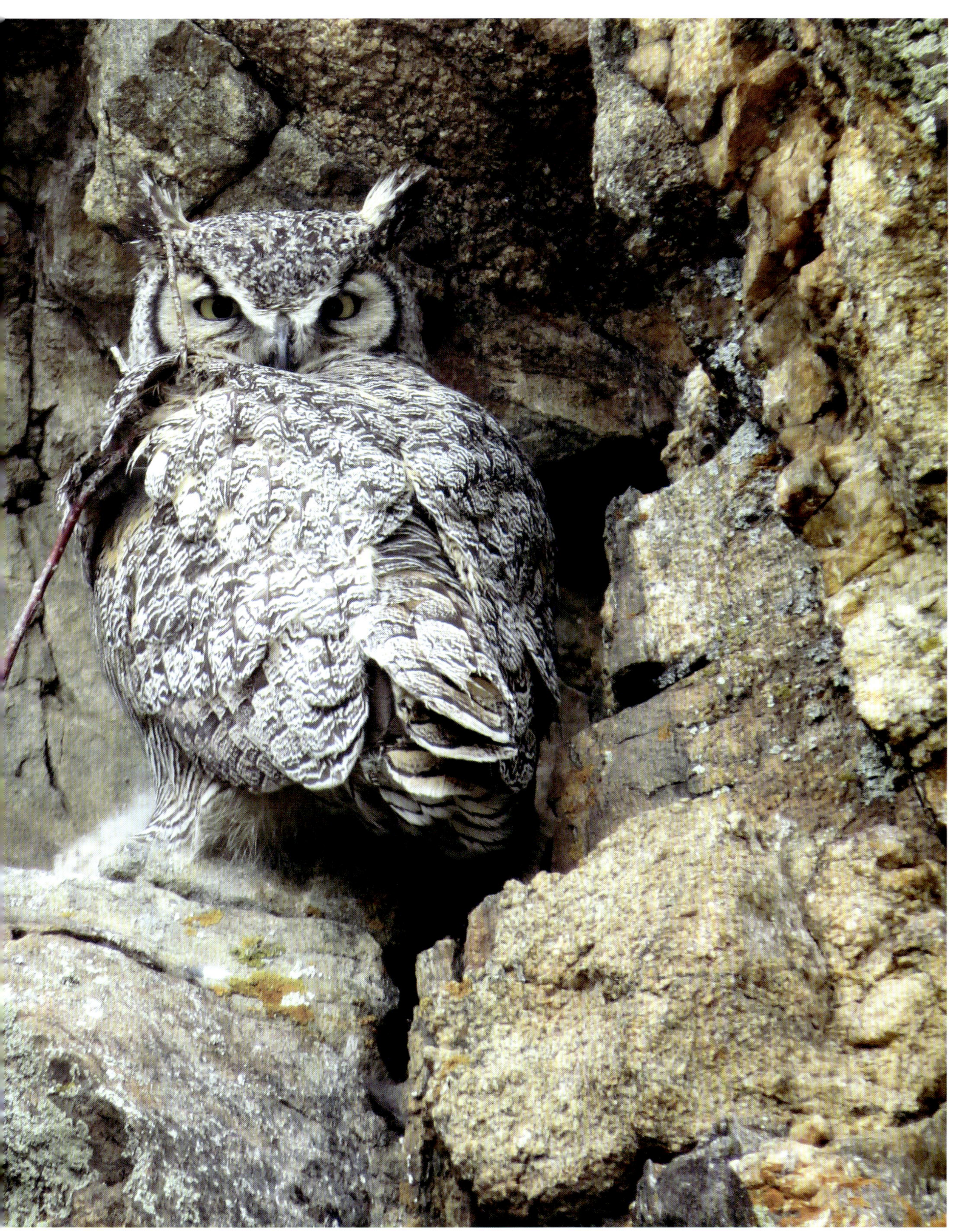

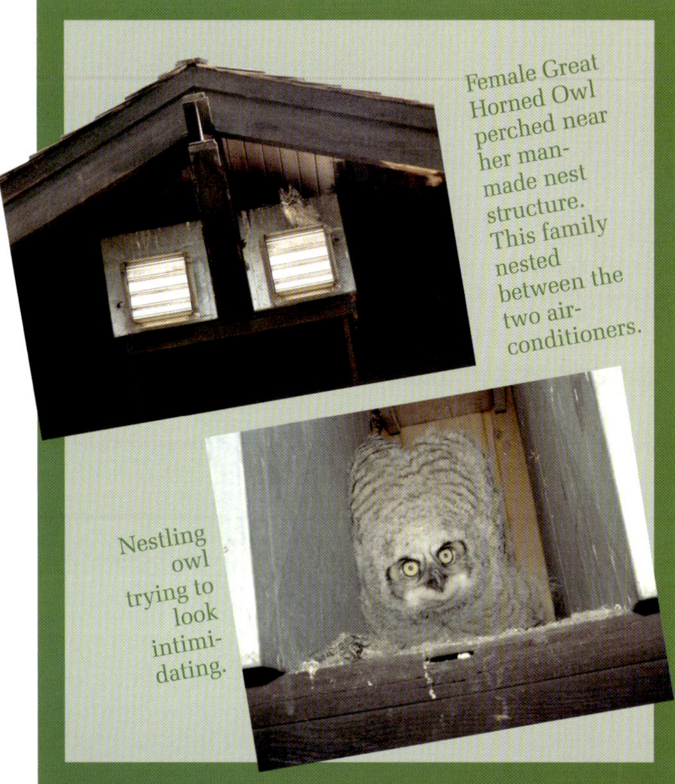

Female Great Horned Owl perched near her man-made nest structure. This family nested between the two air-conditioners.

Nestling owl trying to look intimidating.

In 1995, I was told of a pair of Great Horned Owls that had taken up housekeeping between two air conditioners underneath an eve of a restaurant in Estes Park. These birds added nothing to their nest platform, but routinely had between two and four young. These owls reused the platform for many years until the restaurant was sold and turned into a health club and the landowner didn't want the owls around. Just north of the nest was a large open field that the owls used to hunt. However, that area is now filled with condominiums. The year after the nest platform was removed I received a call from the health club employee at 5:30 a.m. who told me that a large owl was perched on the floor inside the health club. When I arrived at the club, the girl at the front desk told me to walk into the weight room and I would find the bird. A few moments later the bird was spotted. I slowly made my way to the bird and, while talking to it, placed a towel over the owl and picked it up. I took the bird outside, placed a Fish and Wildlife Service leg band on the bird and placed him on the branch of a ponderosa pine.

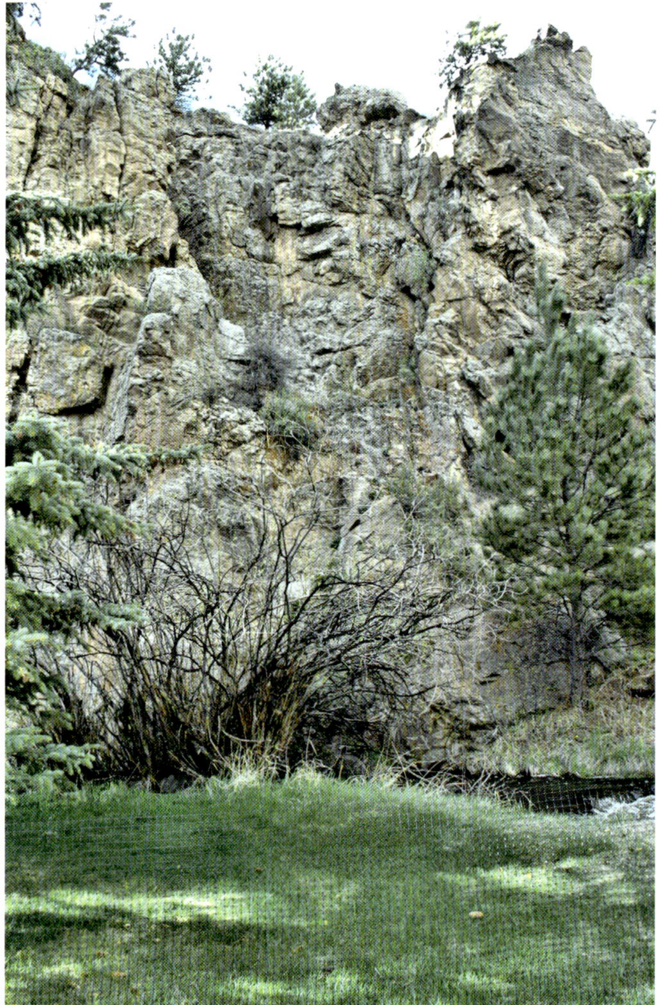

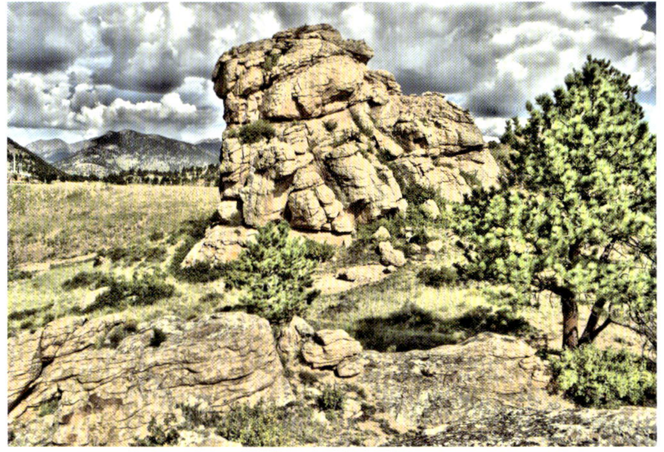

For years, a pair of Great Horned Owls nested in a crevasse of this rock just south of Estes Park, Colorado.

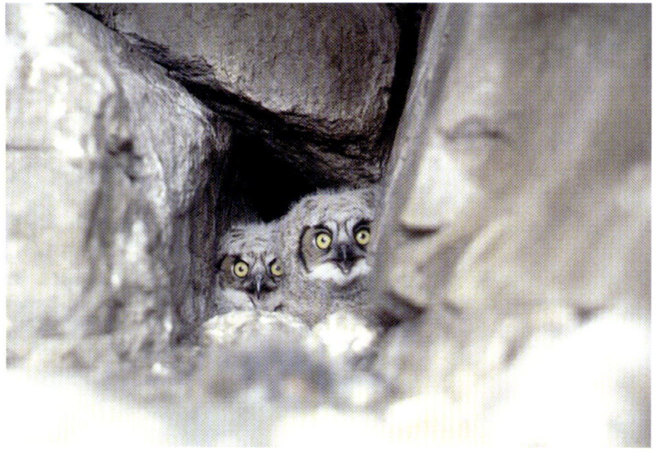

A close-up of two owlets from inside that nest crevasse.

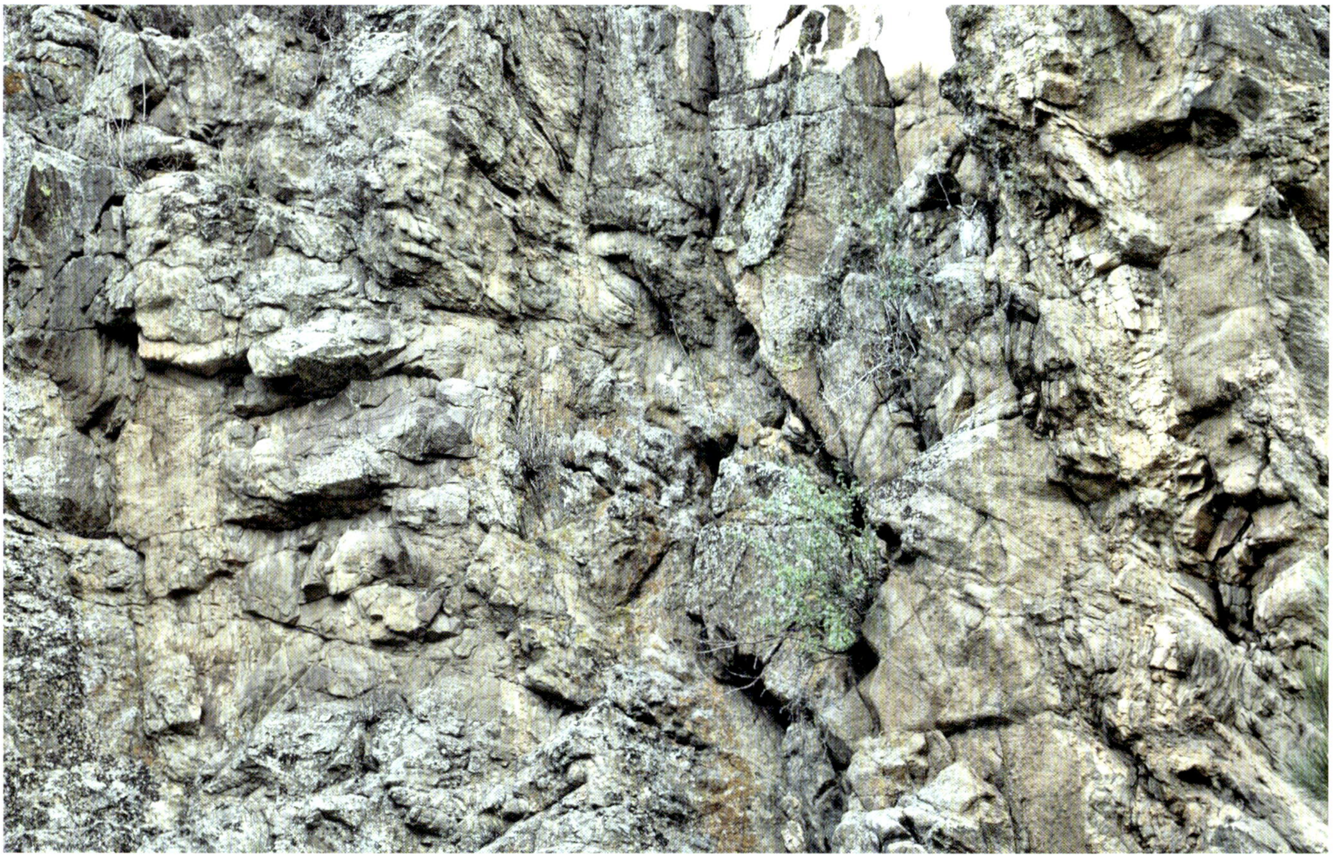

Cliff in Estes Park where Great Horned Owls have nested for years. If you look closely, you will see the female owl perched at the entrance to her nest.

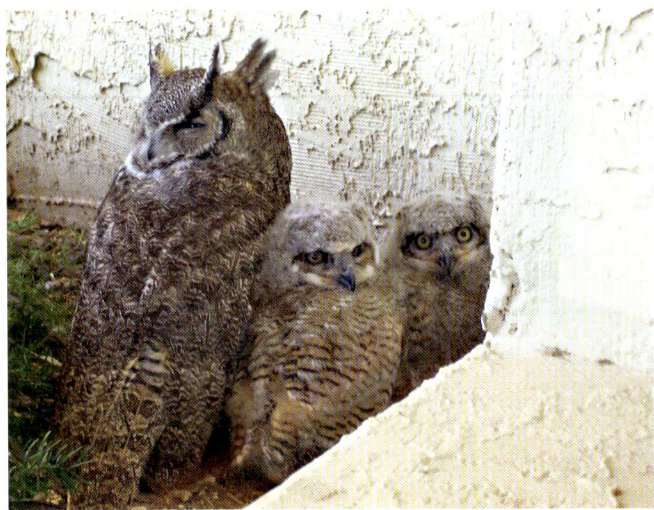

For years, Great Horned Owls nested just outside of a church in Green Valley, Arizona.

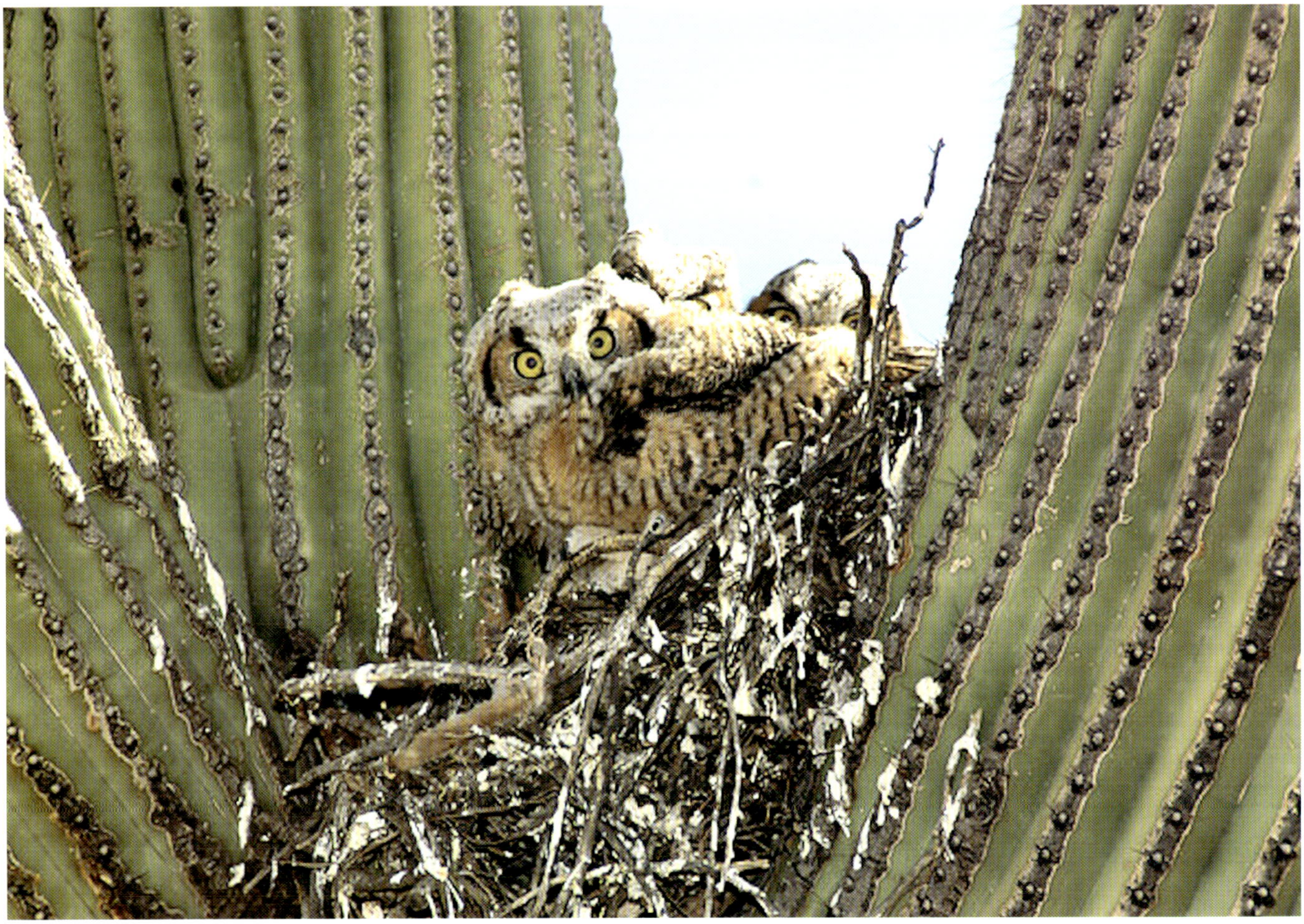

In the desert southwest, Great Horned Owls often use hawk nests on saguaro cactus. *Photo © Young Cage.*

EGGS/INCUBATION

Great Horned Owls lay between one and five eggs, but as a rule lay two to three eggs that are white in color and show little or no gloss, though there are occasional exceptions. They are rounded, oval in shape, and the shell is thick and rather coarsely granulated, feeling rough to the touch (Bent 1939).

According to Bent (1939), Dr. Ralph told Bendire (1892) that in Florida sixty percent of the nests that he found had only a single egg. Bent (1939) wrote that all of the nests that he found in Massachusetts contained either two or three eggs and/or young. In northern Colorado, I have found nests containing between one and four young. I have only found two nests containing four young Great Horned Owls. However, I find more nests with two young than I do with a single owlet. In Saskatchewan, Houston (1971) found that five percent or more of nests contained four young, with twelve percent or less containing only a single owlet.

The eggs measure between 2-3/16 x 1-7/8 inches (56.1 x 47mm), with extremes being 2-3/8 x 2 inches (59.9 x 50mm) and 2 x 1-3/4 inches (50 x 43.2mm) (Bent 1939). The first egg laid is the largest with the last egg laid being the smallest (Houston et al. 1998). Eggs are apparently laid from one- to seven-day intervals (Baumgartner 1938).

Incubation appears to be about thirty-five days (Austing and Holt 1966), with the majority of the incubation being carried out by the female; however, the male will share in these duties (Cameron 1907). Cameron also suggests that the eggs may actually hatch as much as a week apart, meaning that the eggs may also be laid at such intervals. Incubation occurs even when the ambient temperature reaches as low as -14.8°F (-26°C) (Holt and Drasen 2001). In 2011, a Great Horned Owl that nested at the Birds of Prey Foundation incubated for exactly thirty-five days when the first egg hatched.

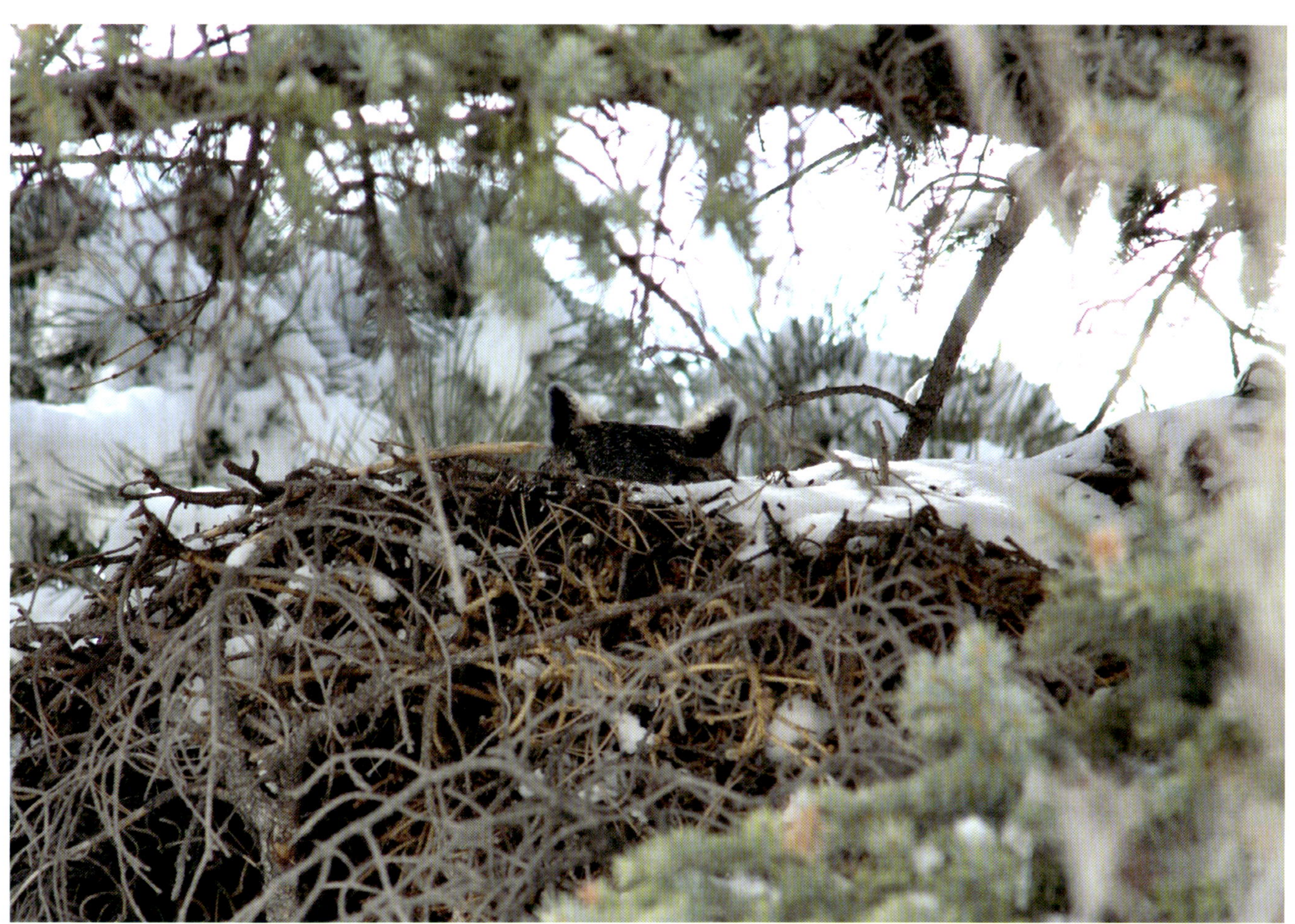

A female Great Horned Owl incubating her eggs during late winter in Estes Park.

The Great Horned Owl is one of the earliest nesting birds in North America. The farther south the birds nest, the earlier the female lays her eggs. In southern Texas, along the Lower Rio Grand Valley, Mulaik (1935) had two eggs brought to him and after looking at the contents of the eggs, it was believed that they were laid about the fourth or fifth of January. Craighead and Craighead (1969) found the earliest date for egg-laying of the Great Horned Owls in Michigan was February 4th; that was in 1949.

Elder (1935) found a Great Horned Owl incubating the first egg of her clutch on January 20, 1935. The owl laid two more eggs, with the first hatching on February 27th. In Arizona, Mader (1973) notes that these owls lay their eggs between the second and third weeks in February, with other individuals laying eggs between the first and second weeks in March.

Holt and Drasen (2001) found a Great Horned Owl nest near Missoula, Montana, in 1996, in which they estimated the eggs to have been laid on or about January 22nd. On the Fort Carson Military Reservation in east central Colorado, Anderson (1996) found Great Horned Owls laid their eggs in early March. In and around Rocky Mountain National Park, I've found these owls to lay their eggs in the first two weeks in March, yet the owls in and around Fort Collins and Loveland lay their eggs three to four weeks earlier. Loveland and Fort Collins are about a hundred miles (161km) north of Fort Carson. Estes Park is about 2,000 feet (610m) higher in elevation than Loveland and Fort Collins, with Rocky Mountain National Park being several thousand feet higher in places.

Dixon (1914) found a pair of Great Horned Owls in the Escondido Valley in California that had laid a set of eggs by January 29, 1911, and February 14, 1907, was thought to be a late date for a full clutch to be laid. He also found a four-day span between the laying of first and

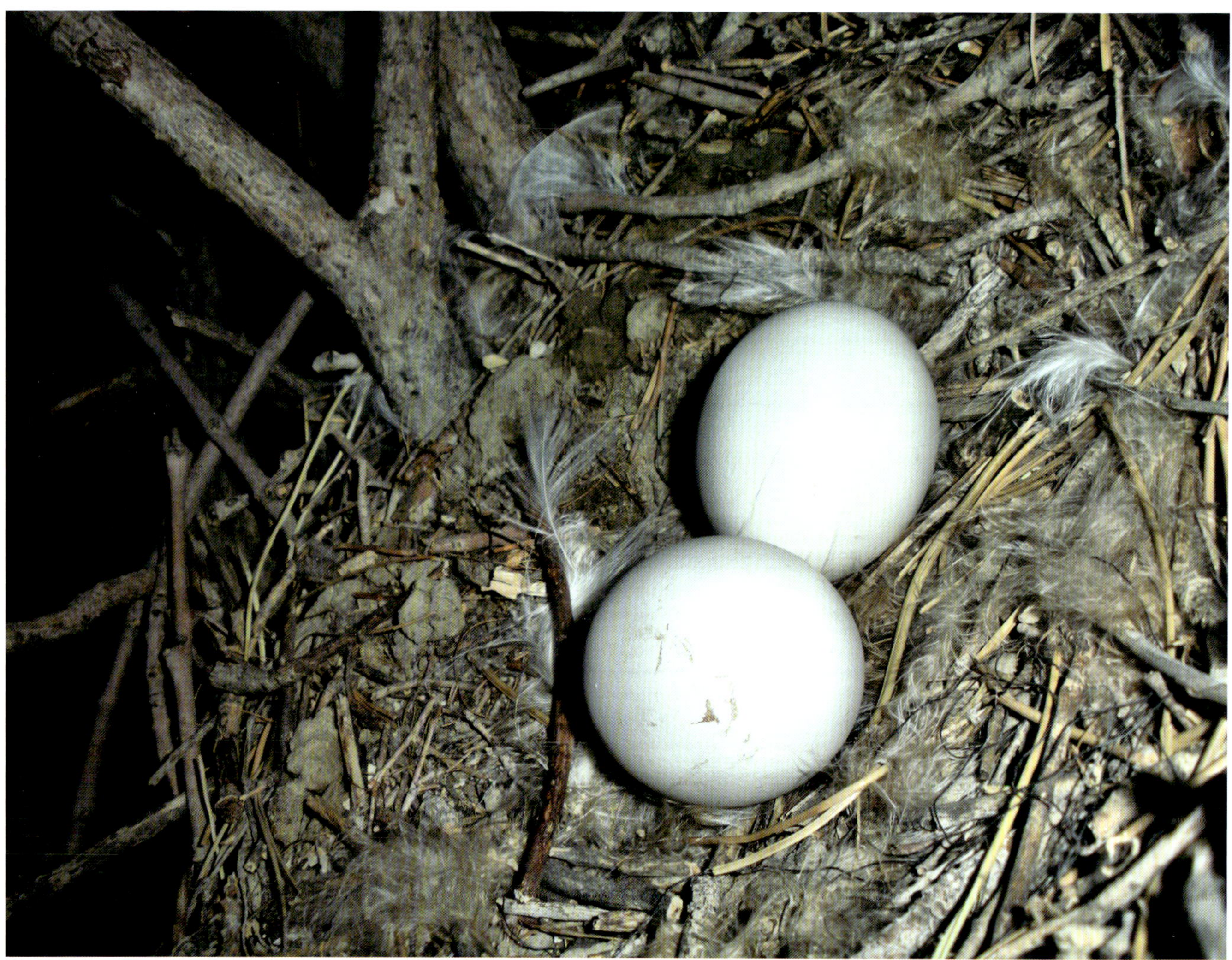

Great Horned Owl eggs.

second eggs. However, incubation began with the laying of the first egg. The females of five different nests laid three eggs each and two other females laid two eggs within their nests. The female owl would lay a second clutch and even a third within twenty-one days if the previous eggs were stolen.

C. Stuart Houston (1975) wrote of some interesting observations about items found within Great Horned Owls' nests in Saskatchewan. With the assistance of several owl banders who banded nestling Great Horned Owls, they found several eggs in the nests. The interesting thing is many of these eggs were not Great Horned Owl eggs. These eggs were from coots, Gray Partridge, Northern Pintail, and an unidentified duck. It was unlikely that the eggs were brought to the nests by themselves, so a better hypothesis is that the eggs were inside the birds that were brought to the nests. As the birds were devoured by the owls, the eggs remained uneaten.

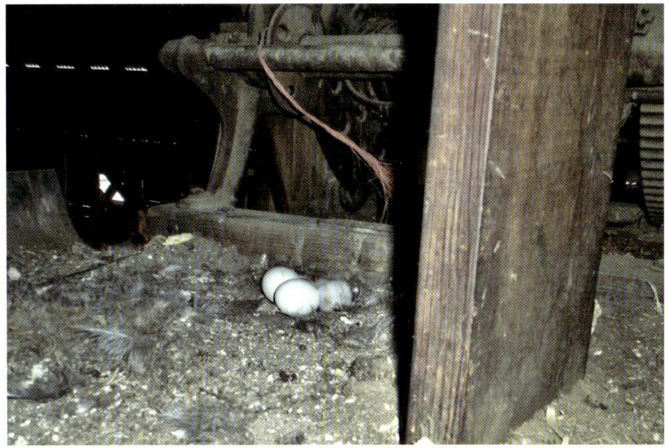

The Great Horned Owl will nest in buildings if the situation arises.

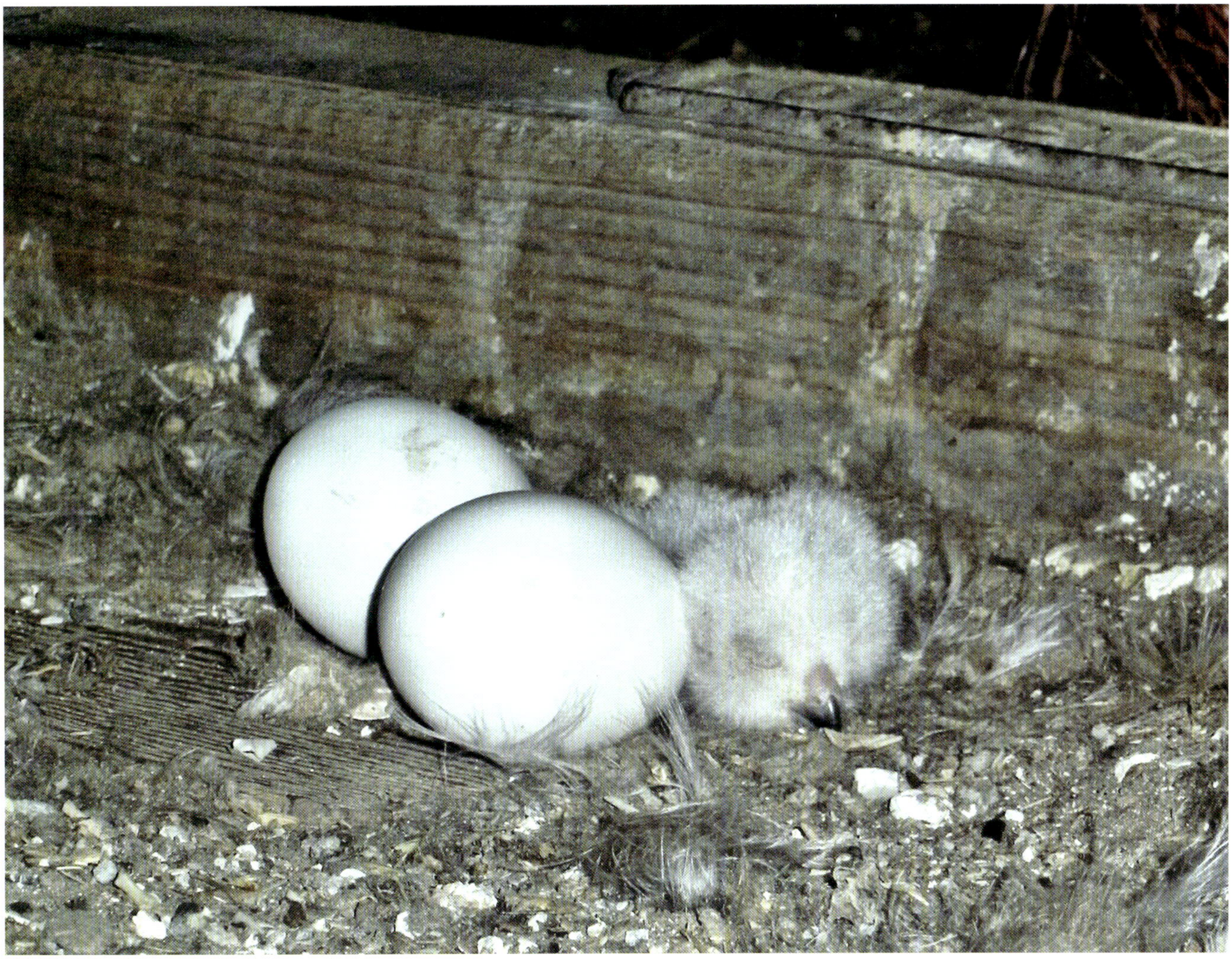

Two Great Horned Owl eggs and a one-day-old owlet.

Chapter 5

HUNTING / FOOD PREFERENCES

The Great Horned Owl is classified by most biologists as a generalist hunter (Austing and Holt 1966) and crepuscular in habits rather than nocturnal (Reed 1925). They will hunt throughout the evenings when the moon is bright enough. The adult owls are voracious feeders, capable of overpowering virtually any small- to medium-sized creature that walks, crawls, flies, or swims — especially those that are nocturnal (Bent 1938). The list of creatures that this species can and has overpowered is probably the longest of any avian predator in North America (Voous 1988). These large owls may take small prey — ranging from earthworms, grasshoppers, and other creatures — weighing less than a pound/gram, to large hares, squirrels, and birds weighing several pounds (Houston, Smith and Rohner 1998). Marti (1974) believes the Great Horned Owl is the owl species with the largest variation in prey size due in part to it having the most pronounced sexual dimorphism. These owls have extremely strong talon strength, as it takes 28-1/2 lbs. (13,000g) of force to open an owl's closed foot (Marti 1974).

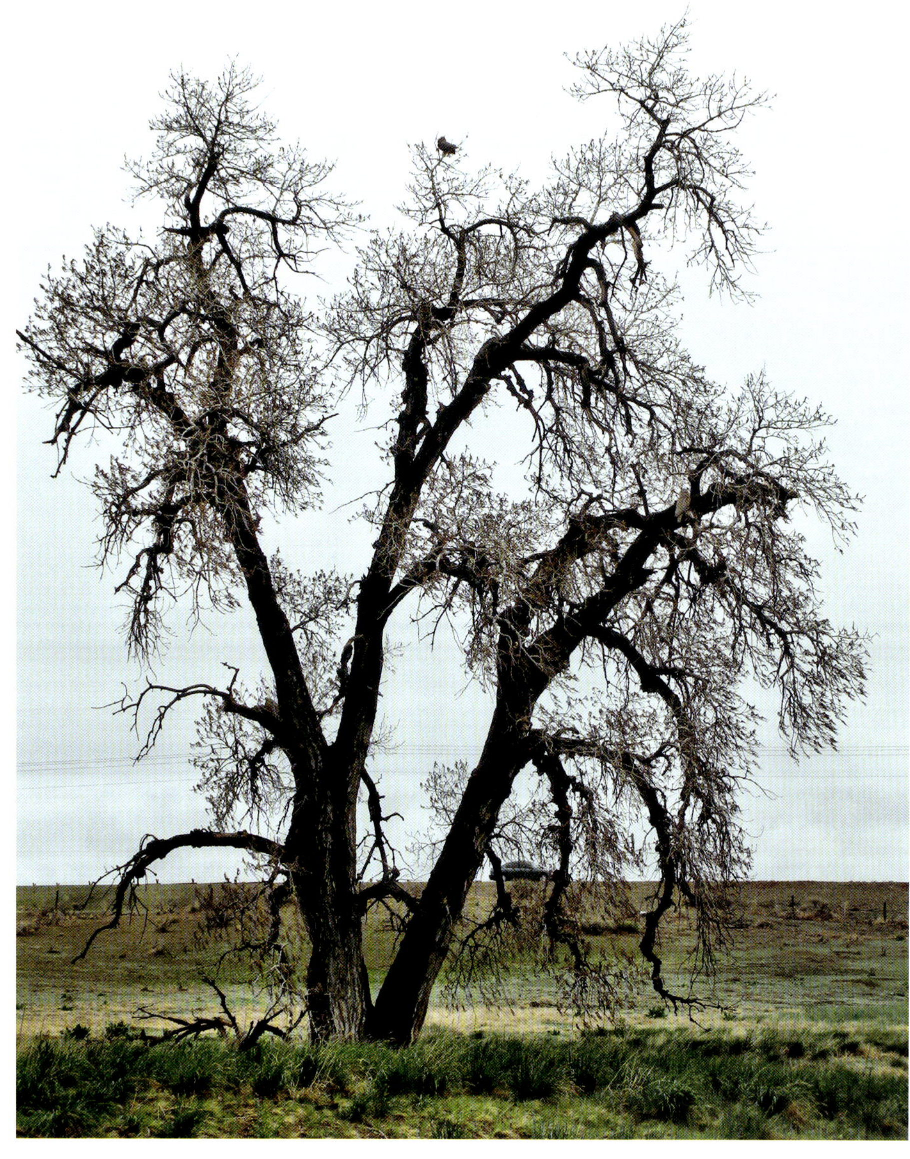

A pair of Great Horned Owls hunting during the day.

I have watched Great Horned Owls hunting on several occasions. They hunt a lot like Red-tailed Hawks, in that both species perch on a telephone pole, rooftop, and/or treetop searching for prey, usually well before total darkness. The only difference is that the owls are often perched searching for prey after the hawks have moved to an evening roost. Marti (1974) describes the methods of hunting: "I observed that Great Horned Owls hunt by perching on vantage points such as cliffs, poles, and trees. Generally, they would remain at one perch for three to five minutes and then move to another. If prey were sighted, a direct, low, rapid flight would be initiated in an attempt to capture it. These flights varied from a little over 55-1/2 to 328 feet (17-100m) in length."

One of the most unusual prey items that end up on the owl's menu is skunks, which can be found throughout most of the owls' range. The Great Horned Owl is one species that routinely attacks, kills, and devours them. G. Norman Wilkinson (1913) in Bent (1938) writes:

> One morning, late in the autumn, I was driving through the woods, when I heard a disturbance in the dry leaves a little distance from the road. As I drew near, I saw clearly the cause of the disturbance. A few feet in front of me was a large Great Horned Owl in a sort of sitting posture. His back and head were against an old log. His feet were thrust forward, and firmly grasping a full grown skunk. One foot had hold of the skunk's neck and the other clutched tightly by the middle of the back. The animal appeared to be nearly dead, but still had strength enough to leap occasionally into the air in its endeavors to shake off its captor. During the struggle, the owl's eyes would fairly blaze and he would snap his bill like the sound of clapping hands. Neither the bird nor its victim paid the slightest attention to me, though I stood quite close. How long since the owl had secured its death grip I do not know, but there was no doubt about his having it. The skunk could no more free itself from the owl's grip than it could have from the jaws of a steel trap. Its struggles grew less and less frequent and at the end of about fifteen minutes they ceased altogether.

I have lived in Estes Park since 1989 and, for the first several years living here, I hadn't seen or even smelled a skunk. Therefore, I presumed we didn't have skunks at this elevation, which is over 7,200 feet (2195m). In 2000, I received a Great Horned Owl that was injured after having been hit by a car. The bird had an unusual smell to it, but it wasn't like the striped skunks that I am familiar with. When I took the bird to the Birds of Prey Foundation in Broomfield, Colorado, for exercise, Sigrid, the director of the foundation, told me my owl had been eating skunks. The smell wasn't what I was used to because the owl was feeding upon spotted skunks, not striped ones. The two species have a different smell, which at the time I didn't know. Since that time I have found evidence of spotted skunks in the area and have even seen a family of spotted skunks in Rocky Mountain National Park.

Oliver L. Austin, Jr. (1932) writes in Bent (1938) of an interesting prey item that a Great Horned Owl had captured:

> "I flushed a Great Horned Owl, which fluttered up ahead of my car and flew laboriously down the road. The headlights showed it was carrying something heavy, something which it could lift two feet off the ground. I gave chase, and the bird dropped clumsily a hundred yards farther on, to crouch defensively atop the prey it seemed to loath to leave. I stopped the car twenty feet away and turned on my strong spotlight. The owl's attention was riveted by the dazzling beam, and while it stood motionless staring into the glare, I crept up cautiously on the dark side, threw my jacket over it, and pinioned it down. After rapping the claws in my handkerchief to prevent accidents, and folding the bird safely into my jacket, I stopped to pick up its prey, which to my surprise (and delight) proved to be a half-grown house cat. The kill had evidently just been made, for the limp body was still warm and quivering."

Another unusual item that the Great Horned Owl has been known to attack is a porcupine. In 1909, the Rev. C.W.G. Eifrig, as described in Bent (1938), had one of these owls brought to him that had tussled with a porcupine. "It was liberally sprinkled over with quills, especially on the soles of the right foot — the quills having penetrated even that horny skin, under the right wing, on the breast, neck, and even two in the left eyelid. Some of the quills had penetrated the thick, solid muscle of the breast, lying against the sternum. Fifty-six quills and parts of quills were extracted from the skin and flesh, with about ten left in."

Baker (1962) watched Great Horned Owls attacking bats at Carlsbad Caverns National Park. Out of all the species that preyed upon the bats, the Great Horned Owl was the most consistent. Apart from the Great Horned Owl feeding on the bats, he also documented Peregrine Falcons, Red-tailed Hawks, Cooper's and Sharp-shinned Hawks, Northern Harriers, American Kestrels, and Swainson's Hawks attacking the bats. Being unable to out-maneuver the bats like the hawks and falcons could, the Great Horned Owl would wait until the stream of bats became thick enough to attract the interest of the owl and then drive through the flock with open talons and striking by setting their wings, rearing back in a sitting position and thrusting out with their talons. Whether or not the owl was successful in the attack, it would land on the opposite side before beginning another attack or consuming its catch. The owl was successful about one out of three attempts.

Throughout the years, I've witnessed owls hunting during the day. On May 27, 2009, while searching for fledgling Great Horned Owls in Rocky Mountain National Park, I came across an adult owl that had just captured a Wyoming ground squirrel. The nest is the well-known site near the Fall River entrance to the park that was described earlier. The owl was on the north side of the road, several hundred yards from the nest. I heard several

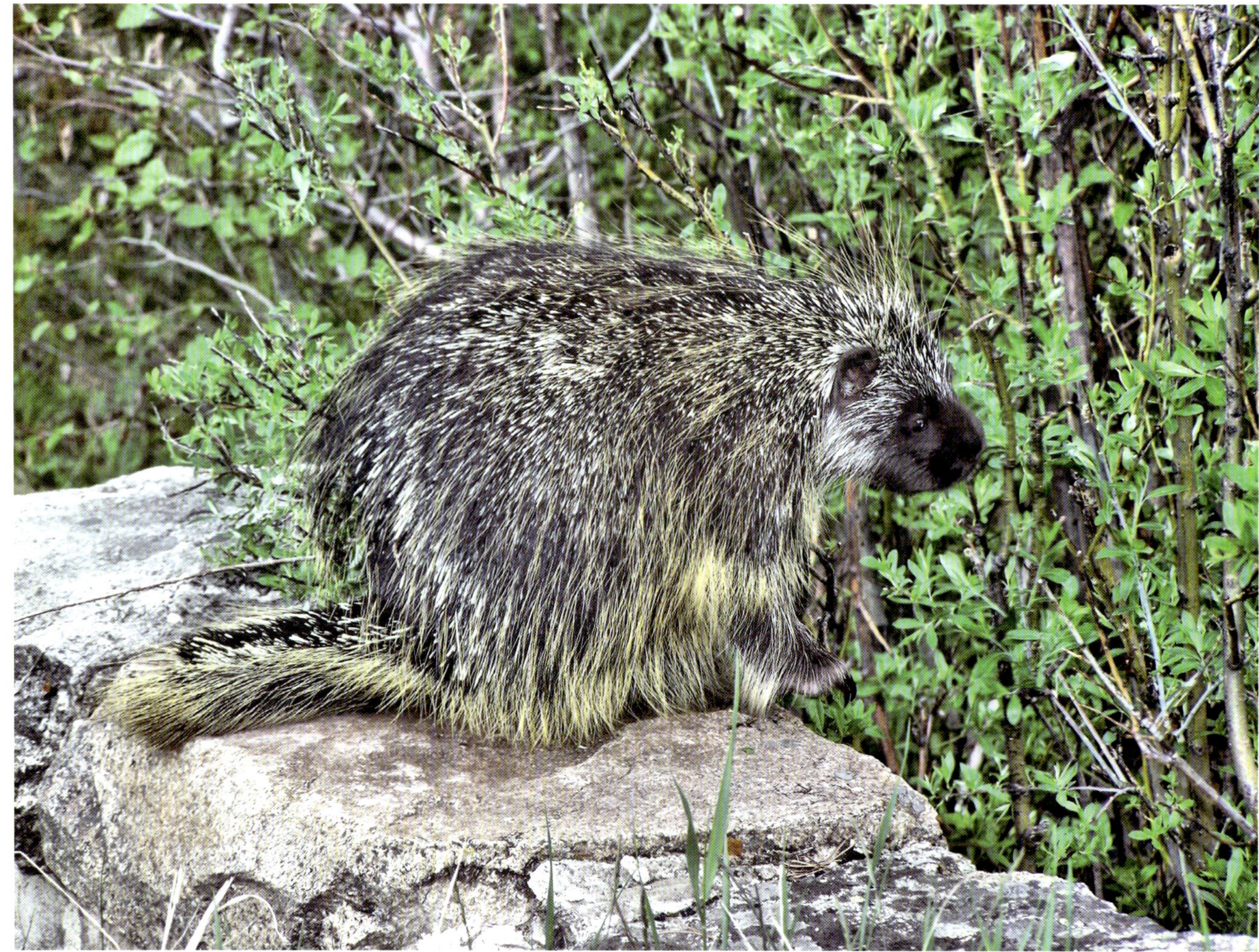

Porcupines are occasionally attacked by Great Horned Owls.

Steller's Jays scolding loudly, so I hiked to the raucous jays and found an adult Great Horned Owl on the ground with something grasped in its feet. While looking thorough my binoculars, I could see the back legs and tail of a ground squirrel. The owl saw me and flew off through the trees, with the squirrel, toward its nest.

On at least three different mornings, I watched an adult Great Horned Owl hunting on the nine-hole golf course in Estes Park. The owl would perch early in the morning, on top of a ponderosa pine, surveying the course. On all three occasions, the owl would perch, seemingly waiting for the ground squirrels to appear. After a few moments, the owl would spring into action, grasping one of the small mammals, and then fly into the woods. The owl was successful on two of the three attempts. The first morning I saw the owl, it was just after 6, as I was walking through the bird sanctuary that is adjacent to the golf course. I looked across the creek that separates the course and the sanctuary and saw the owl perched on top of a spruce near the center of the course. It was scanning the ground with a certain level of intent. From where I was standing, I could see a few ground squirrels scurrying across the course. After a few moments, the owl took off from the spruce, flapped a few times, and then glided to the ground. Just before impact, the owl threw its legs and feet forward and hit the ground feet first. After a second or two, it looked down and seemed to bite something. It then flew off into the trees. As it flew off, I could see the lifeless ground squirrel in the owl's feet.

The second time I saw the owl catch a ground squirrel, the owl was perched on a branch of one of the cottonwoods that line the north side of the creek. At one point, the owl saw a ground squirrel and took off gliding low towards its intended target. Just before the moment of impact, the owl threw its legs and feet forward and hit the squirrel and the ground at the same time. After a few moments, the owl bit the squirrel and flew off.

Northern pocket gophers are a staple of the diet of Great Horned Owls in and around Rocky Mountain National Park.

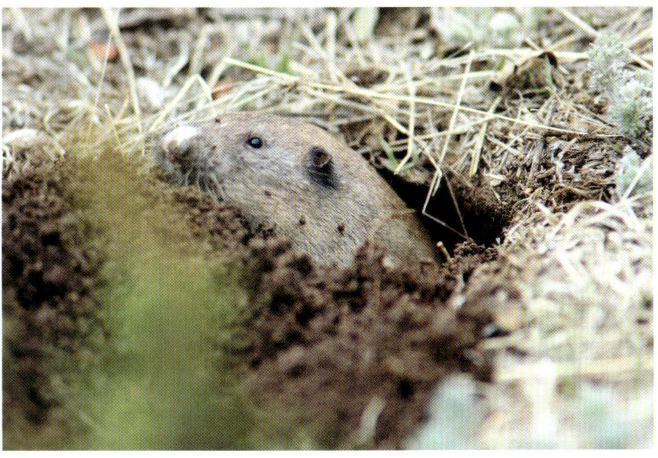

Snakes, including rattlers, are occasionally taken by Great Horned Owls.

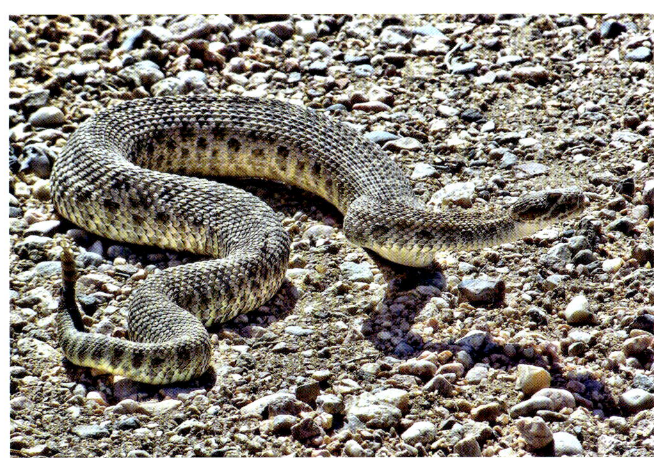

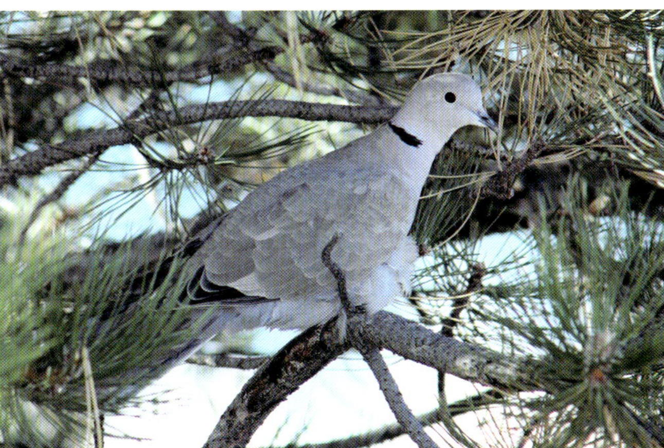

Where plentiful, Eurasian collared doves are frequently consumed by Great Horned Owls.

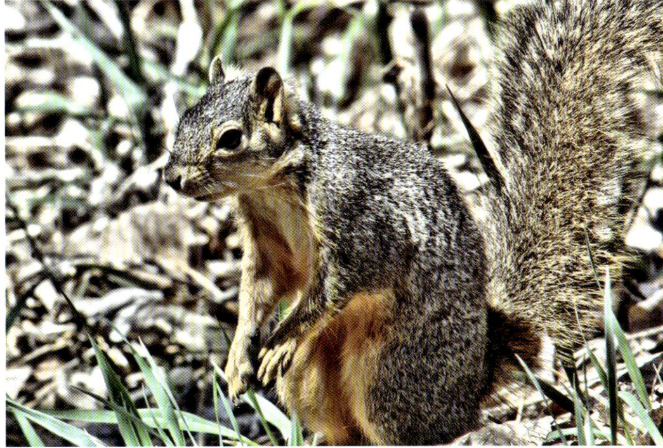

Great Horned Owls frequently take both ground and tree squirrels like this fox squirrel.

Vaughn (1954) watched a Great Horned Owl foraging during the day and on one occasion found an owl pellet with the skull of a Chuckwalla (*Sauromalus obesus*) — a large lizard — in the pellet. This species of lizard is only active during the hottest part of the day, which means that the owl most likely captured it during the day.

In and around RMNP, we have lots of ground squirrels and fewer rats than other areas of the Great Horned Owl's range. However, in some parts of the species' range they seem to prefer rats. To illustrate this, O.E. Niles writes in Bent (1938): "In the nest where he captured the young owls he noticed several full-grown Norway rats, with their skulls opened and their brains removed. On descending to the ground he also noticed the bodies of many rats around the tree, and out of curiosity counted them, and found the bodies of 113 rats, most of them full grown. Looking at the decayed appearance suggested that the rats were all captured within the previous week to ten days." This, to me, is quite exciting, because it shows that the amount of prey the Great Horned Owls are delivering to the nest is due to the abundance of prey available, not the number of mouths they are feeding.

The Great Horned Owl is not above eating other birds of prey when the situation arises. Many researchers believe the Great Horned Owl and the Red-tailed Hawk are complementary species, each hunting the same areas for similar prey, but one during the day and the other after dark (Austing and Holt 1966). As one might expect, with these two species nesting, often in close proximity, there are going to be times when they meet — with one or the other getting "the short end of the stick." Bent (1938) writes: "In the middle of a bright day in April, while we were hunting for nests of the Red-tailed Hawks in the woods of Plymouth County, Mass., we saw a pair of Red-tailed Hawks sailing above over a large tract of pitch pine timber, half a mile or so in the distance. Half an hour or so had elapsed before we began a systematically search for the nest, when only one of the hawks were seen circling back and forth over the woods and evidentially looking for something. We had not gone far into the pines before we saw a Great Horned Owl fly from a small pitch pine; on closer inspection, we saw apparently the owl's feeding roost, as there were feathers and droppings on the ground beneath. I climbed up to investigate it and was surprised to find the wing of an adult

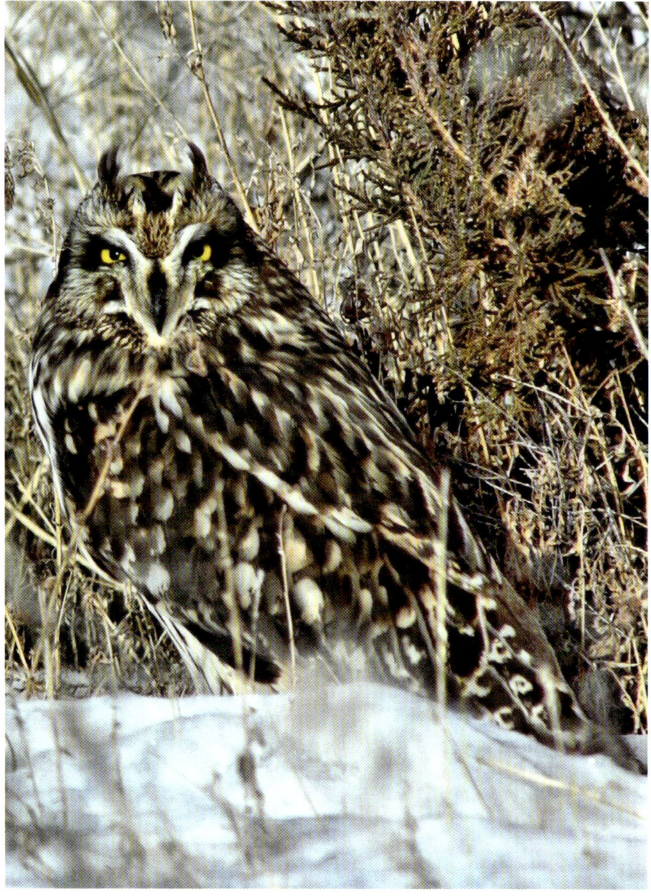

Short-eared Owls and other birds of prey are often eaten by Great Horned Owls.

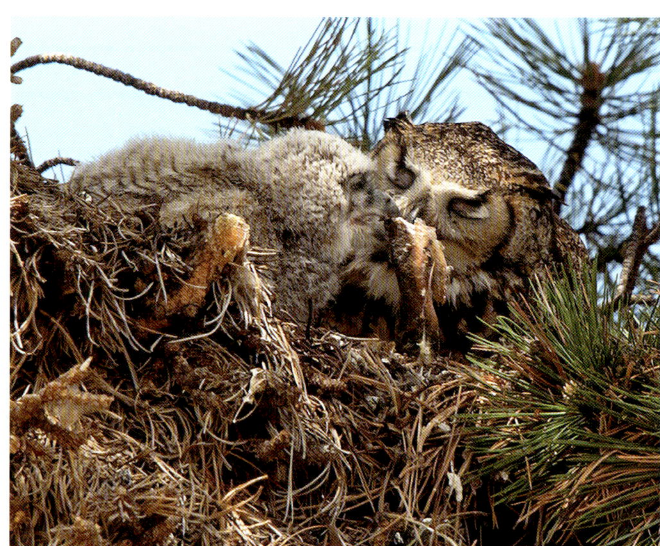

Fish are one of the more unusual items that Great Horned Owls feed upon. *Photo © Gene Putney.*

Rabbits are the favorite prey of Great Horned Owls. *Photo © Wayne Johnston.*

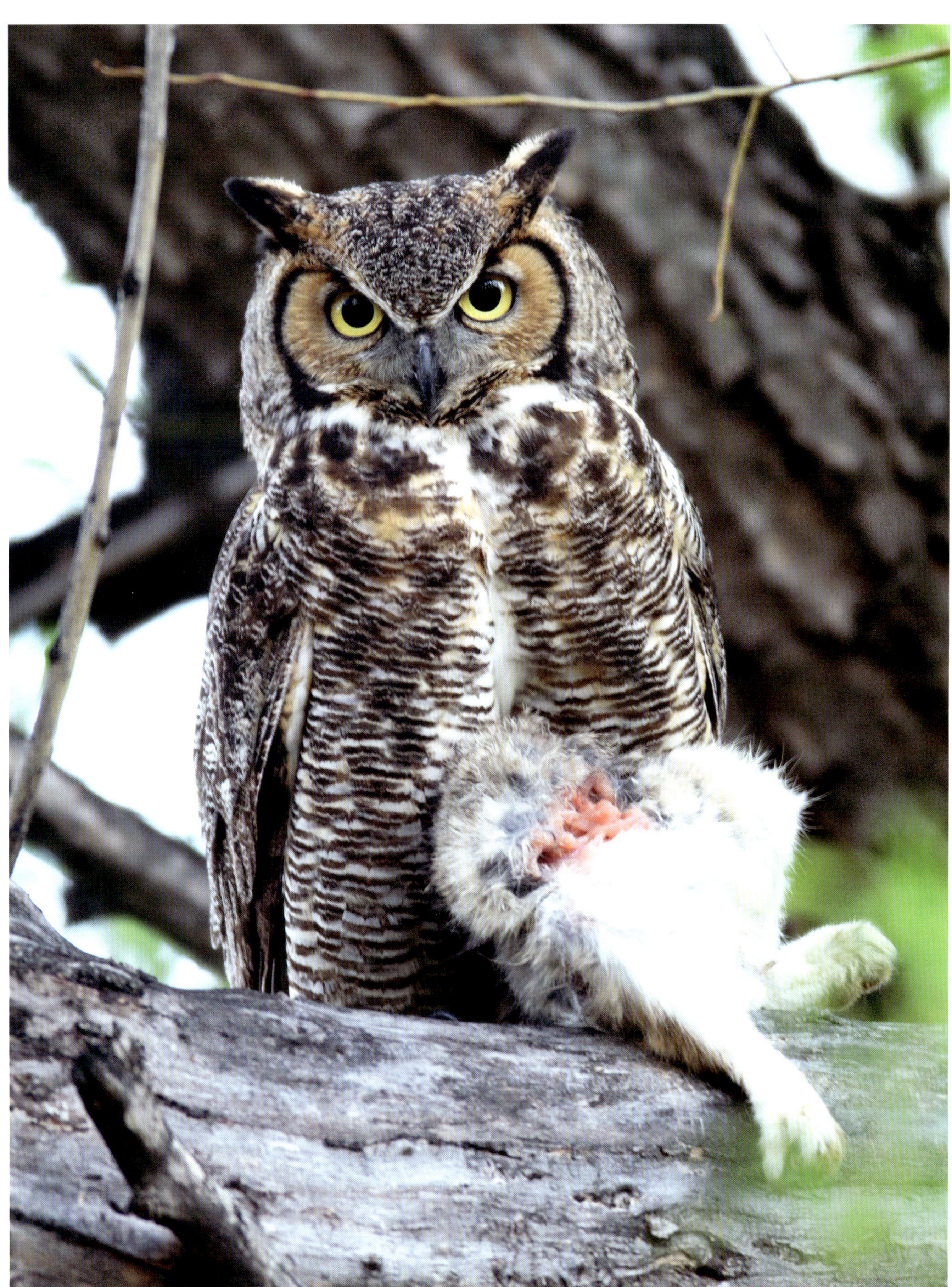

Red-tailed Hawk, which had recently been torn from the body of the victim; the flesh was still warm and fresh." In 1928, Arthur H. Norton found Red-tailed Hawk remains in a Great Horned Owl nest in Maine as well (Bent 1938).

I know that there are several accounts of Great Horned Owls feeding upon other raptors, but actually witnessing the end result is another thing entirely. Dr. Ronald Ryder and I went to the Meadow Springs Ranch in Northern Colorado on the morning of June 15, 1998, to band Ferruginous Hawk nestlings. This part of the country is very open, rolling hills, just a few trees scattered throughout. It is a perfect place for these grassland hawks to nest, and in fact, may be the only place for them to nest outside of the birds nesting on the ground.

We had a pretty good morning banding nestling Swainson's and Ferruginous Hawks — until we arrived at a particular Ferruginous Hawk nest. There were two large cottonwoods in the center of the seemingly endless meadow, both of which had large nests in them, presumably made by the hawks. Apparently, the adult birds would trade off using one of the two nests in different years.

A few weeks prior, on May 27th, we arrived at the Ferruginous Hawk nest to find a brooding female hawk. The second nest had an adult Great Horned Owl, presumably a female, with two approximately two-week-old owlets. I climbed to that nest as the female flew off. After taking a few photos, I placed the two owlets in a large canvas bag and lowered them to the ground, where Ron banded them. After that, I placed them back into their nest. We left the area with the intent to return in a few weeks to band the young hawks. We returned to the hawk nest two weeks later to find an adult Great Horned Owl perched on the hawk nest with hawk feathers strewn about the nest and ground beneath. The owl had apparently killed the adult female hawk and the nestlings and either ate them herself or fed them to her owlets.

Craighead and Craighead (1969) found two nests of Red-shouldered Hawks and one of the Red-tailed Hawk that were destroyed by Great Horned Owls. They found two young Red-shouldered Hawks killed and partially eaten on their nest, with several owl feathers on the nest.

Rohner and Doyle (1992) found a Northern Goshawk dead beneath one of the nests that they had been studying. On June 25, 1991, they found several breast feathers and the left wing of an adult goshawk, along with four Great Horned Owl feathers, 6-1/2 feet (2m) from the base of the nest tree. They also found the right wing and several more breast feathers under a log about 40 feet (12m) from the nest. By measuring the length of the wings, they determined the hawk to be a female.

In early January 1947, Guillion (1947) found the remains of a Cooper's Hawk in a pellet of a Great Horned Owl. He also found what he believed to be the remains of a dead Northern Harrier, whose deaths were attributed to a Great Horned Owl as well.

The Great Horned Owl are often found nesting near other species of owls, including the Short-eared Owl, but due to the nocturnal activity period of the two species, any interaction is seldom witnessed. On July 14, 1978, Bluhm and Ward (1979), while driving along the north shore road of the Delta Marsh in Manitoba, Canada, saw a Great Horned Owl perched on top of a freshly-killed, adult Short-eared Owl. Due to the plumage of the Great Horned Owl, they determined it to be a juvenile. Bruce Wolhuter (1968) also found that a Great Horned Owl had killed and fed upon a Short-eared Owl. In his case, he found the "posterior half" of the smaller owl in a nest of the larger one.

Over the years, I've located prey from several nests in and around northern Colorado. The owls that live in and around RMNP have fed upon muskrat, Wyoming ground squirrel, mountain cottontail rabbit, snowshoe hare, red squirrel, Abert's squirrel, northern pocket gopher, domestic house cats, and skunks. The bird remains I've found in and around Great Horned Owl nests include parts of the American Robin, Brown-headed Cowbird, Northern Flicker, Steller's Jay, Black-billed Magpie, Rock Pigeon, White-faced Ibis, Mallard, Canada Goose, Barred Rock Chicken, and European Starling. I've also found bones and scales of fish. In the foothills of northern Colorado, the Great Horned Owls that I've monitored fed on Ring-necked Pheasant, Northern Flicker, Rock Pigeon, Eurasian Collared Dove, Mourning Dove, American Robin, Blue Jay, Common Grackle, Northern Flicker, and the previously mentioned Ferruginous Hawk. The animals include skunk, fox squirrel, mountain and prairie cottontail, and prairie dog.

Great Horned Owls killing and eating squirrels is well documented (Seidensticker 1968, Hamerstrom and Mattson 1939, Errington 1932), however the owls attacking the squirrel nest is a bit less documented. "At 10:30 in the morning on 19 November 1983, Mr. Packard observed a Great Horned Owl circling slowly above the trees of the University of Kansas Natural History Reservation. Suddenly the bird glided downward at approximately a forty-five degree angle toward a yellow oak. When the owl was within about 10 feet (3.05m) of the upper branches, it extended its feet and legs and then struck a squirrel leaf-nest in a periphery of the tree. A fox squirrel emerged, climbed down the supporting branch to the trunk of the tree and crouched there facing the nest." The owl was unsuccessful obtaining a squirrel meal that day.

The extensive list of animals taken by Great Horned Owls, according to Bent (1938), include hares and rabbits or various species, gray, red, and fox squirrels, chipmunks, various rats and mice, voles, muskrats, ground squirrels, pocket gophers, minks, weasels, large and small skunks,

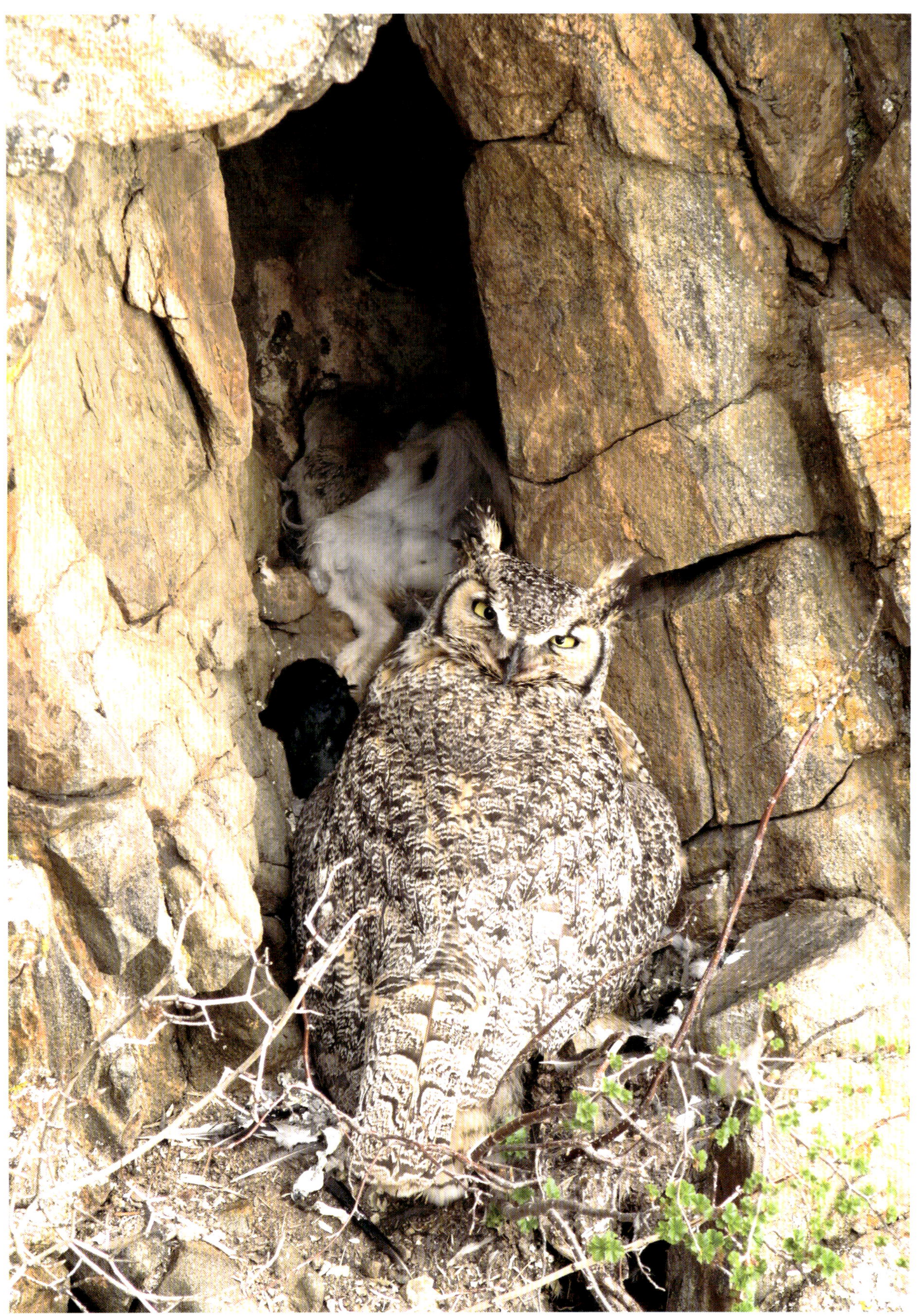

A Great Horned Owl nest on a cliff in Estes Park. Behind the owl are the remains of an American Crow, a Snowshoe hare, and a Northern pocket gopher.

prairie dogs, woodchucks, opossums, porcupines, domestic cats, shrews and bats.

The list of birds the Great Horned Owls have fed upon is much more extensive and, according to Bent (1938), includes grebes, several species of ducks, Canada Goose, tame ducks and swans, herons including Great Blue Herons, American Coot, Purple Gallinule, king and Virginia Rail, Red Phalarope, Wilson's Snipe, Greater and Lesser Yellowlegs, Woodcock, various quail and grouse, pheasants, domestic poultry (including turkeys, hens, Guinea fowl, and pigeons), Mourning Dove, marsh, Cooper's, Red-tailed, and Red-shouldered Hawks, Barn, Barred, Long-eared, and Screech owls, Northern Flicker, sapsuckers and other woodpeckers, jays, crow, starling, blackbirds, meadowlark, Snow Bunting, juncos, and other sparrows, mockingbird, and various thrush species.

Other avian species on the menu of the Great Horned Owl include Cave Swallow (West 1987), Killdeer (Knight and Jackman 1984), Double-crested Cormorant, Common Eider, Herring Gull (Morse 1971), California Gull (Aigner et al 1994), Common Nighthawk, Whip-poor-will, Sharp-shinned Hawk, Northern Saw-whet Owl, Boreal Owl, warblers, vireos, kinglets, wrens, creeper, nuthatches, titmice, Horned Larks, Black Tern, Foresters Tern, Bonaparte's Gull (Errington et al 1940), Common Raven (Fortman pers.com) and Leach's Storm Petrel (French 1979), and Harris's Sparrow, Purple Martin, and American Woodcock (Olmstead 1950).

Due to these large owls being such excellent hunters and providers for their families, they often catch much more food than either they or their young can consume. During the nesting season, the male most often just keeps bringing food to the nest and piling it on.

Outside of the nesting season, the owls will still store excess food. They will store the food in the coolest place they can find to keep the food as fresh as possible. At the Birds of Prey Foundation, there is a large log in the middle of the flight cage. The owls often store partially consumed rabbits under this log—out of the sun—since under the log is a little cooler than anywhere else in the cage. Not only have there been partially eaten rabbits under the log, but the fur was folded over the meat to keep it as fresh as possible. When I first saw that, I asked if the employees did that for the birds and, of course, they hadn't. To me, that shows the intelligence of the owls.

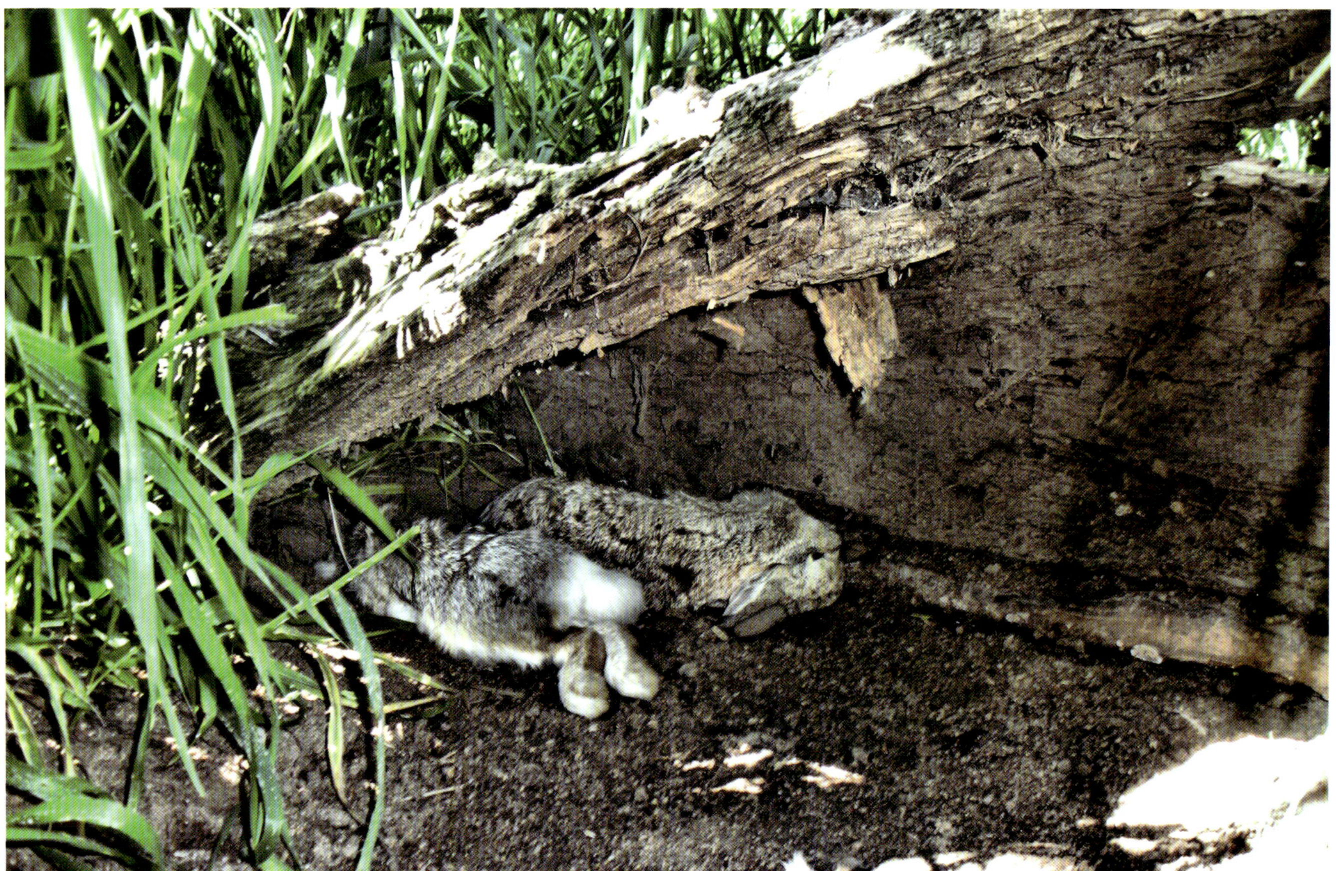

When owls, including Great Horned Owls, have excess food, they often store it in a cool place to keep it fresh.

CASTING PELLETS

One good way to identify what a bird of prey has fed upon is to dissect its pellets. Pellets are indigestible portions of the item that the owl has consumed. These indigestible portions consist of bones, fur, feathers, hair, and, to a lesser extent, scales of the prey that the raptor had fed upon. After the owl has swallowed their prey, the sphincter between its proventriculus (glandular stomach, and ventriculus (the gizzard)) closes. The prey remains are then compressed into the smaller space in the ventriculus within two to three hours, with the maximum compression completed after about ten hours. The pellets are then ejected after about sixteen hours (Houston et al 1998). The pellets of Great Horned Owls are often rather large, with some being as large as 4 to 6 inches long (10-15cm) and an inch (2.5cm) or so wide.

Discerning owl pellets from hawk pellets is quite easy. Owl pellets are comprised of both fur/feathers and bones, while hawk, eagle, and falcon pellets have few, if any, bones in them. Owl pellets are often found under the owl's favorite perch. Furthermore, when defecating, owls drop their feces strait below them, whereas hawks and eagles shoot their feces out behind them.

Reed (1925) found that if an owl needed to cast a pellet, the bird would not eat until the pellet was regurgitated first. Like Mr. Reed, I've noticed this as well, but I saw it with Northern Pygmy-Owls, not Great Horned Owls. The situation is as follows: On the morning of June 8, 2012, while I was watching an adult female Northern Pygmy-Owl near her nest, her mate brought her a chipmunk. She took the chipmunk from him and flew off, landing on a pine

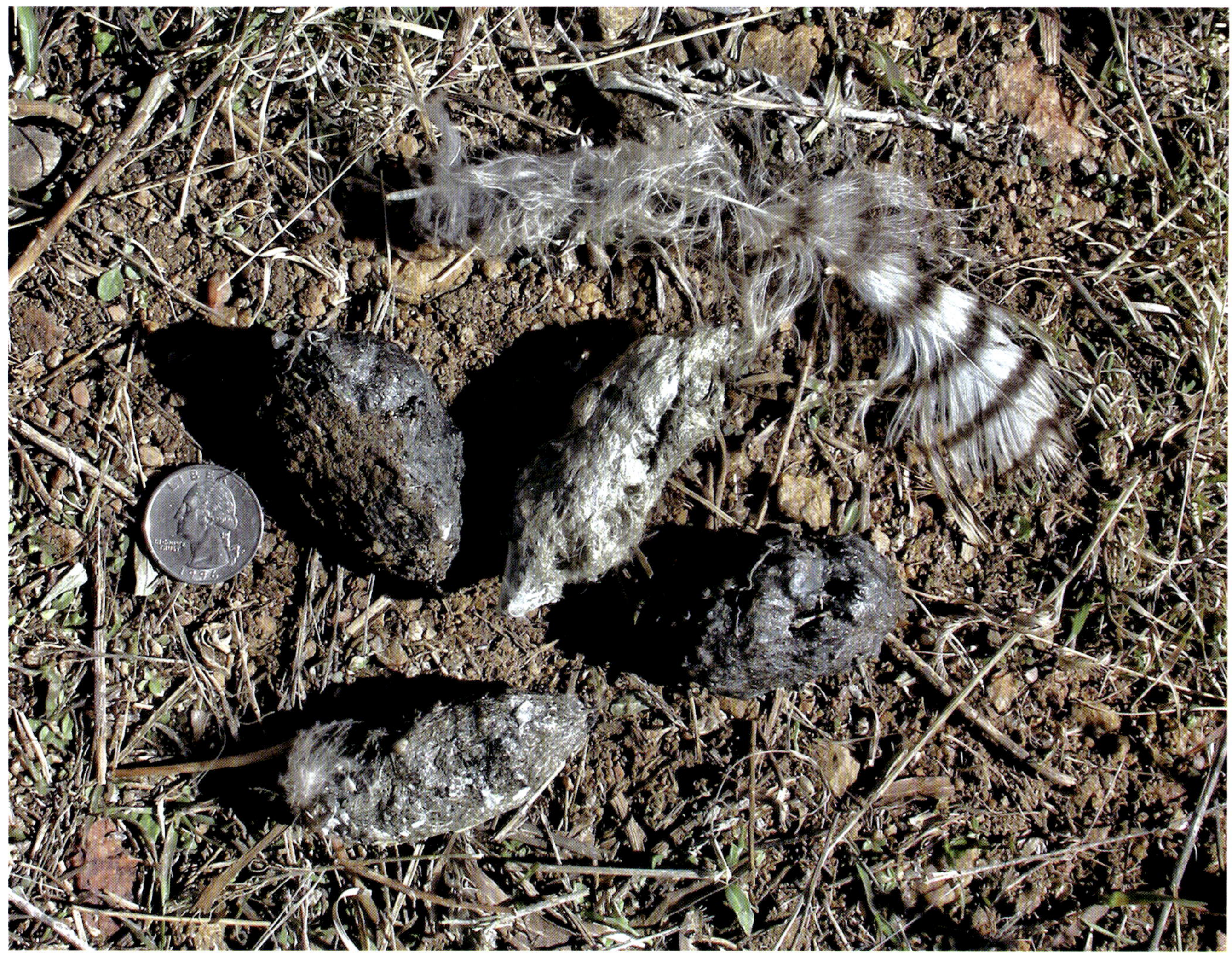

Great Horned Owl pellets with a quarter for size comparison.

a few yards from her nest cavity. She looked round for a few minutes and then, with what appeared to be a bit of difficulty, coughed up a pellet. A short while later, she began eating the head of the animal, after which she took the uneaten portion to her nestlings.

The owls often regurgitate a pellet before leaving their day-roost to hunt for the evening. The pellets of wild owls are often gray or brown. Captive Great Horned Owls being fed white rats produce white pellets. Sometime after the owl has consumed a meal, a pellet of indigestible portions of the prey is formed by muscular contraction in the bird's gizzard (muscular stomach). The pellet passes from the gizzard into the glandular stomach (proventriculus), where it remains until the bird gets stimulated to regurgitate it. This stimulus is most often more food. The bird then needs to eject the pellet to make room for the item it is about to consume (Terres 1982).

A dissected Great Horned Owl pellet. Owl pellets have bones in them.

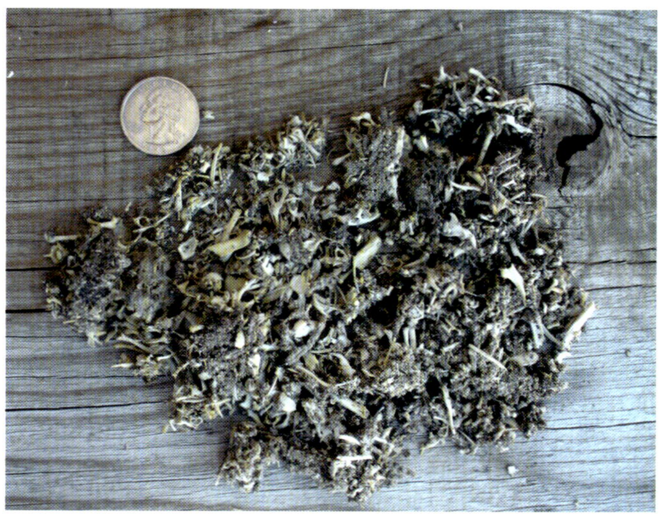

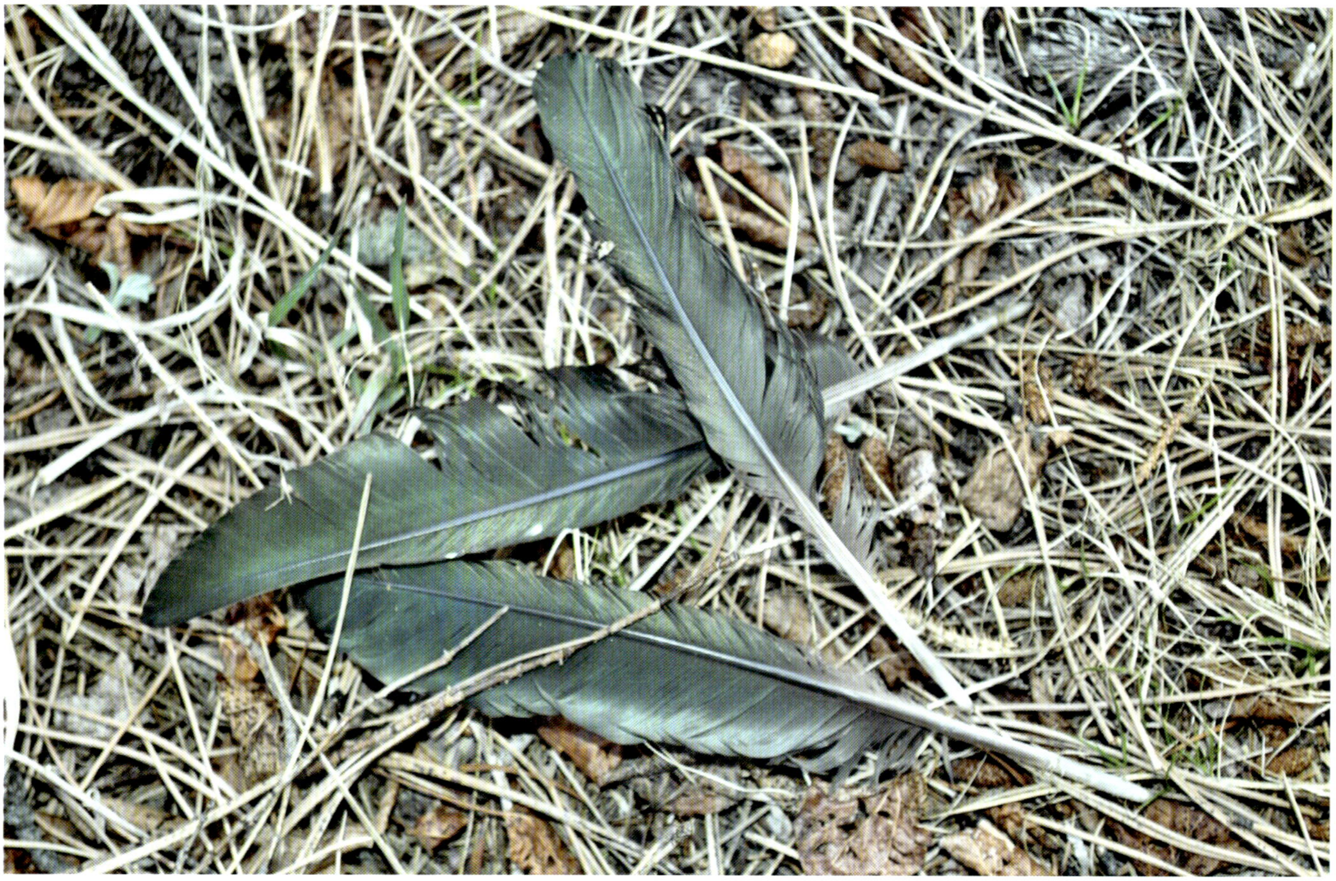

Feathers from a White-faced Ibis that a Great Horned Owl preyed upon at the YMCA south of Estes Park.

Chapter 6

MONITORING NESTING / GROWTH OF THE YOUNG

Monitoring the activities of a nesting Great Horned Owl is a bit more difficult than monitoring the nest of a diurnal raptor, such as a Red-tailed Hawk or Northern Goshawk. This is because Great Horned Owls do very little during most days. Throughout most of the nesting season, especially during incubation and when the chicks are young, the adult female broods the owlets and moves very little. When brooding the young, the female owl lies with the owlets between her legs, yet under her breast feathers. This keeps the young warm and dry. When watching the female, you will often see her feathers move under her. This is her owlets moving about, possibly trying to find a comfortable area.

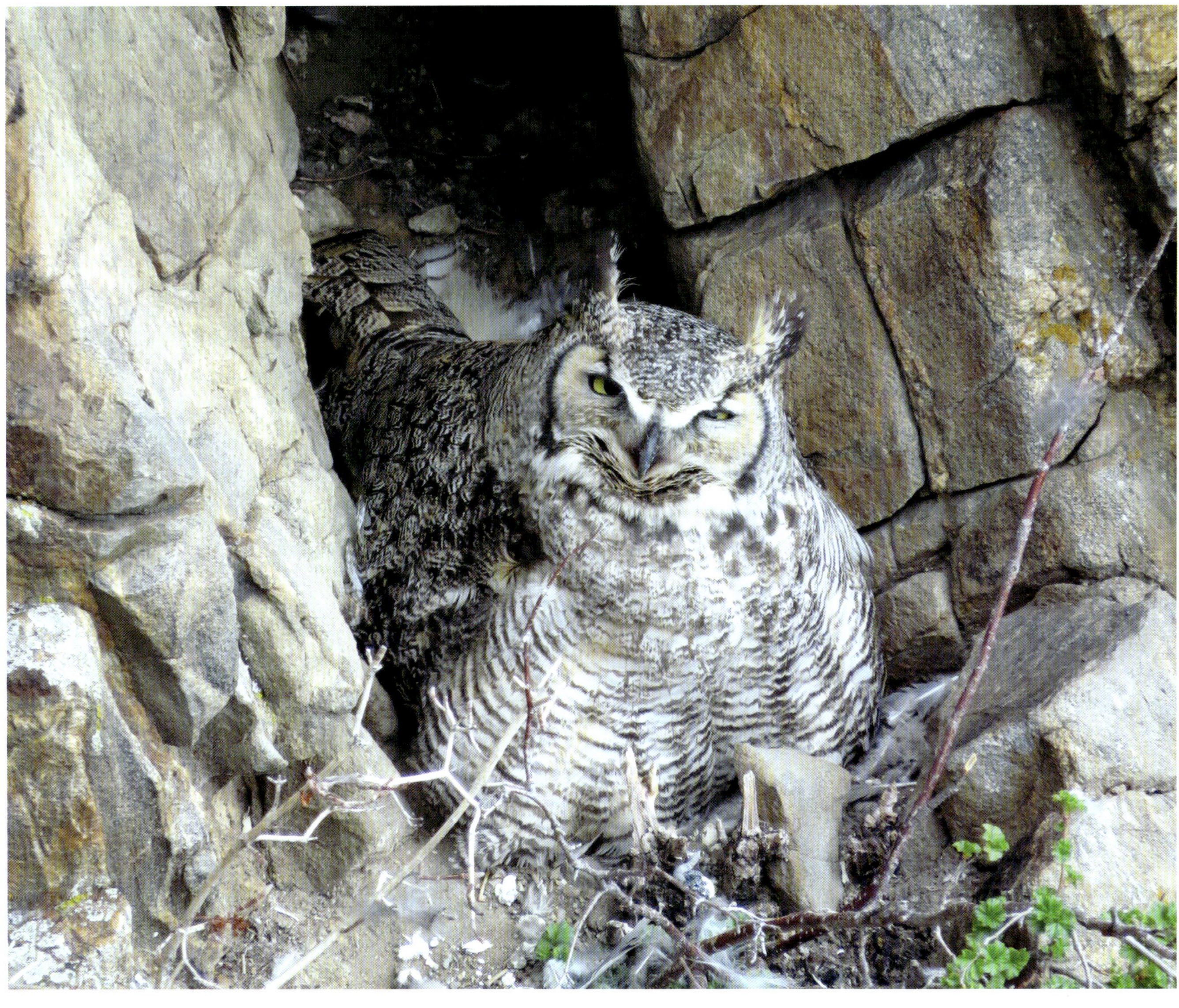

A female Great Horned Owl brooding very young owlets.

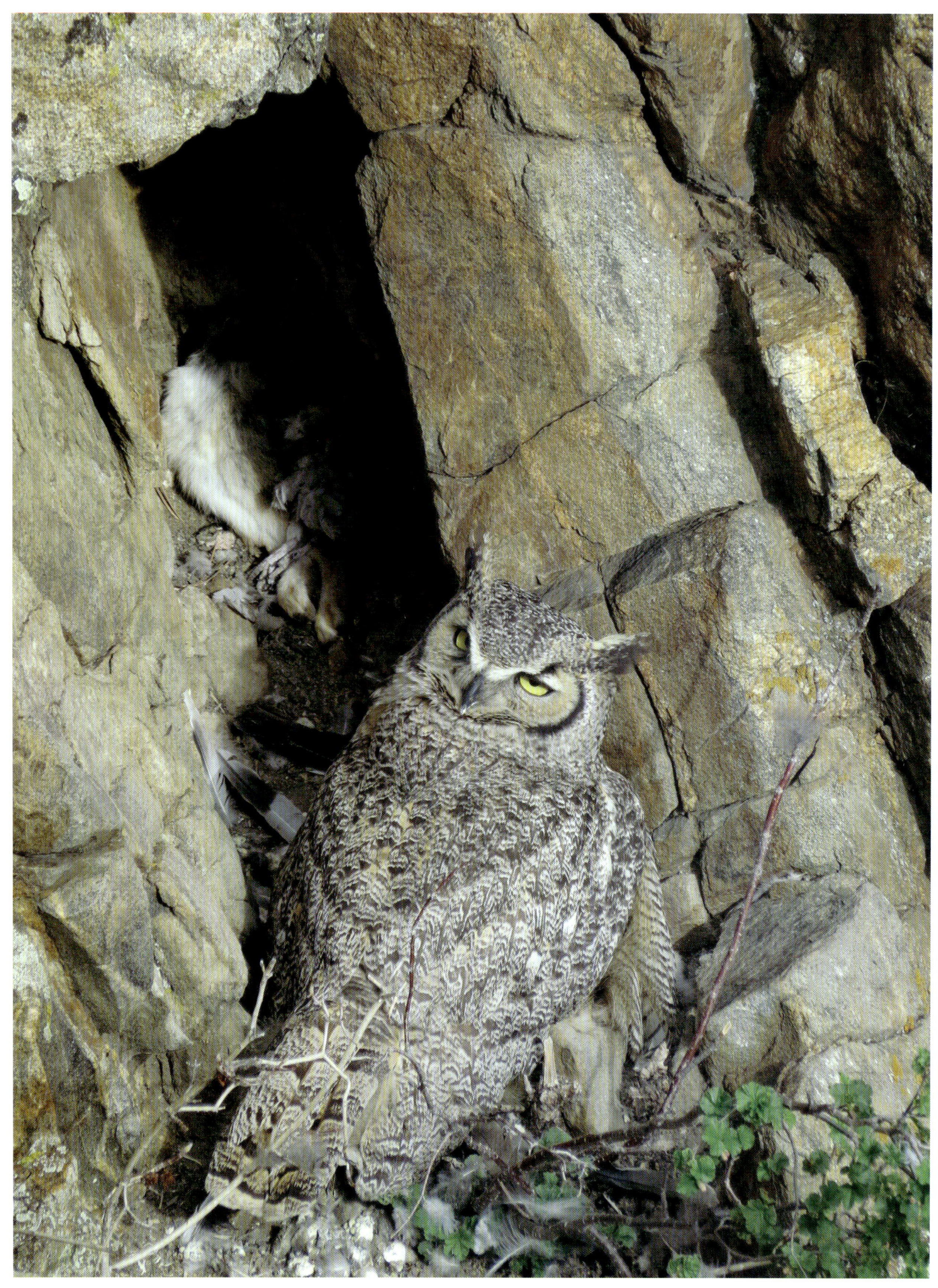

That same female on her nest with the remains of a domestic chicken, an American Crow, a rabbit and a Eurasian collared dove behind her.

After dark, but on occasion during the day, the male will deliver food to the female. As he approaches the nest, he will hoot and the female will respond. In my opinion, this is the way the male lets his mate know he is coming near the nest. I presume that if he arrives unannounced, he may be killed and eaten by his larger mate by accident. Dr. Ron Ryder told me of a female Great Horned Owl that was seen feeding an adult Great Horned Owl to her nestlings; he presumed the nestlings were fed their father.

Fredrick Baumgartner (1938) spent an evening watching a Great Horned Owl nest. He tells of both the male and female owls incubating the eggs early in the nesting stage. "The female came in at 11:45 p.m., when I heard hoots and twittering notes like those a young owl makes when being fed. The female had come to the nest carrying part of some mammal, and apparently her mate was begging for food. She shared the kill with him and flew off again." Yet, later in the incubation process and closer to the hatching date, the female incubates and remains on the eggs until they hatch. "At a later stage in the incubation period the schedule of the two birds seems to have been different. Then the female was on the nest all night with the exception of a short period toward morning."

Baumgartner also explains how the male of a mated pair of owls came to the nest one morning to lure harassing crows from the incubating female. "On several mornings I noted that the male bird usually flew in close and hooted a few times shortly after sunrise. This invariably aroused the crows and when they besieged him he flew off to a hemlock tree a few hundred feet deeper in the woods. One morning after the owl had flown into the conifer to roost, the crows began to harass his mate on the nest. Finally she uttered a few low hoots and immediately her mate appeared, alighting on a branch close to the nest. The crows at once shifted their attention to his more conspicuous enemy. After a short period of ducking and dodging, this owl flew into the top of an adjacent tree in an even more conspicuous spot. Gradually he led them off through the woods by short flights and the incubating bird settled down on the nest again free of her tormentors."

A female owl resting during the day with a downy white owlet next to her.

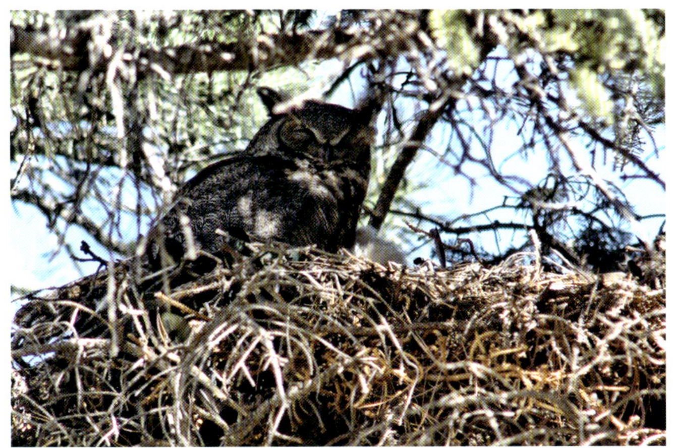

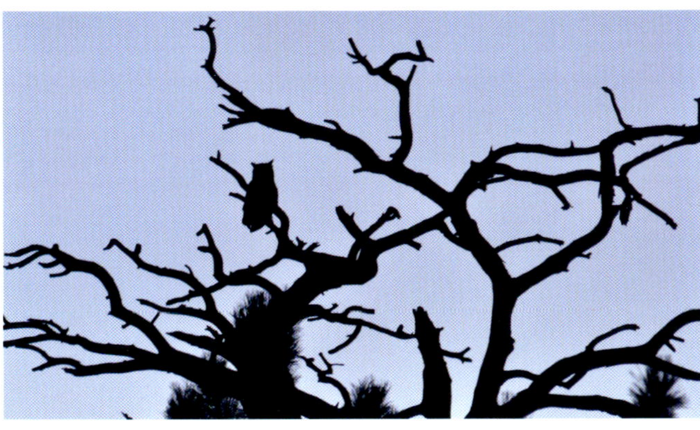

At dawn, Great Horned Owls can be seen silhouetted against the early morning light.

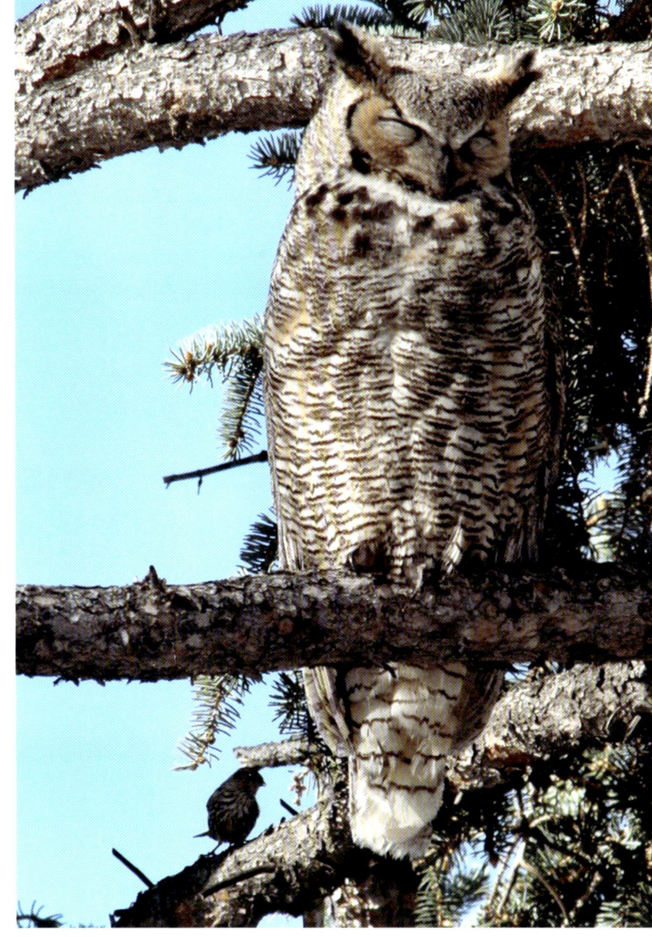

A male Great Horned Owl being harassed by a House Finch. However, the owl doesn't appear to care.

GROWING BOYS AND GIRLS

When the young first hatch, they are blind, helpless, and completely dependent on their mother for warmth and protection. At this stage, the female will add her own saliva to the small bits of food that she feeds the young. This additional saliva aids in the young owl's digestion (Kay Mckeever, pers. com). When feeding her young, the female sits up in the nest with the young owls between her legs. As she stands up, the owlets lift their heads, placing the backs of their necks against the belly of their mother. The adult female tears small bits of food from the carcass of what the male has brought to her and leans down, giving small bits of food to the closest owlet. As that owlet eats its full, the next in line gets to eat and so on, until all owlets are fed to their content.

Bent (1938) raised a couple of young owls and describes their growth: When the owlets are two days old, they are a little larger than a newly-hatched chicken, covered with white down and eyes closed. They are able to hold their heads up and make soft peeping sounds. At about two weeks of age, the owlets are about one-third grown; the owl's first coat of white down is replaced by a coat of dirty, buff-colored down feathers. Their eyes are open at this age and the irises are a pale yellowish-hazel. At twenty days of age, the iris of the young owls begin getting brighter yellow and clearer from day to day. The ear tufts appear when the owlets are about twenty to twenty-five days of age. At a month old, the owlets have a heavy coat of fluffy down; their eyes are light yellow and their primary flight feathers are partially out of their sheaths.

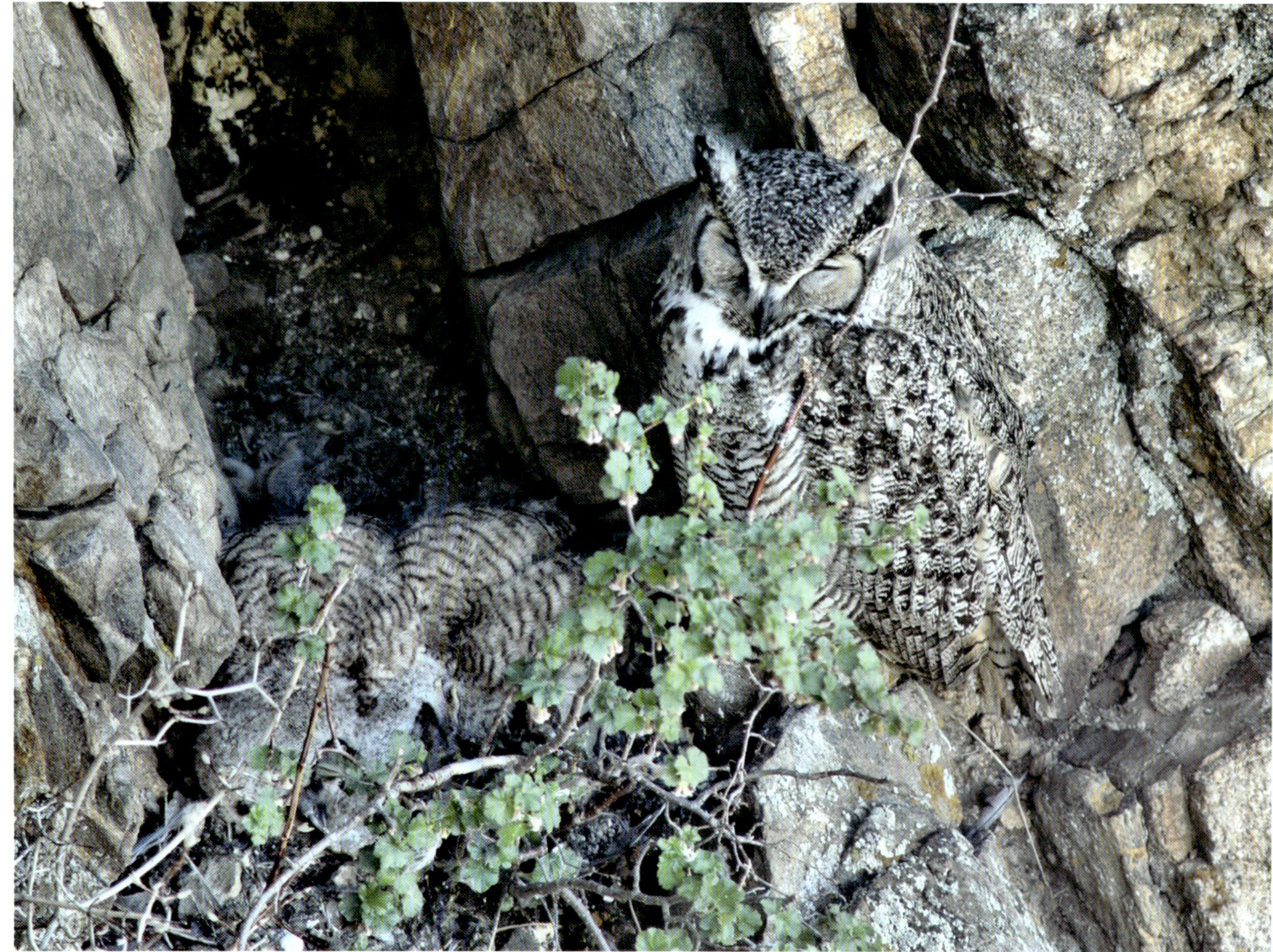

When approaching nesting owls quietly, you can sometimes catch the owls napping.

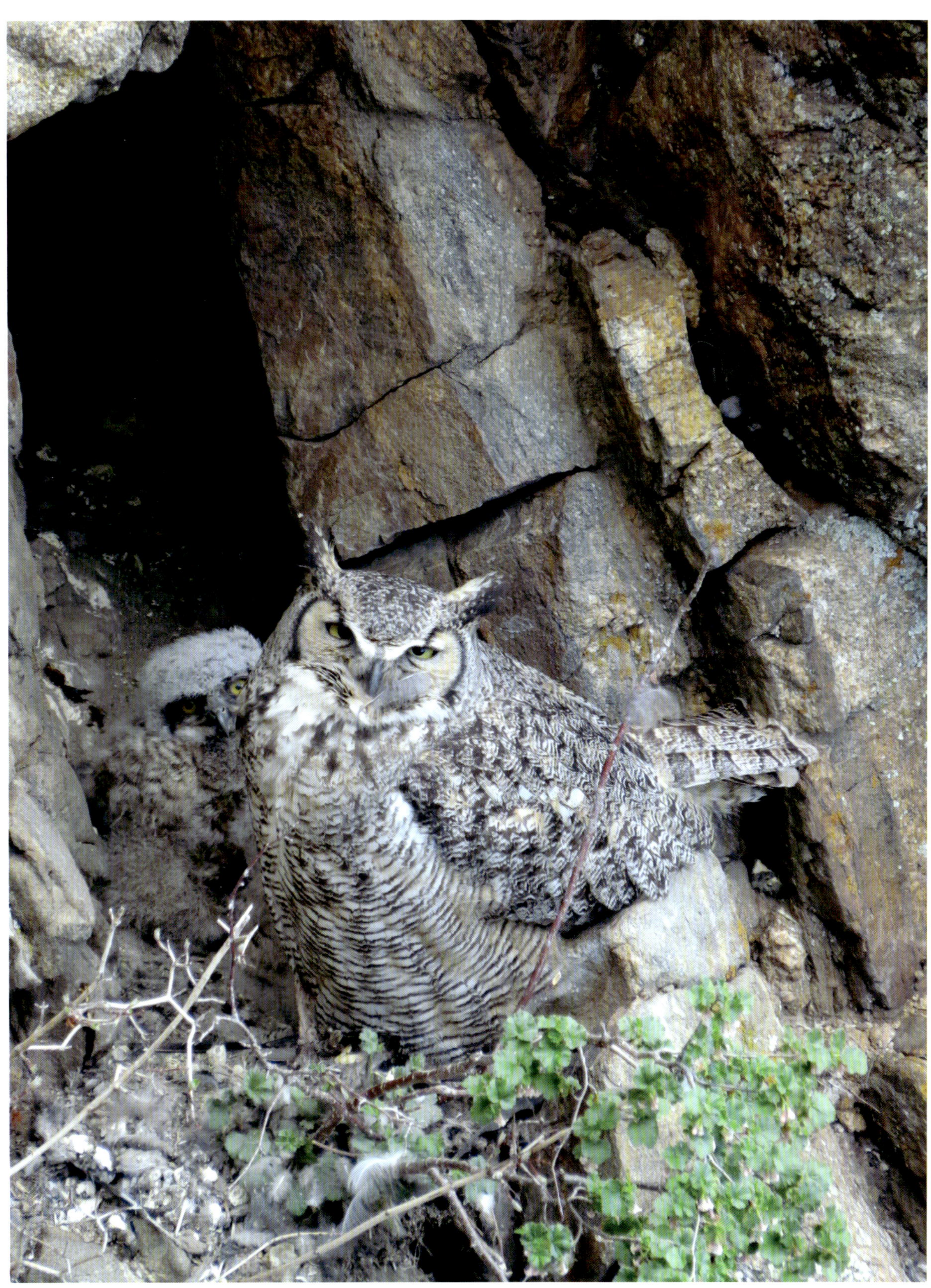

A female owl is at her nest with her three-week-old owlet.

Five weeks after hatching, the owlets are about 12 inches (30.5cm) high and often become quite defiant, hissing and bristling, snapping their bills and threatening to attack when approached. Their ear tufts stand about a 1/2-inch (13mm) high. At this stage, their wings are still undeveloped and their tail is just beginning to burst from the sheaths. Depending on the size and structure of their nest, some individuals will fledge their nest at this age. However, with the majority of the nests that I have monitored, the young fledge from between six and ten weeks of age, depending on the size of the nest and how much room they have when on it. One nest that I monitored in Fort Collins, Colorado, was in a broken limb of a cottonwood. The young from that nest fledged at about ten weeks of age. This was due, I believe, to the placement of the nest, which did not allow the owlets to walk from the nest to an adjacent branch. Therefore, in order for those particular owlets to fledge, they needed to have flight feathers that were developed enough to allow the owlets to make the estimated 100-foot (30.4m) flight to the nearest tree. In 2010 and 2011, the adult female owl would perch away from the nest as the owlets were about five weeks and older; she was always in view of the owlets though. At week nine, she would sit in the nest with the owlets, making it uncomfortable for the little ones to remain happily in the nest. It was as if she was trying to force them to fledge.

It always amazes me how these birds pick nesting sites that enable them to remain camouflaged.

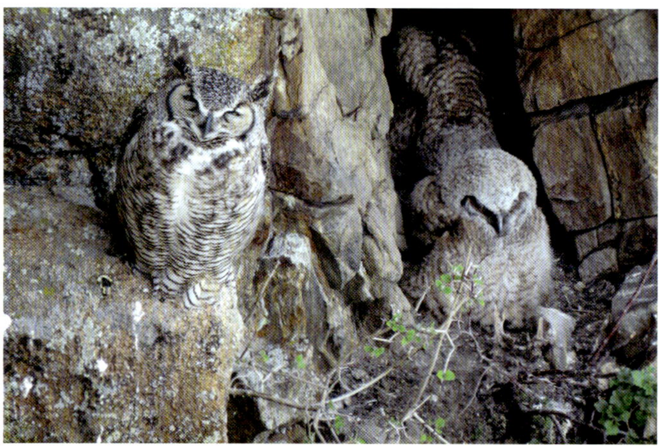

Great Horned Owl nestlings at about nine weeks old.

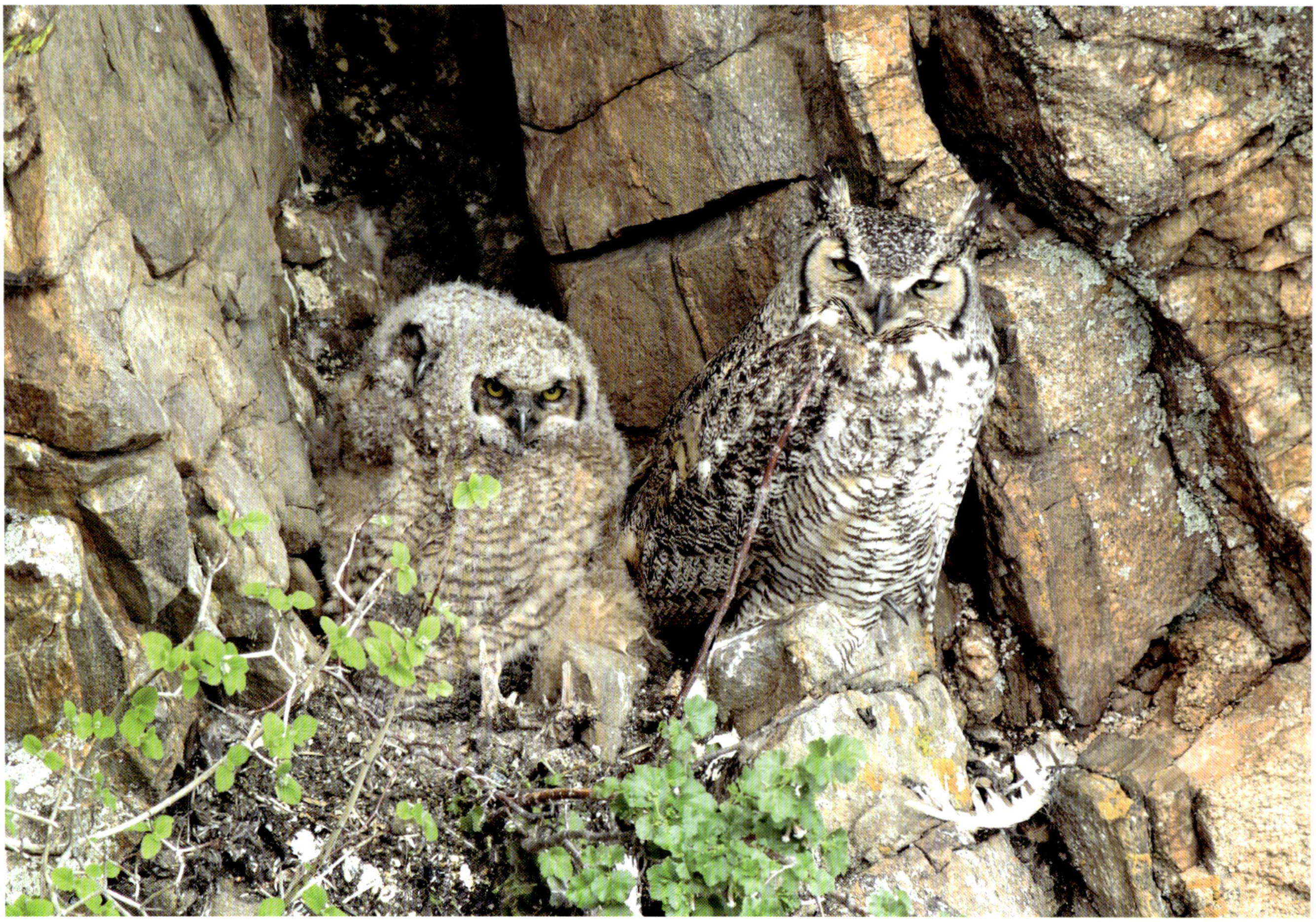

BANDING NESTLINGS

Banding nestling Great Horned owls can be an eye-opening experience when the parent birds decide to defend their young. Many researchers have been brutally attacked by adult Great Horned Owls when trying to climb the nest to band the young. In their book *The World of the Great Horned Owl*, Austing and Holt tell of such adventures. It appears to be a bit more advantageous to bring reinforcements when climbing Great Horned Owl nests to band the young. The more people you have around you, the less likely the female owl will try to attack.

I have climbed a handful of Great Horned Owl nests to band the young and, thankfully, have never been attacked by the adults. My first experience banding a young owl was May 27, 1998. I was assisting Dr. Ron Ryder. We were on the Meadow Springs Ranch in northern Colorado to band nestling Great Horned Owls. There was a nest that he knew of in a low cottonwood tree. In that part of the country, there are few trees, so the owls often use the nests of the large hawks and Golden Eagles that have previously constructed nests. This nest was in one of three well-spaced cottonwoods that were several hundred yards apart. As we got within a few hundred yards of the nest, the female, who was perched on a limb near her two owlets, flew several hundred yards to the nearest tree and landed.

I leaned the ladder against the tree, climbed until I reached a large branch just under the nest, and lifted myself up to the nest's edge — I found two approximately seven-week-old owlets perched on the back side of their nest, one directly behind the other. As soon as the owlets saw me, they began clapping their bills, to

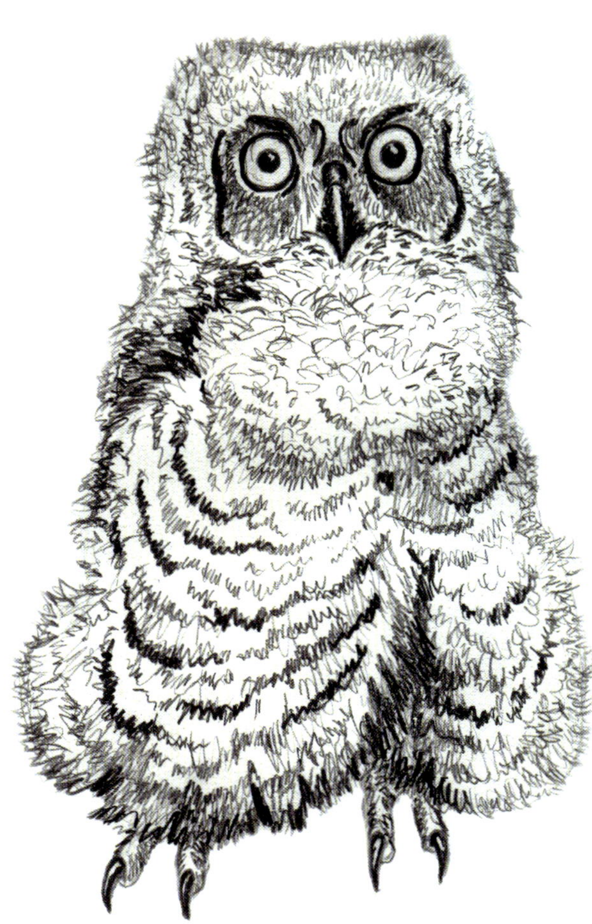

A two-week-old Great Horned Owlet.

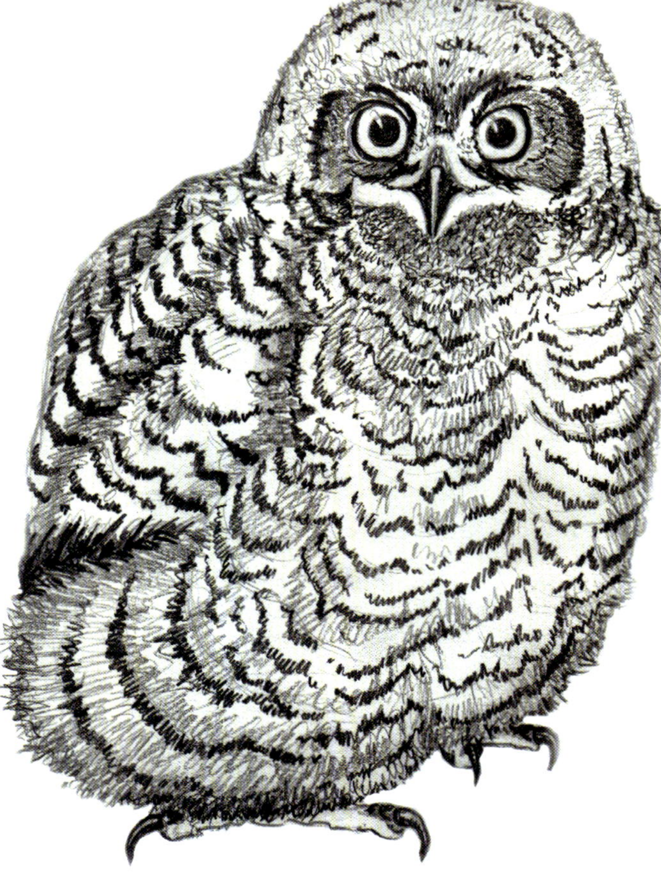

A four-week-old Great Horned Owlet: Note the barring on the owl's belly, breast, and back.

hopefully scare me off. Owls often clap their upper and lower bills together as a way to let you know that they are upset with the situation. When a small owl, such as a Northern Saw-whet Owl, claps its bill together, it sounds like someone snapping his fingers. When a Great Horned Owl claps its bill together, it often sounds like someone clapping his hands.

I reached across the top of the nest and grabbed the first owlet by the legs and placed it into a large canvas bag, and then I grasped the second owlet the same way and placed it in the bag as well. I then lowered the bag to Ron, who was waiting on the bottom of the ladder so the owlets could be banded. Nestling owls are quite harmless. They often just lie in your hands and snap their bill a few times. Luckily for us, at that age, owlets don't have any idea that soon their feet and talons will be effective weapons. Ron banded the first owlet and allowed me to band the second. I then placed the owlets back into the bag and lifted them up the tree and placed them back into their nest. They really didn't seem to care much.

The following year, a pair of owls had chosen to nest in the back of a restaurant, under the eve on a platform between two air-conditioners in Estes Park. I had previously spoken to the restaurant owners and decided the owlets would be banded on May 3rd. I arrived at the restaurant that morning and, after a short greeting, several of us moved to the back of the restaurant to find the female owl perched in a ponderosa pine and four owlets between the two air-conditioners. I placed the ladder against the building and climbed to the owlets. The owlets began clapping their bills, as someone from my group told me the female owl had just landed a few inches from my head. What amazed me was that I never heard the owl coming toward me — I just heard its claws hit the roof as it landed. I leaned back and looked up to see the female owl just a few inches from me. We were face-to-face for a moment before she flew back to the ponderosa.

I placed all four owlets in a large canvas bag and lowered them to the ground. I banded all four owlets as the female watched me intently. After the birds were processed, I returned them to their nest. Before I placed them back onto the platform, I checked the nest for prey remains. I found an uneaten muskrat, along with the remains of mountain cottontails, various blackbirds, American Robins, pigeons, and Black-billed Magpies. I placed the owlets back onto the platform and left. As I mentioned earlier, the following year, the building was sold and turned into a health club; the air-conditioners were removed and the owls moved elsewhere to nest.

That same year, a pair of owls had chosen to nest in a cliff near Mary's Lake, south of Estes Park. Retired veterinarian Dr. Rick Dill told me of this nest and assisted me by holding the ladder as I climbed to the entrance of the nest to find two owlets. As with the other owl nests, this female flew to a nearby ponderosa pine and hooted at us. When I reached the opening in the cliff, the two owlets had moved to the back of the nest and began snapping their bills. I reached in and grabbed the first owlet, placing it in the canvas bag. I then grasped the second owlet, placed it in the bag, and lowered them to Dr. Dill. I checked this nest for prey remains and found remnants of various animals, magpies, pigeons, and even fish bones and scales. After I had banded the owlets, I returned the owlets to their home and left.

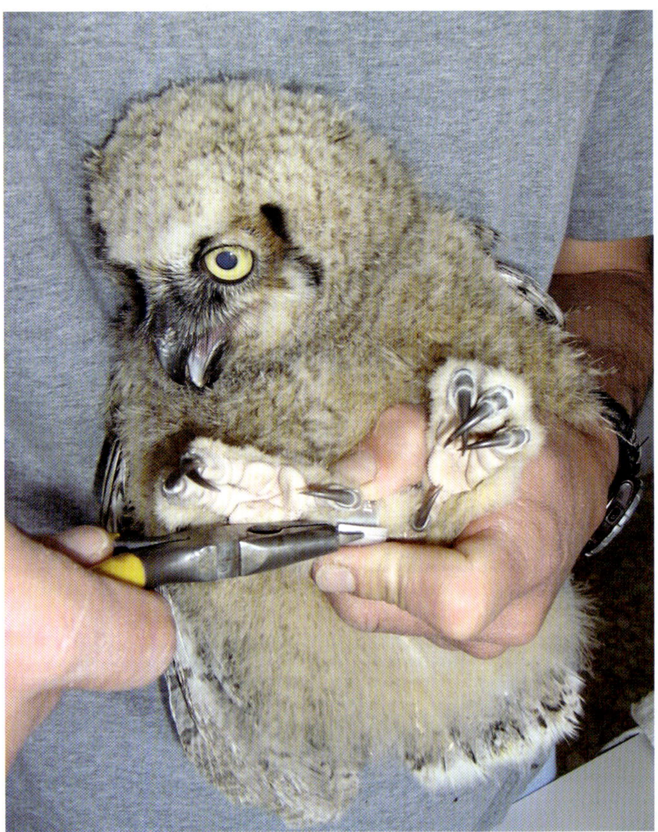

The author banding a young Great Horned Owl. *Photo by Susan Rashid.*

POST FLEDGING

For the first few days after the owlets become mobile, they can often be found perching conspicuously, with two or more owlets leaning against one another or at least perched near each other, and one of their parents perched within view of them. The fledglings readily become tired, as their legs are not yet strong enough for the young birds to perch for extended periods of time. When the young owls become tired, they often lay down on a horizontal branch, resting on their chests. Kay McKeever of the Owl Foundation termed this "sternal recumbency." As the owls become stronger and more mobile, they move farther from their nests and are often found during the day perched besides their mother, high in a large tree. At dusk, the mother will go off to hunt while the young most often move very short distances or just stay where they are, waiting for their parents to bring them something to eat.

Bent (1938) continues describing the owls. At eight weeks, Great Horned Owlets have adequately developed wings and tails, making them capable of short flights. Their body is still covered with down feathers, though. Young owls are often fully capable of flight by twelve weeks of age. Usually by October, in central and northern latitudes, the owlets reach their adult plumage.

A ten-week-old owl in captivity ate fourteen House Sparrows and a quarter-pound of beef kidney in a single feeding. This is a great example of how much these owls can consume. It also illustrates how beneficial these owls can be in the wild by depleting species that are over-populating certain regions.

By their first winter, the young owls are very much like the adults, but their plumage is more rufous throughout and their underwings have a pink cast. Their ear tufts are smaller and their white throat patch is less extensive than in adults. Prior to their tenth month, the owls can and often have some downy feathers around the neck and underparts. Adult birds have a partial molt and, according to Pyle (1997), can be aged to three years (until August of the third year) because they have an incomplete wing molt and only molt a few flight feathers each year. A complete molt would enable an owl to molt all of its flight feathers each year. A Northern Pygmy-Owl is a species with a complete molt.

As one can imagine, the first lesson that any young bird needs to learn is how to choose the proper perch when landing. Most young owls tend to land on the tips of branches or limbs that cannot hold their weight. On occasion, I have seen young owls hanging upside down from a limb that was too weak to hold them. This is most often followed by some aggressive flapping just prior to the owl releasing its grip and flying off a few feet.

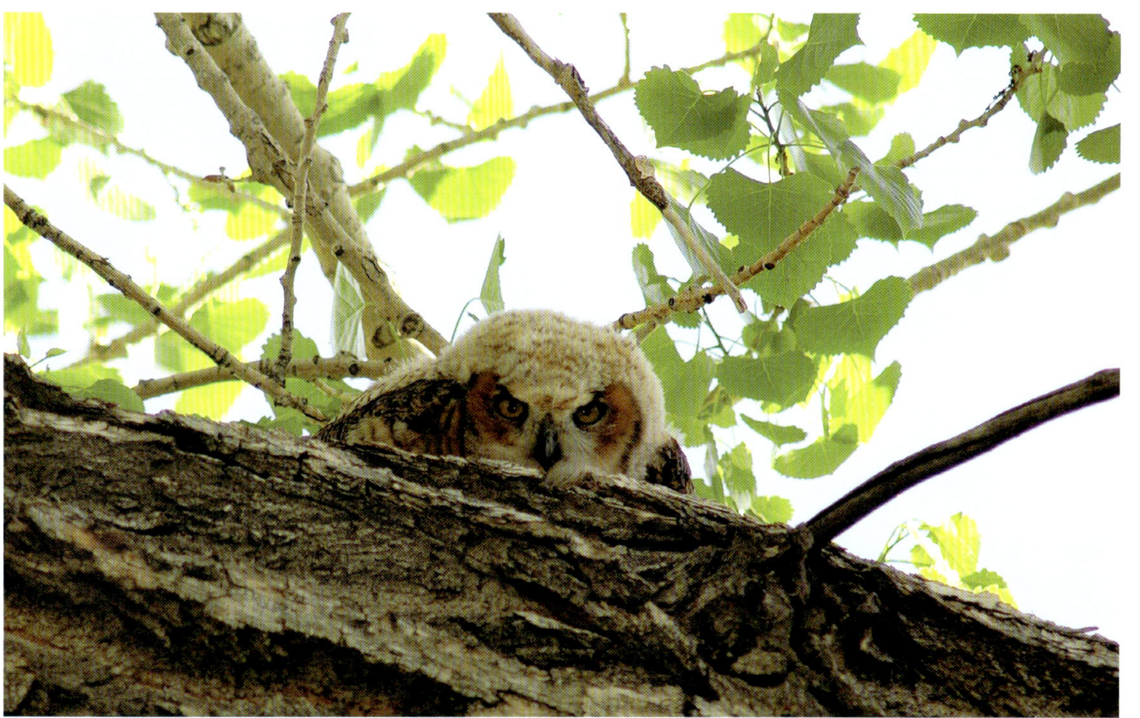

When young owls are tired, they often rest on their sternums, a term known as sternal recumbency.

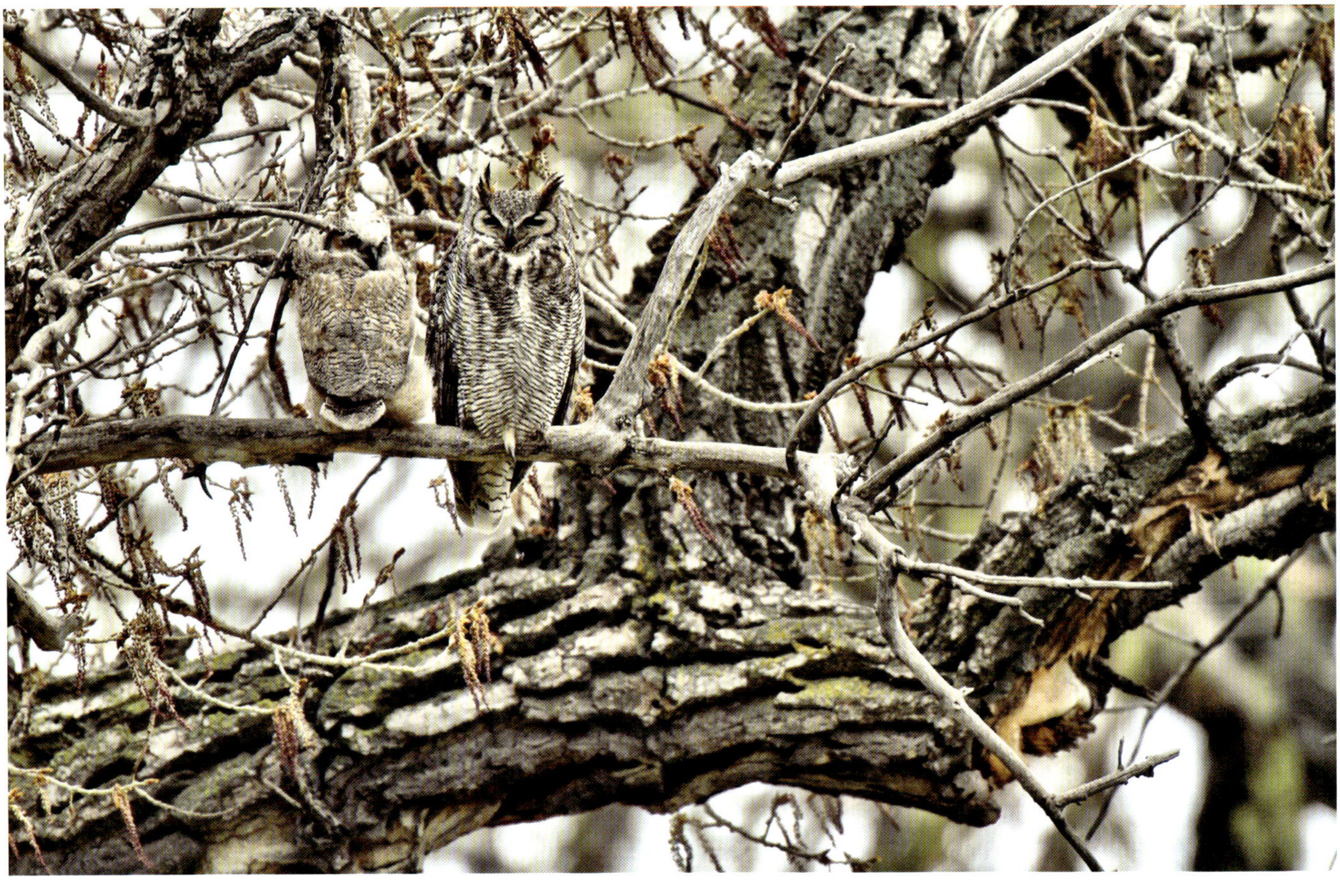

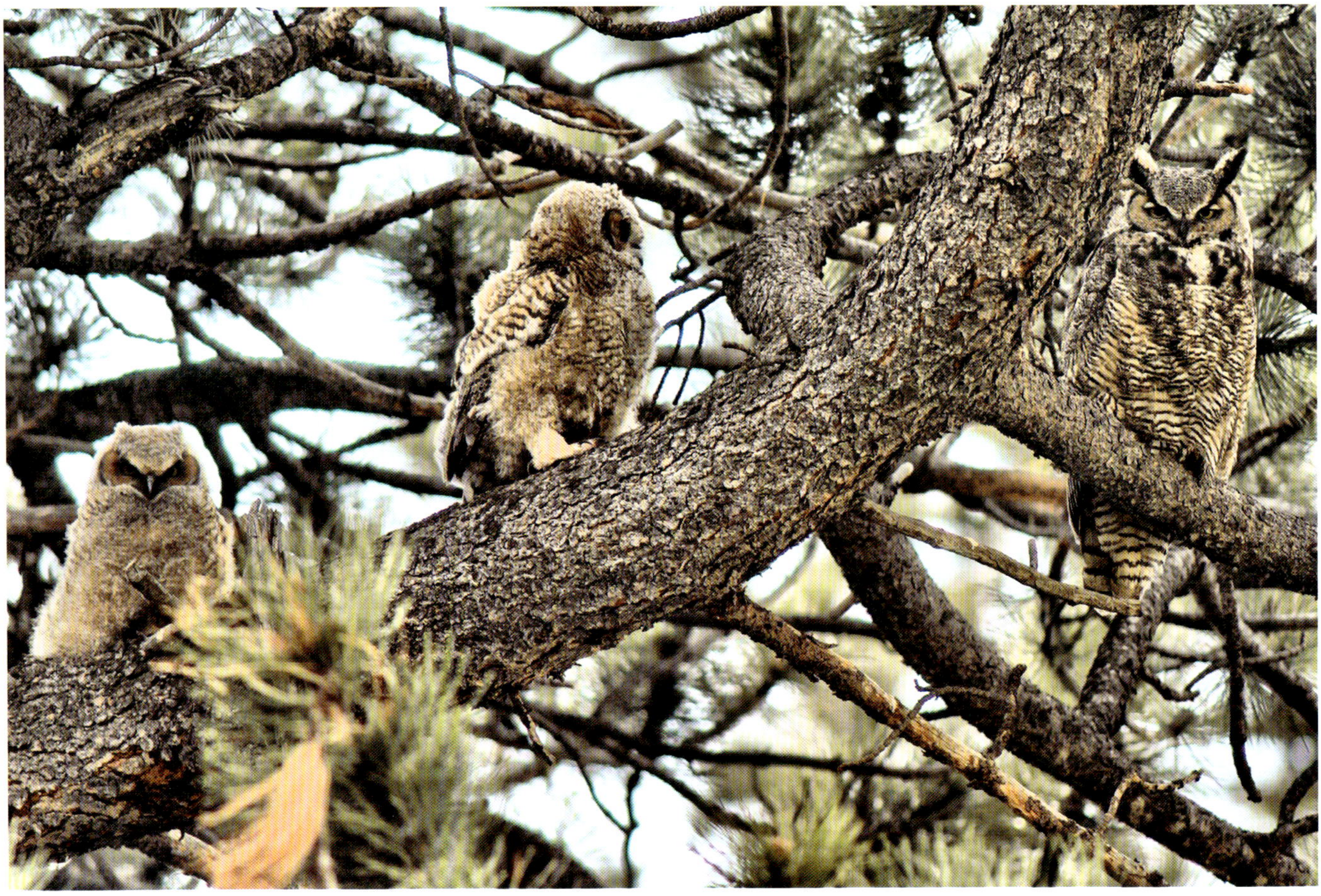

An adult owl and her owlet are well camouflaged in the spring before the trees leaf out. Photo taken in Longmont, Colorado, in May.

A female owl and her two owlets in Rocky Mountain National Park.

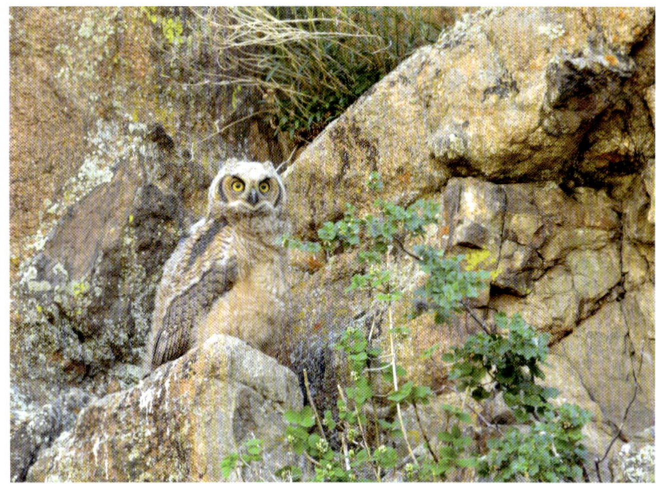

At twelve weeks old, the owlets have fully developed flight feathers but have not yet developed their contour feathers.

Two ten-week-old owlets. Where the owls choose to nest often determines at what age the owlets fledge. Note the remains of a Black-billed Magpie to the right of the owlets.

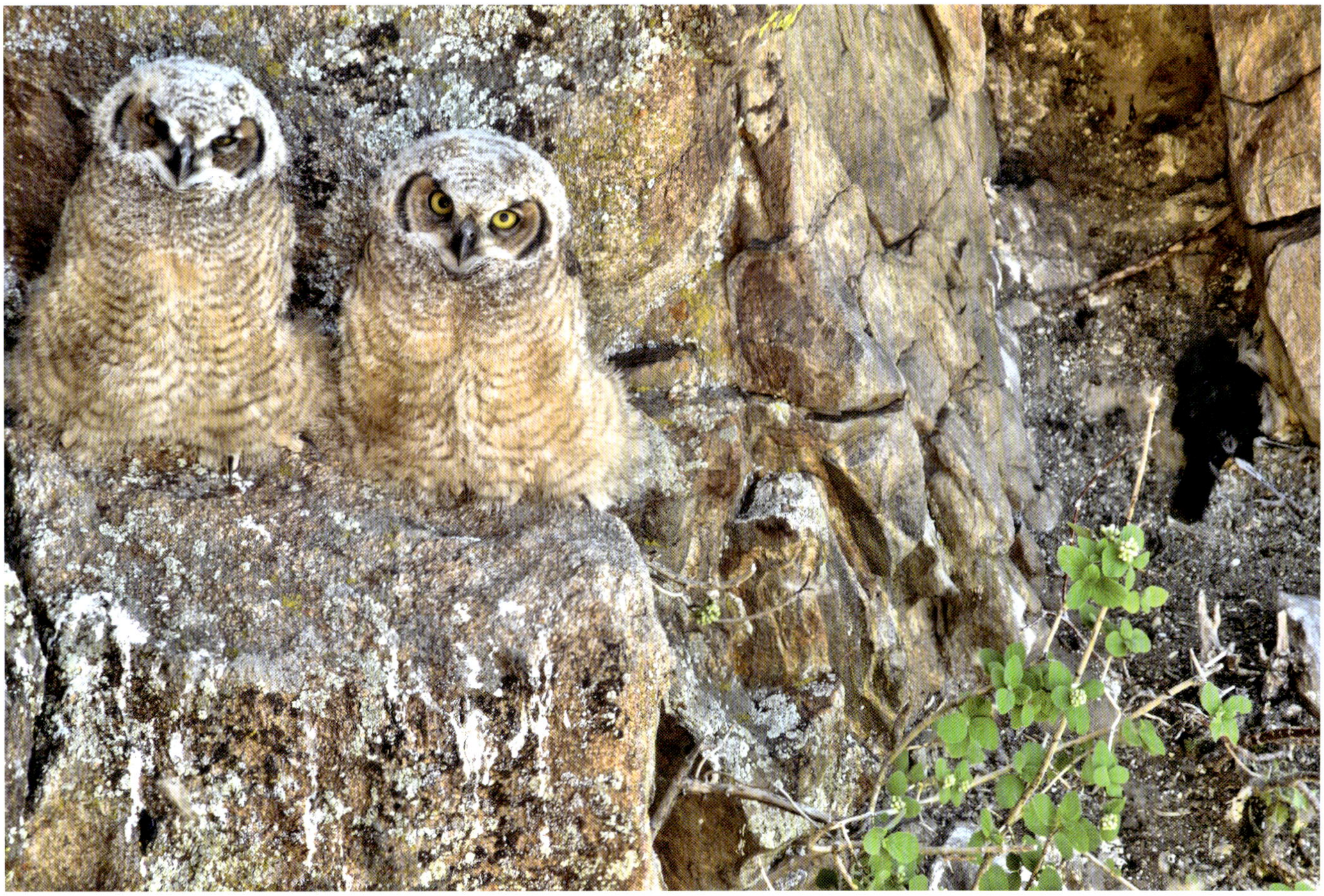

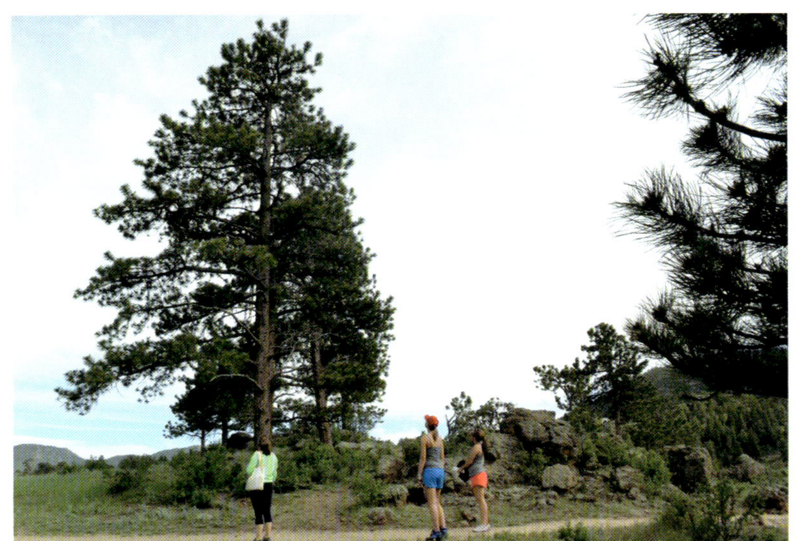

Fledgling Great Horned Owls frequently draw attention when they nest near people.

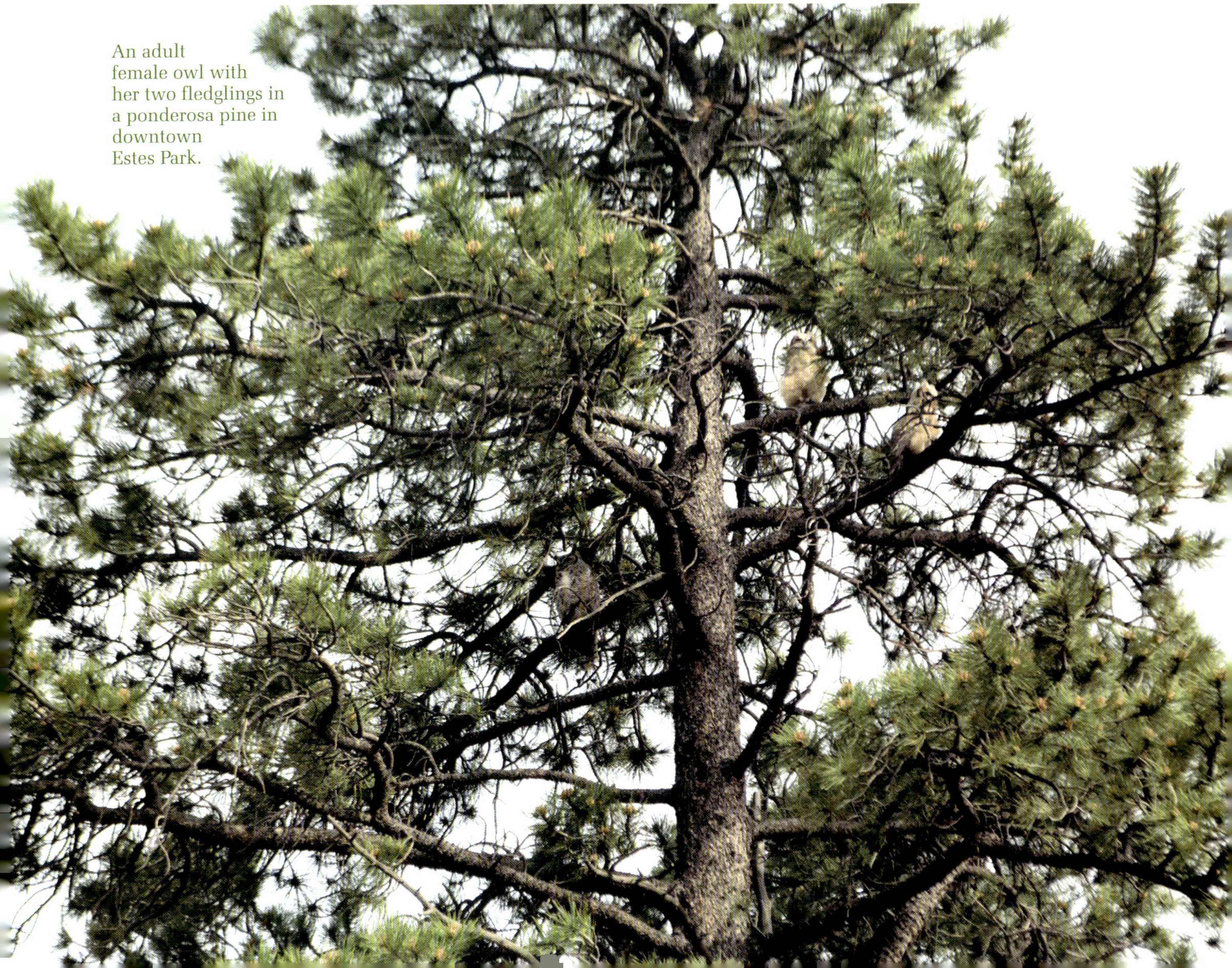

An adult female owl with her two fledglings in a ponderosa pine in downtown Estes Park.

When both young and adult Great Horned Owls are confronted by what they believe is a threat, they often go into a defense posture. When this occurs, the owl leans forward, lifting its wings over its back and extending them out about halfway. This makes the little bird appear three times its actual size. The owl often sways side to side and snaps its bill loudly. More often than not, this is sufficient to scare off most potential predators.

Smith and Smith (1972) followed two fledgling Great Horned Owls for eighteen evenings in central Utah, from June to August, in 1971. By August, the owls were approximately 6-3/4 miles (10.4 km) from their nest and a little over 3 miles (5.1km) from each other. The young owls roosted in the same spot for several days unless they were disturbed. They always began hunting after sunset, but always ten to twenty-five minutes prior to total darkness. The young owls routinely began hunting from a height of 42 to 59 feet (13-18m) from the ground, and then moved to a lower perch, 13 to 23 feet (4-7m), before attacking. He found the young owls frequently hovering for a few seconds prior to the attack. The young owls would often cease an attack prematurely. They also found that the two young owls had a combined successful rate of 17.8%. One owl was successful 22.5% of the time while the other owl was only success 13.3%. Most of the animals captured were small rodents, with the largest being a rabbit.

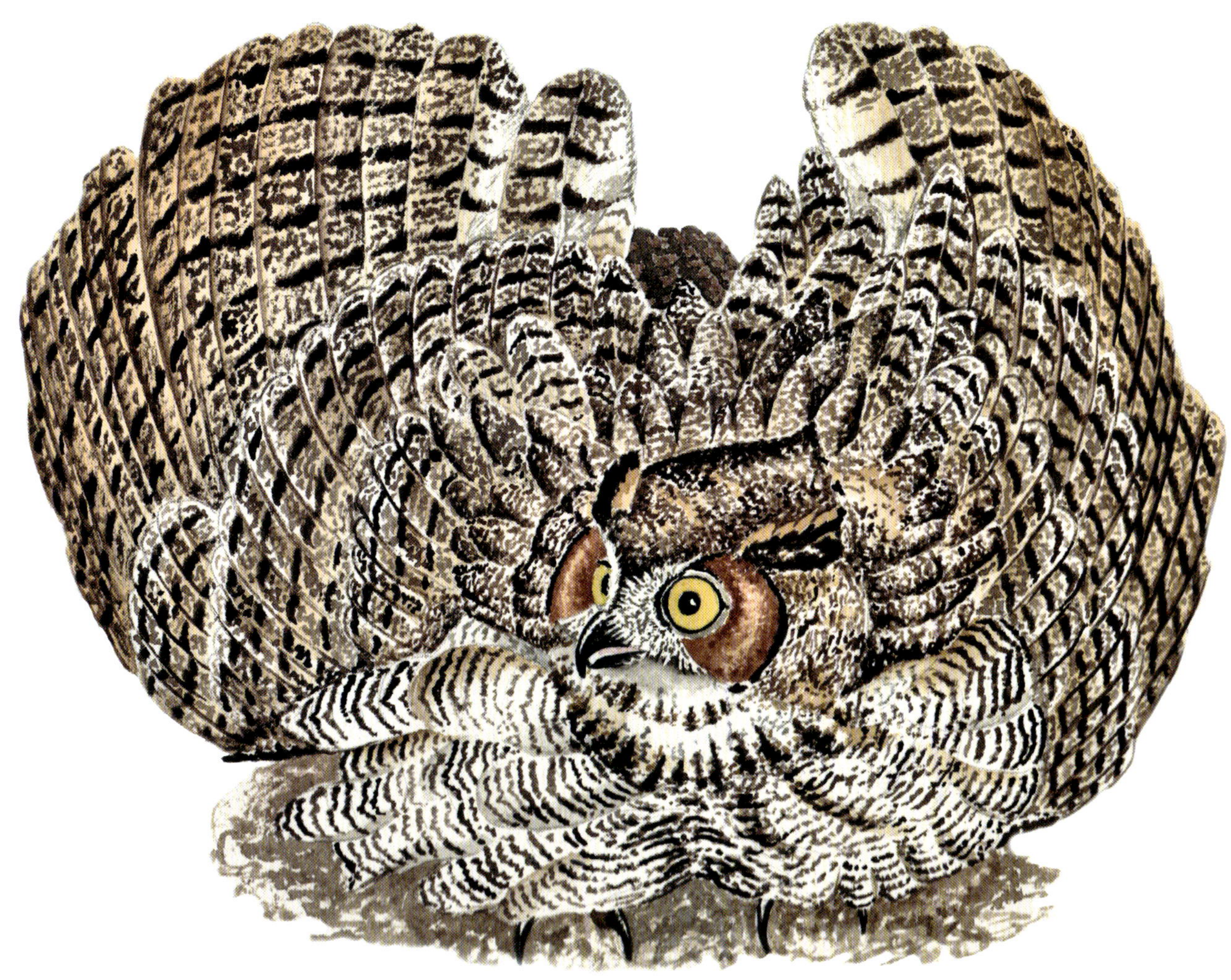

When a Great Horned Owl feels threatened, it moves into this posture to make itself appear larger than it really is in the hopes of scaring off any potential predator.

By August, the fledgling owls can often be heard making a kind of "tschreeeek" call at dusk. This vocalization is their food-begging call. The young owls give this call because, apparently, they don't want to hunt for themselves and have, presumably, become impatient waiting for their parents to bring dinner. I've heard the young owls calling in this manner from late summer through spring. The young owls have all the tools to locate and capture their own prey, but seemingly just don't feel like it.

In September 2000, I received a call from Tom Smith, a local resident, who was convinced that he had Great Gray Owls calling at dusk. He told me the birds would sit on the telephone poles along his driveway and give a loud tschreeeek call. The call the birds were making was not the typical "Whoo....Whoo....Whoo. Whoo....Whooo. Whooo" of a Great Horned Owl, so he was convinced it had to be Great Gray Owls that were calling. Even after I explained to Tom that fledgling Great Horned Owls have very small ear tufts and Great Gray Owls give very deep resonating hoots, he still wasn't convinced.

A few evenings later, I drove to Tom's house at dusk and found two fledgling Great Horned Owls on telephone poles giving their loud tschreeeek calls. I had brought a flashlight to illuminate the owls as they perched on the poles. While the light was on the owls, I explained to Tom why these birds were young Great Horned Owls and *not* Great Grays. I told him that Great Gray Owls live farther north in a different habitat. Before I left, he was convinced I was right about the birds being Great Horned Owls.

Around our house, we have Great Horned Owls, and every year, from about August through February, we can hear the food-begging tschreeeek of the young owls. The fact that we hear these young birds for so many months suggests that the young stay within their parents' territory until the following nesting season, which begins in March. This is one reason that Great Horned Owls are so numerous — their parents are good teachers and tolerant of the young being within their territory, hunting and feeding on prey, until the parents begin to raise another family. Beginning in February and March, the food-begging calls of the young are seldom, if ever, heard.

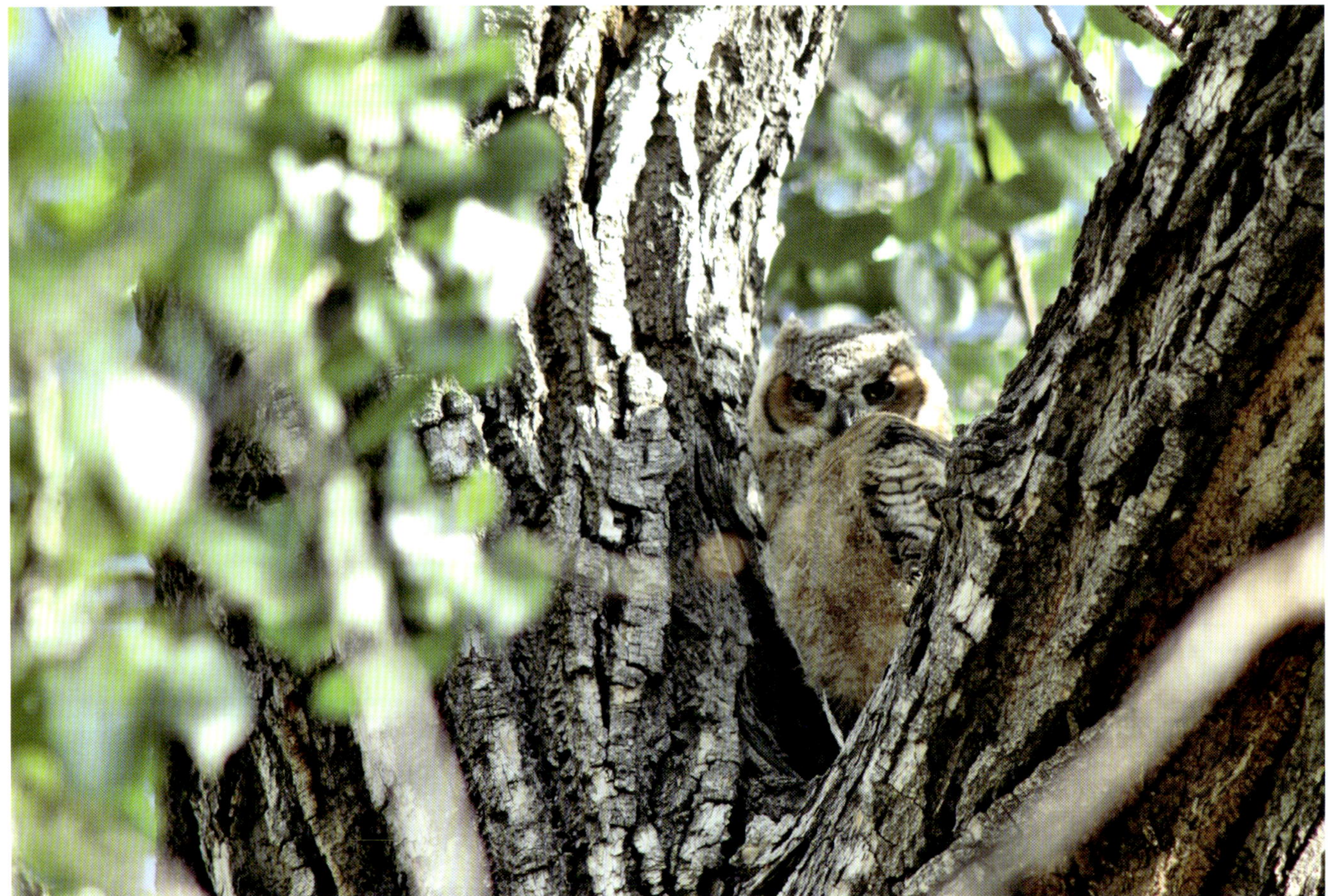

A fledgling owl perched on a cottonwood branch in Loveland, Colorado.

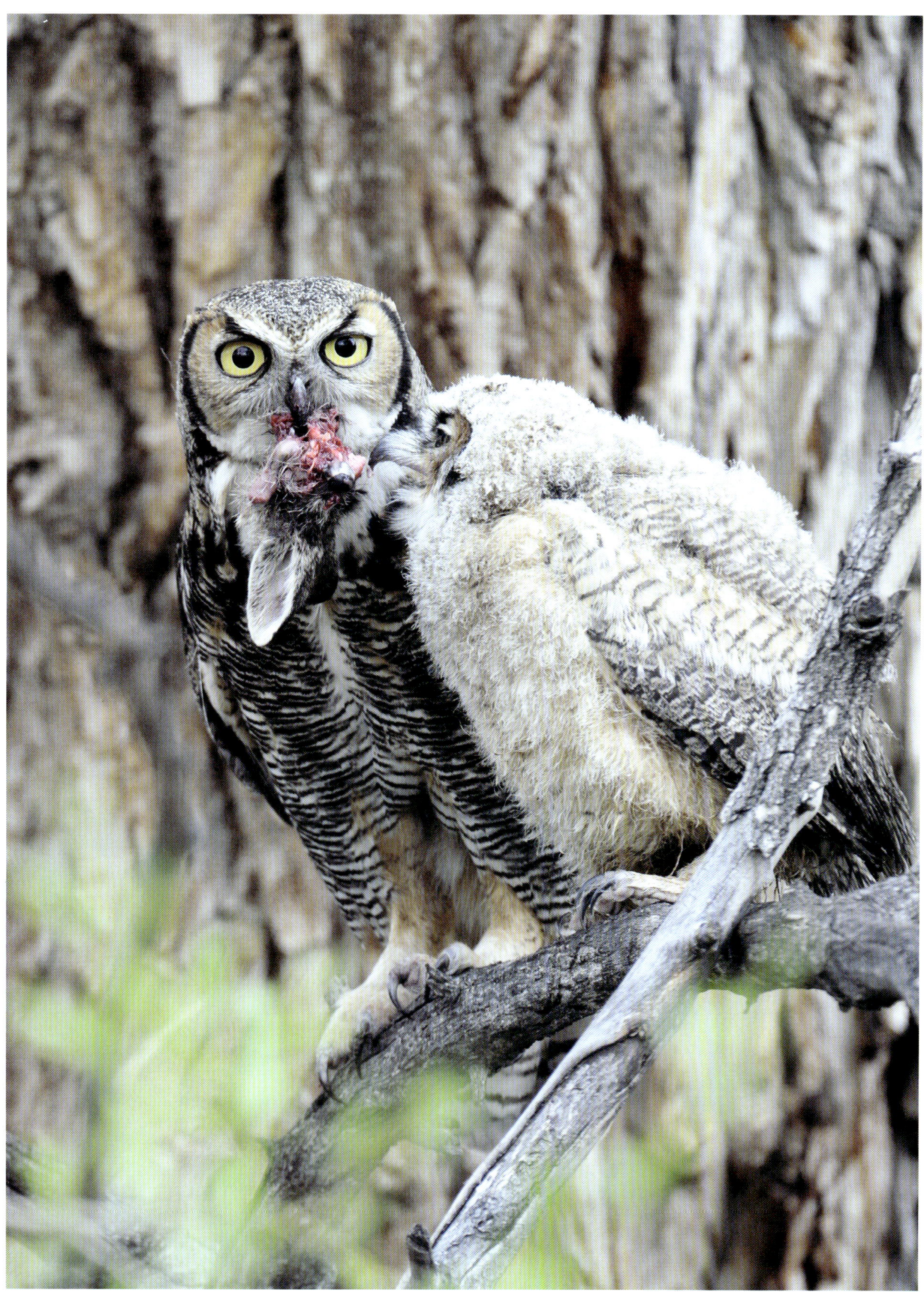

Adult Great Horned Owl feeding a rabbit to one of its young. *Photo © Bill Schmoker.*

A recently fledged owlet at the YMCA of the Rockies.

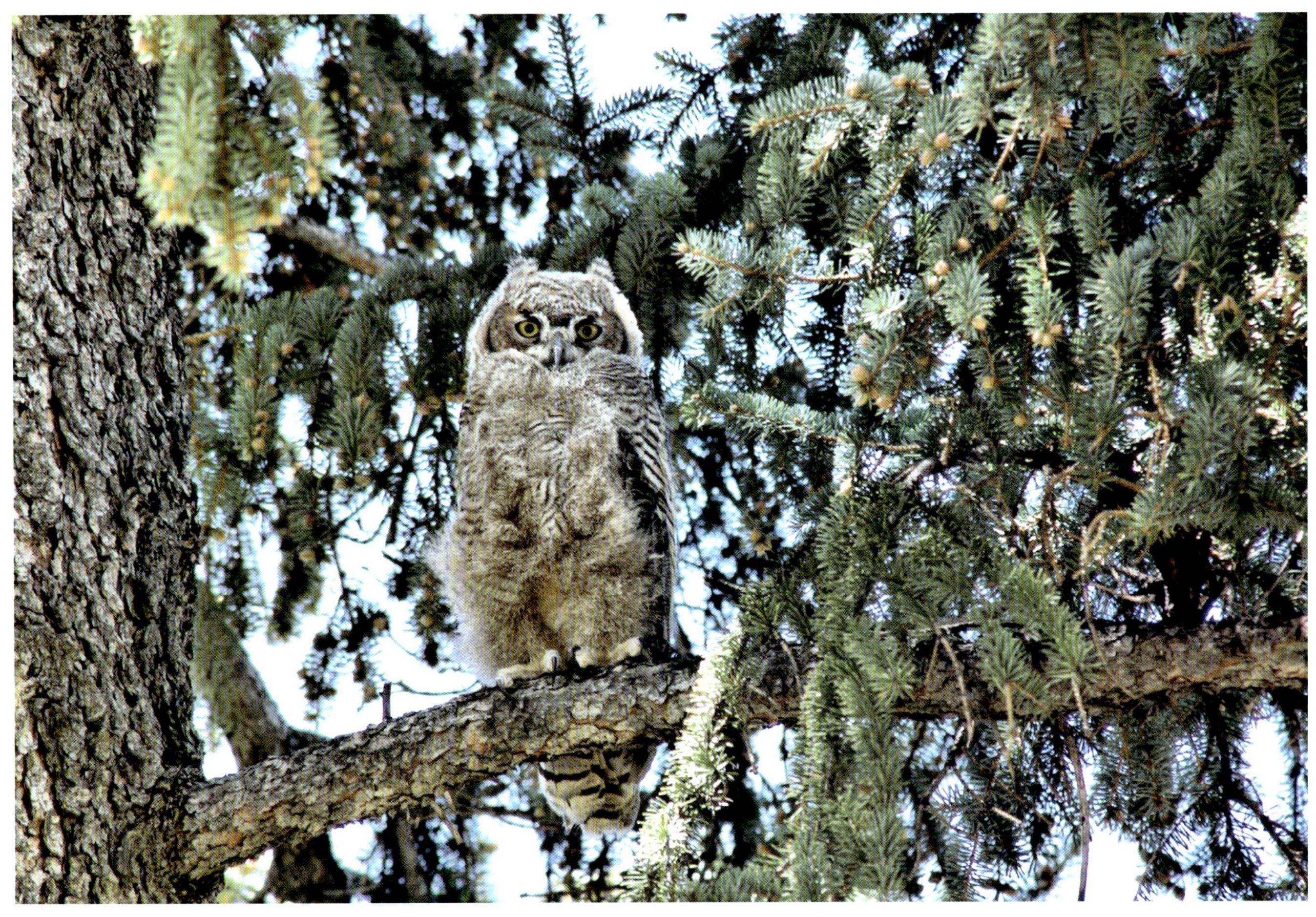

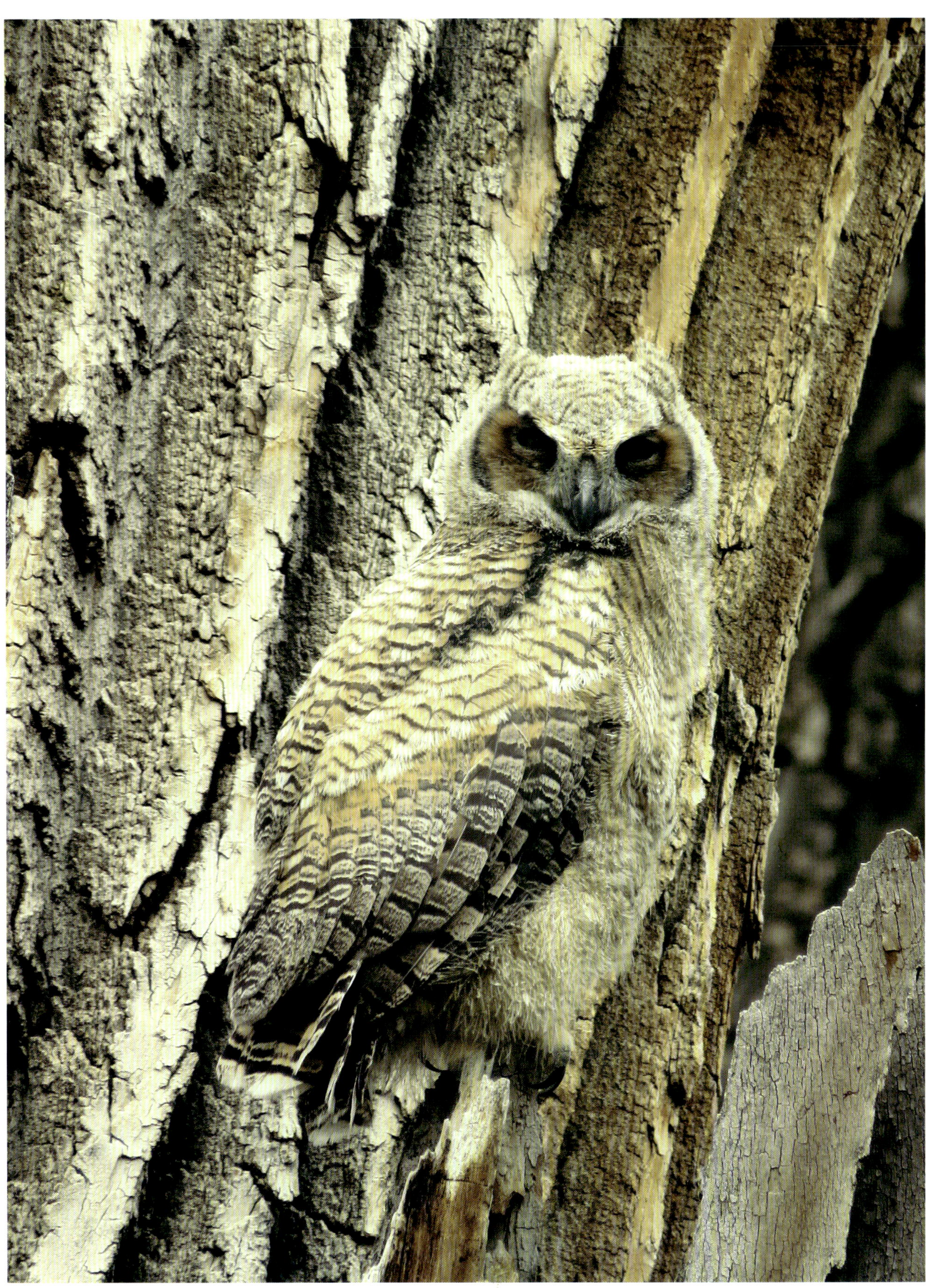
Look how well a fledgling owl blends in with its habitat.

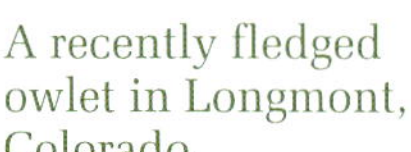

A recently fledged owlet in Longmont, Colorado.

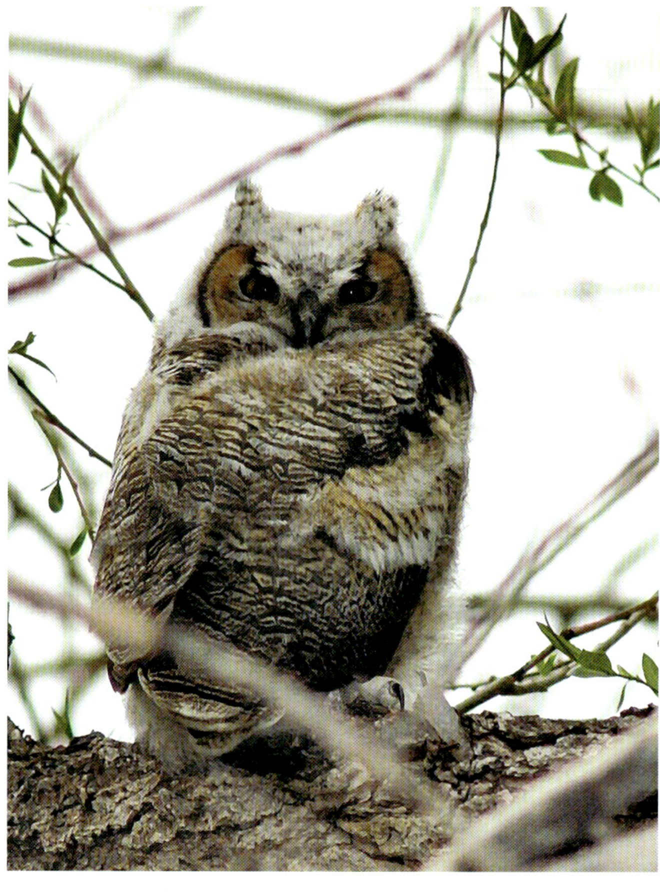

Two fledglings sit close to each other. At this age, they will often lean against each other for balance.

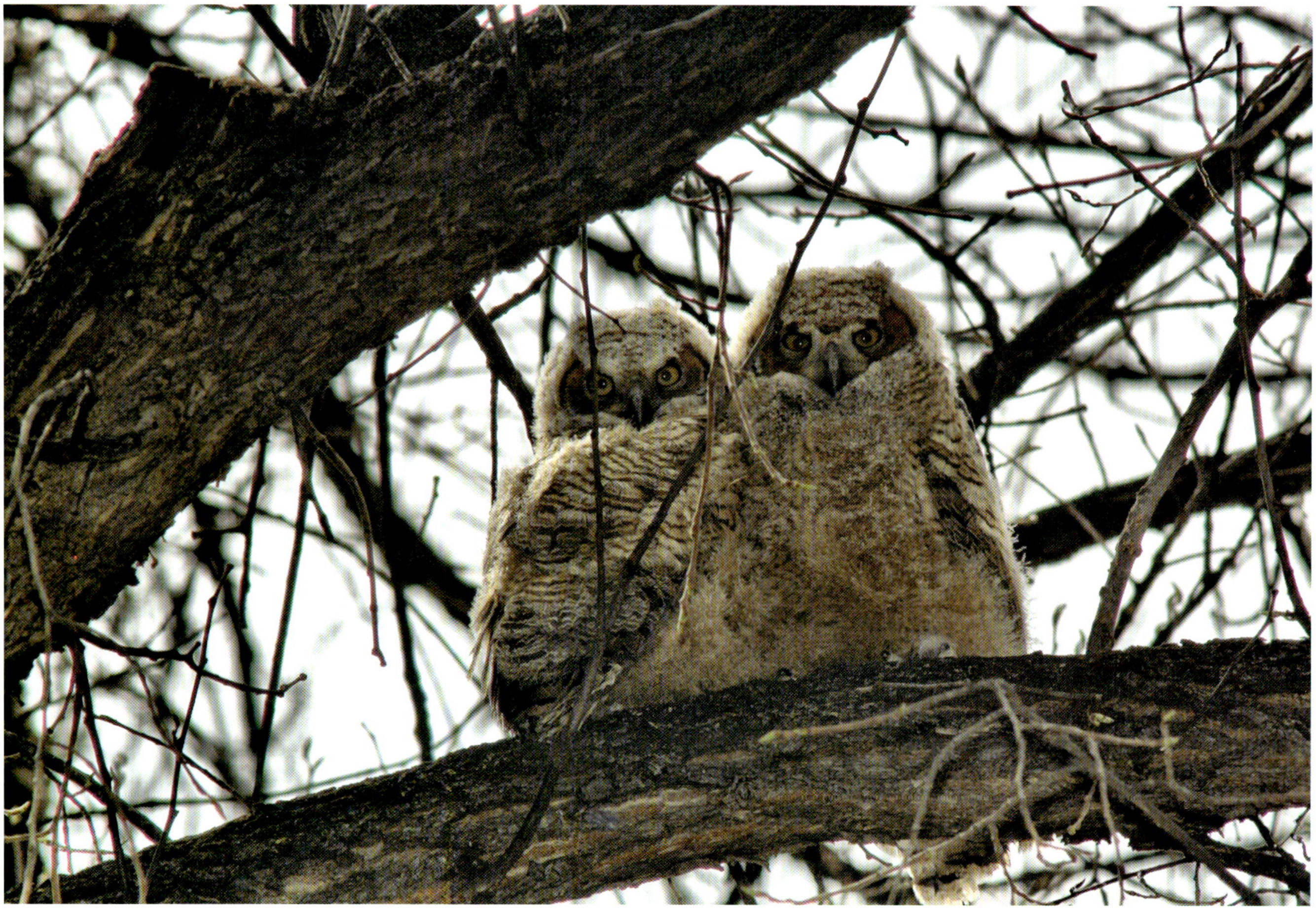

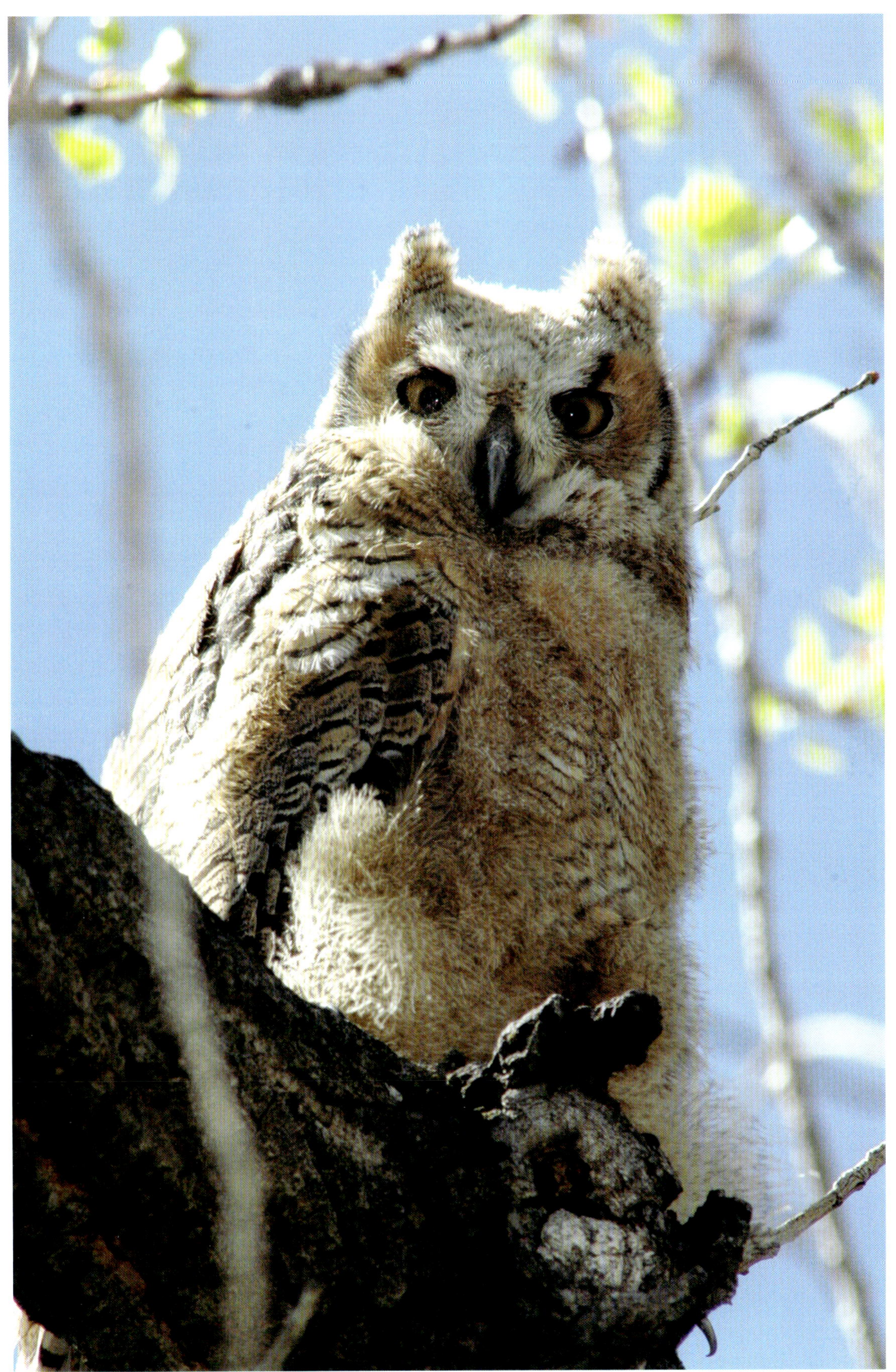

A fledgling Great Horned Owlet photographed in Fort Collins, Colorado.

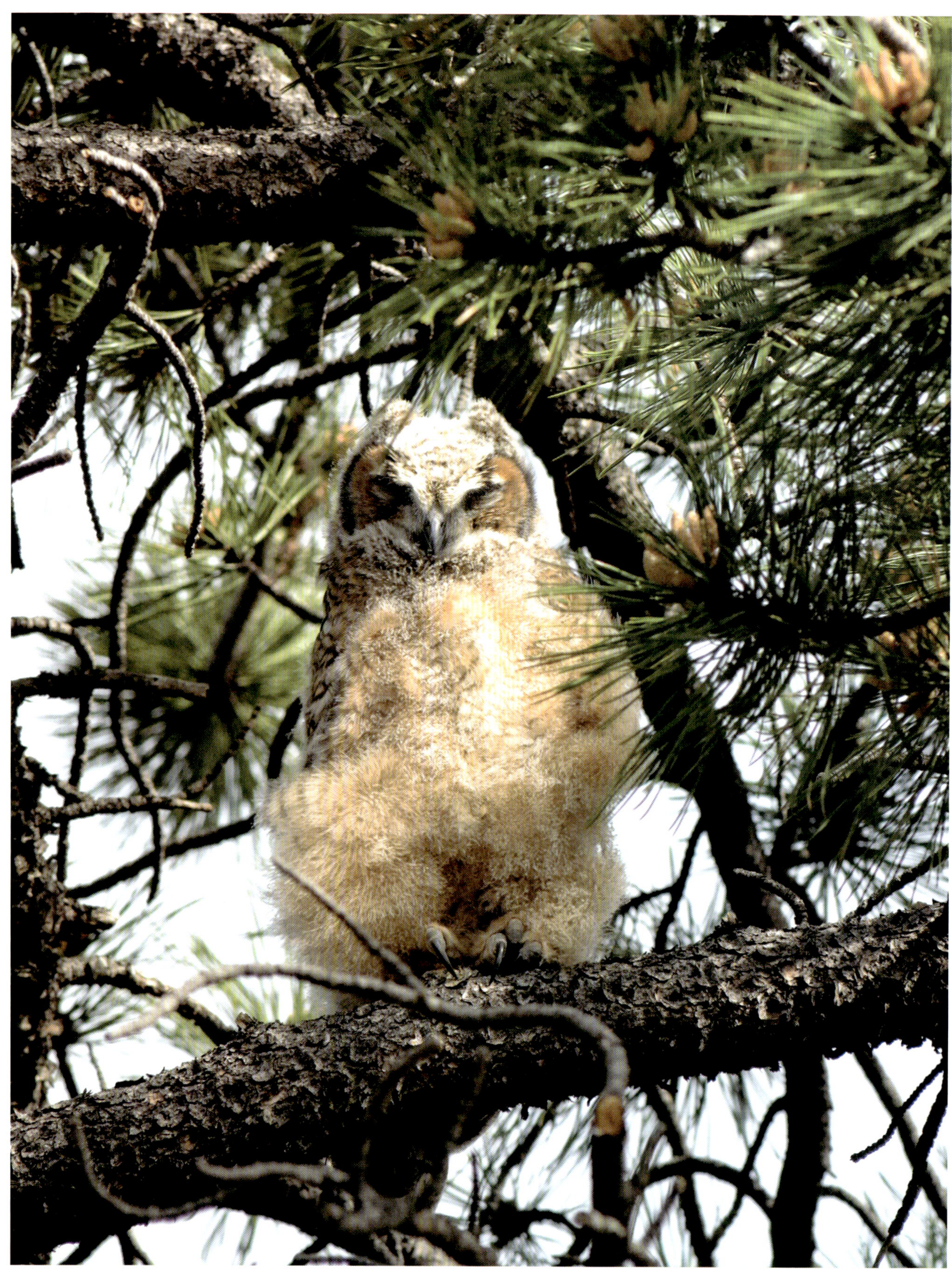

A fledgling owl taking a nap in the sun in Estes Park.

Chapter 7

PUBLIC ENEMY NUMBER ONE

Over the years, I've located hundreds of Great Horned Owls during the day, most of which were found because some bird or birds were scolding or harassing a perched owl. When I'm in the field and hear birds giving their distress calls, I always make my way to the cacophony to identify what the birds are upset about. When I find raucous birds, they are not always scolding predatory birds. One morning several years ago, while on my way to work, I heard Black-billed Magpies and American Crows scolding something. As I drove up the road, I found several corvids in the ponderosa pines vocalizing loudly. I scanned the trees and found nothing, besides the birds. I then noticed that the birds were all looking at the ground. I picked up my binoculars and saw a bobcat on the ground with a magpie pinned between his front paws.

I have to admit…that was a first for me. Most of the time when I find scolding birds, it is a bird of prey that is making the birds so upset. The Great Horned Owl is one of those birds that seem to get birds — like crows, magpies, and jays — extremely upset.

In 2011, there was a Great Horned Owl pair that chose to nest in a witches' broom on the YMCA of the Rockies property. This nest site was very visible to any passers-by, and I often wondered why the owls would even decide to nest in an area with so many people watching them. They don't nest there every year; however, the year they did nest on that platform, they successfully raised young. One afternoon, while driving past the nest, I heard several Steller's Jays calling loudly. I stopped my truck and walked to the Steller's Jays and found that they were scolding the adult male Great Horned Owl. The owl did not move from its perch, but it did keep an eye on the jays.

Several minutes into the calling bout, American crows began arriving, to seemingly assist the smaller corvid. As they began vocalizing near the owl, the jays moved off. It appeared that the jays called to attract the crows. The jays had moved off to continue feeding. By having the crows there and harassing the owl, the jays knew where the owl was and continue feeding without being potentially attacked and eaten by the large owl.

I have also found chickadees do this when they find a Northern Pygmy-Owl or Screech Owl, with similar results. The chickadees find the owl and call vociferously. Other birds come in to see what the chickadees are upset about and, as the other birds harass the owl, the chickadees will move off to continue feeding.

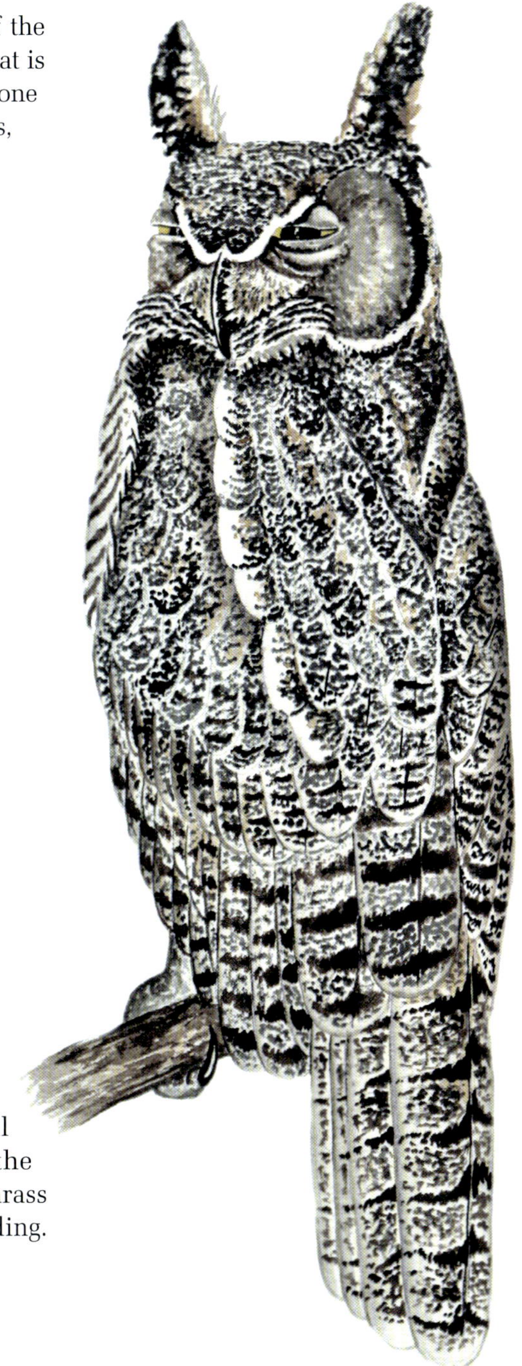

A Great Horned Owl in its concealment posture.

Presumably, the chickadees then know that the calling birds have the owl at bay, which allows the chickadees to go off and continue whatever they were previously doing.

When an owl thinks it has been seen or doesn't want to be seen, it will often move into its concealment posture. I've seen this many times in Northern Pygmy-Owls, Eastern Screech Owls, Great Horned Owls, and Long-eared Owls. The posture that the birds end up in is similar in all four species. The owls move into this posture in a single motion. The individuals pull their feathers tightly against their bodies, raising their ear tufts and squinting their eyes. This often makes the birds appear like a branch, enabling them to remain undetected, as the individual passes by. If the bird feels that you are too close, it often takes flight and moves to another perch.

Occasionally, the birds will fly off when detected. Great Horned Owls are heavy birds, so when they take flight, they swoop low and then, as they flap their wings, they gain elevation. Unlike hummingbirds that can just take off from a perch and fly in a straight line, the larger and heavier birds — such as the Great Horned Owl — have to drop and gain elevation as they flap their wings.

Many times I've been in the woods and come upon a Great Horned Owl. More often than not, the birds fly away from me, but on occasion, they fly past me and land behind me. Many people have said that they have had an owl fly at them and they believe the owl was trying to attack them. I always tell them the same thing: "If the owl was truly trying to hit you, it would have. A Great Horned Owl can catch a moving target much smaller than an average sized human. If an owl wanted to hit you, it would do so with ease."

A Steller's Jay harassing a male Great Horned Owl.

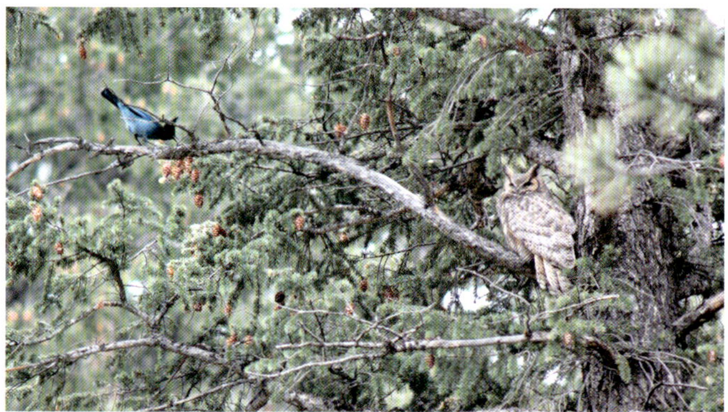

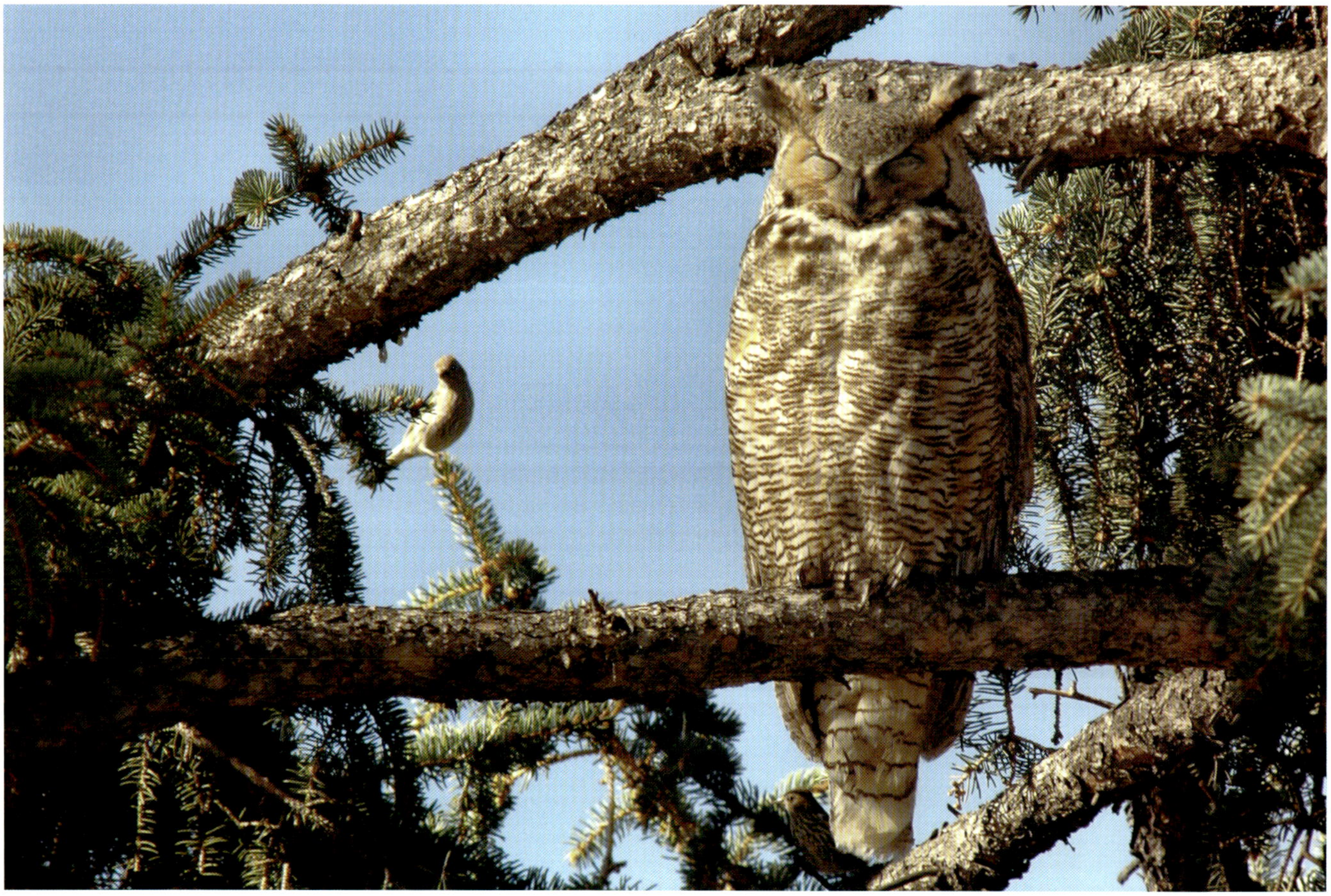

A House Finch tries to harass a Great Horned Owl to no avail.

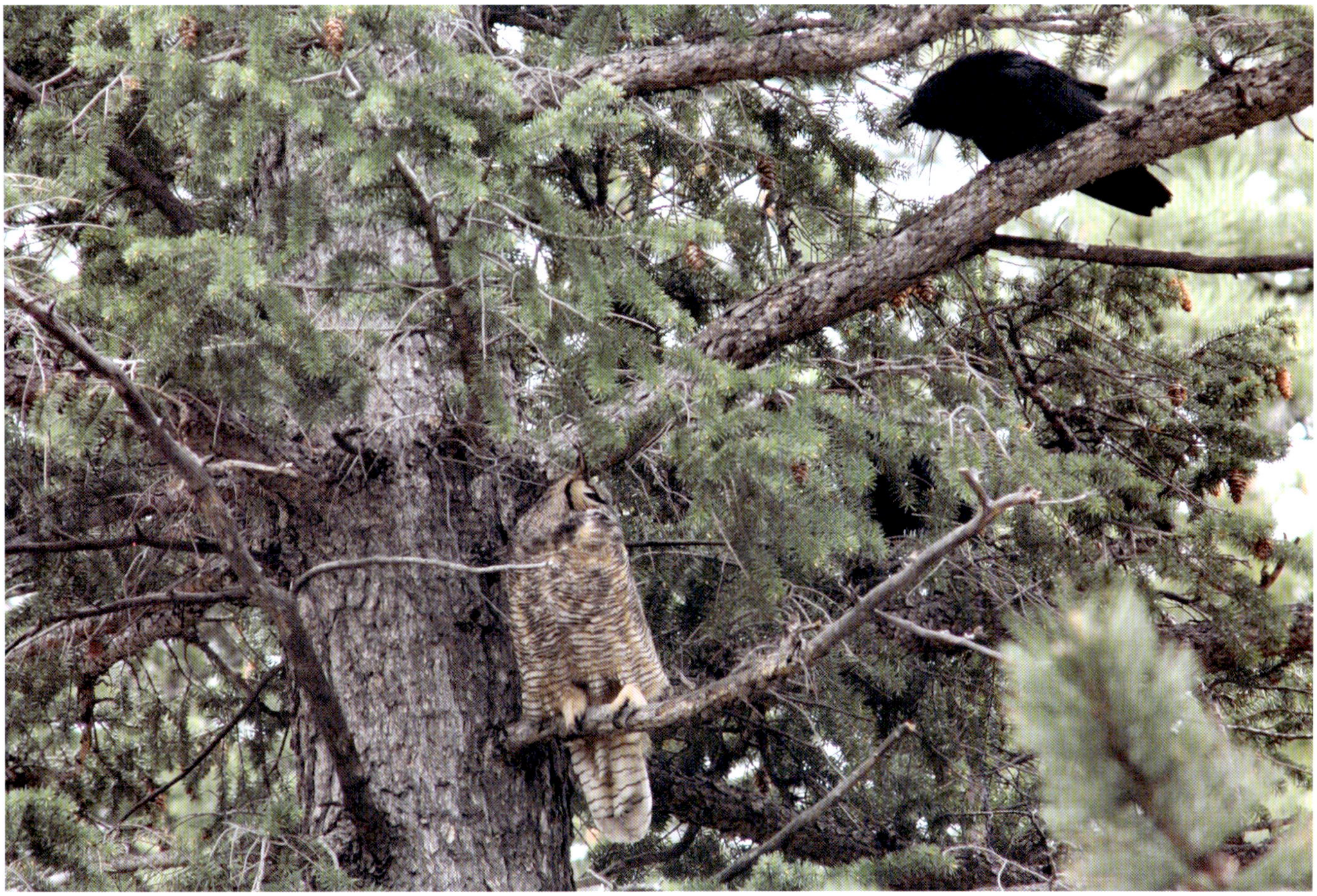

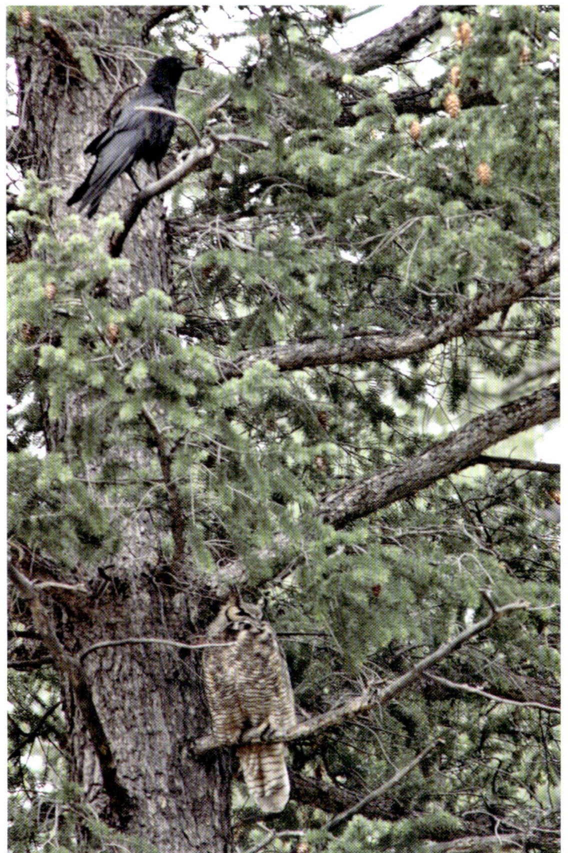

American Crows are notorious for harassing Great Horned Owls.

OWLS IN WINTER

With the exception of the Great Horned Owls of the far north, adult Great Horned Owls remain in their territories year-round (Austing and Holt 1966). The young of the year will often wander away from their natal areas. Some, though, may remain with the parents until the beginning of the following nesting season, at which time the adults will drive off any young owls from their territory. This is due to the adult Great Horned Owls seeing their offspring as competition for food; by chasing them away, they remove the competition so they will have enough food for the next set of young owls.

Young owls without a territory can have a very difficult time during a severe winter. Many young owls will starve before their first spring, due to their inability to find an adequate territory with an ample supply of food and cover. On the other hand, those young birds that find an adequate to superb territory can live twenty or more years in the wild. In areas such as the Pawnee Grasslands in northeastern Colorado, some Great Horned Owls have few places to hide in winter. There have been many winters when I've found these large owls perched low in a leafless tree during the day. I remember I was with Professor Nune, doing the Christmas count in 2008, when late in the day, we came upon a large cottonwood near the edge of a road. There a Great Horned Owl and a Red-tailed Hawk were perched in the same tree at the same time — the hawk was facing north as the owl was facing south. We witnessed no interactions between the two raptors.

On three different occasions in January 2012, while searching for Short-eared Owls in an area south of Greeley, Colorado, I found a Great Horned Owl perched about 6 feet (1.83m) from the ground in the crotch of a leafless cottonwood tree. I thought the owl was perched there by accident. However, on subsequent visits, the owl

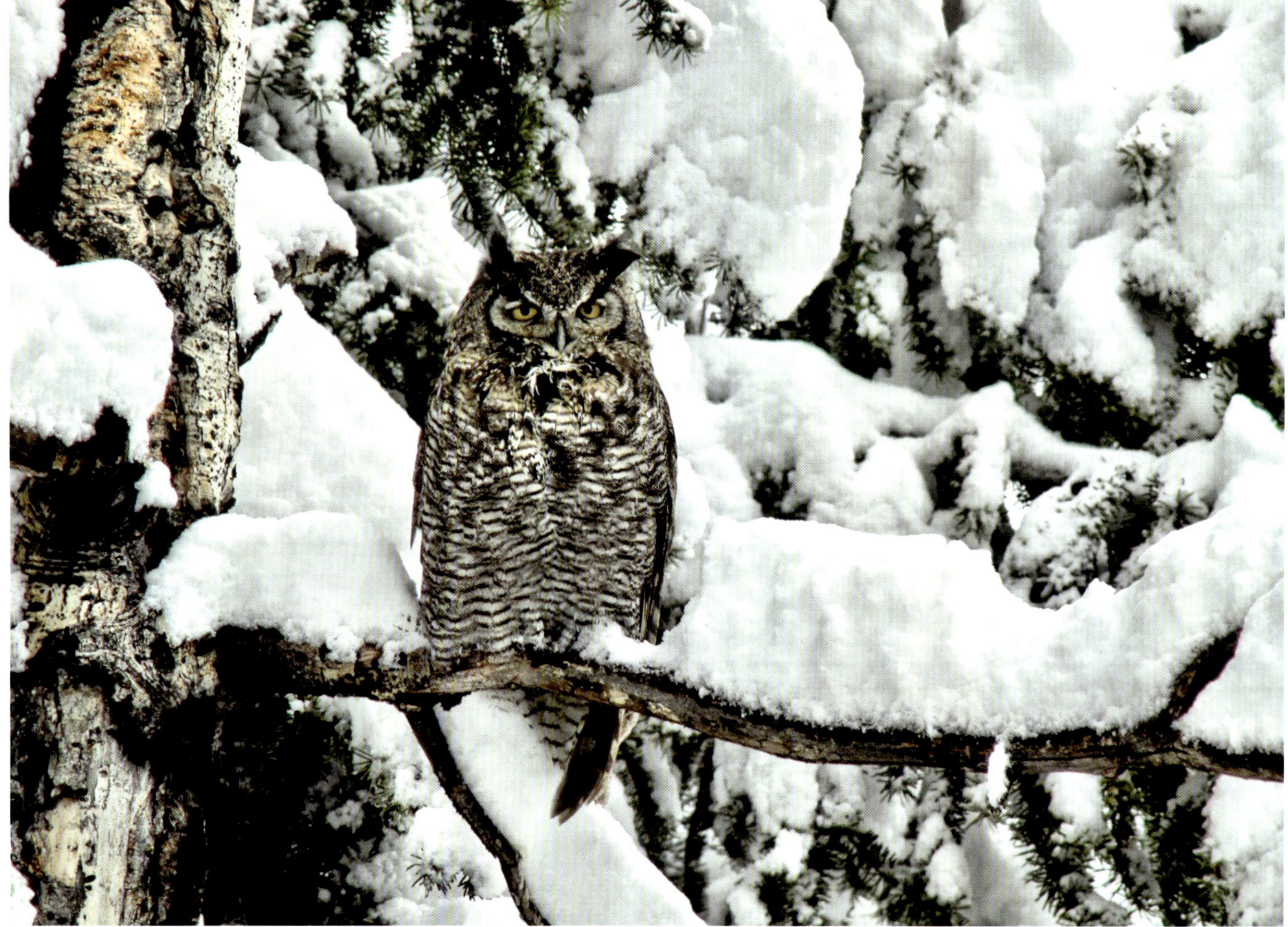

A male Great Horned Owl, in Rocky Mountain National Park, is perched after several inches of snow had fallen.

(presumably the same bird) was seen in that same tree. On one afternoon, there was an adult Red-tailed Hawk perched on the top of that tree, with the owl just a few yards below. I'm not sure that the hawk even noticed the owl, because I saw no interaction between the two species. It was obvious to me that this particular tree was the apparent winter perch for that owl. Interestingly enough, we had seen the Short-eared Owls on three different occasions before the end of the year. However, the first week of 2013, the Short-eared Owls were nowhere to be found. I wondered if the Great Horned Owl had killed and eaten the smaller Short-eared Owl, or if the vole population decreased in such a way that there just wasn't enough food for the Short-ears and they simply moved to better hunting grounds.

On thc night of January 29, 1918, Mr. Hunt (1918) in Bent (1938) writes, "A Short-eared Owl was perched on a rock, which crops from the steep gravelly slope on the campus Berkeley. Suddenly the dark form of a horned owl pounced upon it and crunched it into a gravelly crevice of the ledge. For a few moments there was a lively tussle and a great beating of soft feathers on rocks. Then the talons of the Great Horned Owl closed on the breast of the Short-eared Owl, at once piercing the vitals. The Horned Owl, bearing the body of its victim in its claws, flew across the canyon toward a grove of trees."

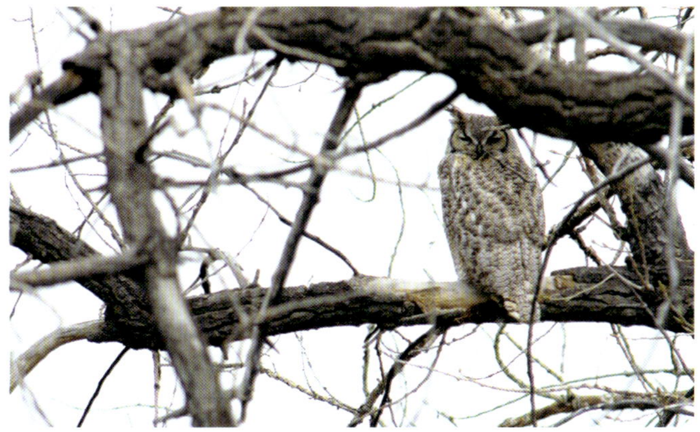

An owl looking very much like the cottonwood branch it is perched on.

When conifers are absent, Great Horned Owls will use trees like this Russian olive for a day-roost. Note the owl in the tree.

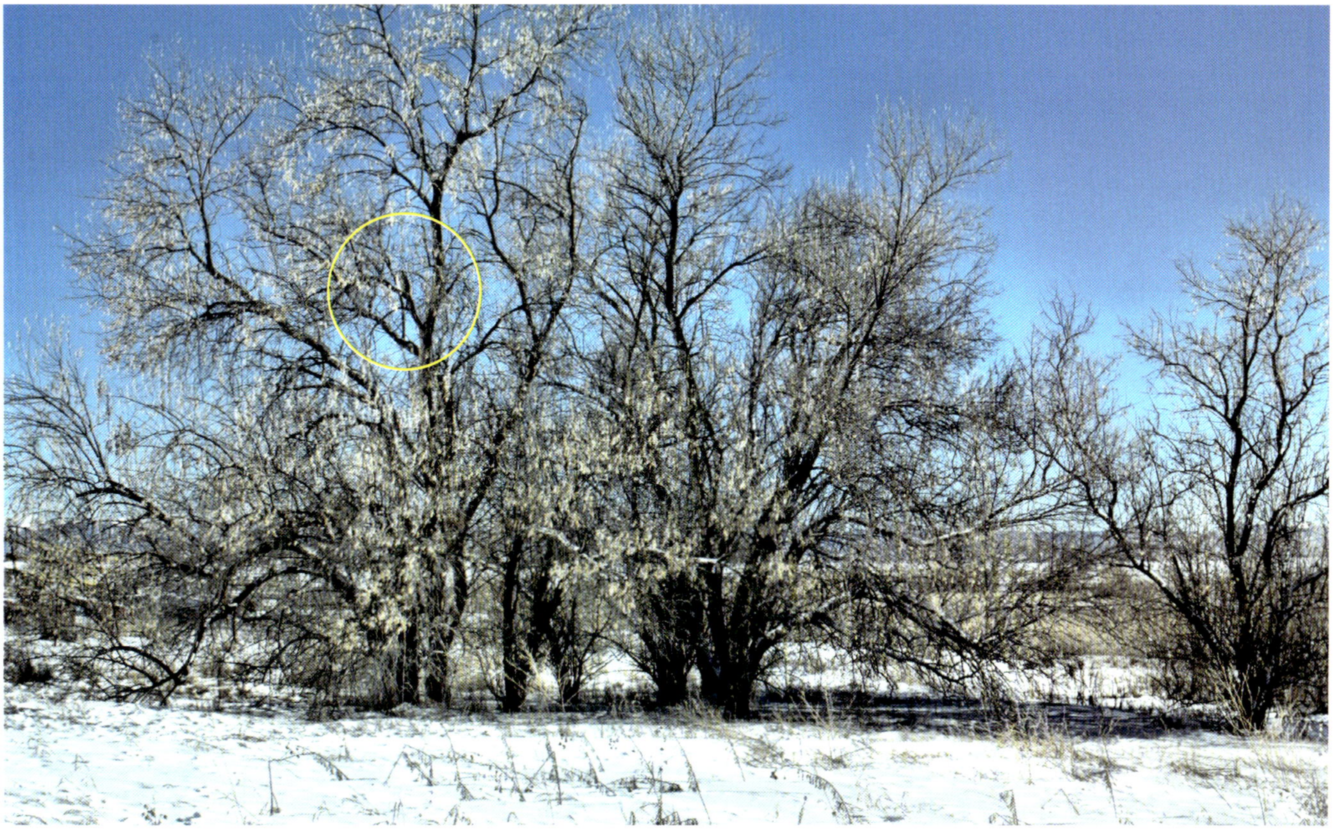

LONGEVITY AND MORTALITY OF GREAT HORNED OWLS

According to the Patuxent Wildlife Research Center, Bird Banding Laboratory in Patuxent, Maryland, the oldest wild Great Horned Owl lived to be twenty-eight years old. The bird was originally banded in Ohio and later encountered there.

Great Horned Owls are very tough birds. However, as far as mortality goes, these large owls have met their demise in innumerous ways. Several are hit by cars each year, while others get shot. (Shooting any birds of prey has been illegal for many years.) Some are caught in traps set to capture fur-bearing animals, while others are poisoned. Again, these and all owls are protected and it is against the law to willfully poison any protected species. Some owls, particularly young birds that have just been released from their parents, end up starving, due to their lack of experience in finding an adequate territory before spring.

Prior to the power company in Estes Park, Colorado, retrofitting their power poles, many Great Horned Owls were electrocuted. At one point, 90% of the Great Horned Owls that I had banded were killed by electrocution. The power company figured out that it was less expensive to retrofit their power poles instead of fixing the poles after a large bird had been electrocuted and there was a power failure.

Northern Goshawks and Golden Eagles have both preyed upon Great Horned Owls (Renyolds and Meslow 1984). Several years ago a friend of mine was out hiking and came across a Northern Goshawk feeding upon a Great Horned Owl fledgling near Colorado Springs. Bloom (1982) found the remains of a Great Horned Owl in a Golden Eagle nest in the western Great Basin of northern California and northwest Nevada. In central Arizona, Eakle and Grubb (1986) also found the remains of a Great Horned Owl in a Golden Eagle nest. Furthermore, in the late 1930s, C.J. Henry (1939) documented a Golden Eagle carrying off an injured Great Horned Owl after he had shot and wounded the owl.

Starting in 2003, many Great Horned Owls have died from the West Nile virus in Colorado. This disease seemed to move through the country from the east to west. As the virus made its way through the state, several Great Horned Owls were admitted to various rehabilitation centers, with several of them dying from the disease.

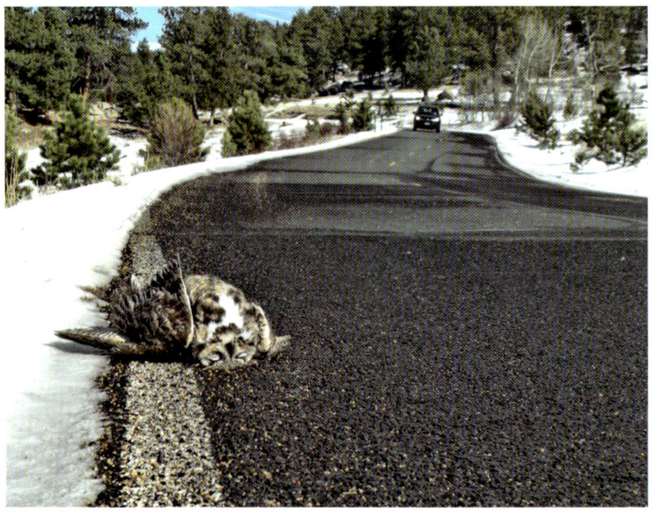

Many Great Horned Owls are hit by cars and killed each year.

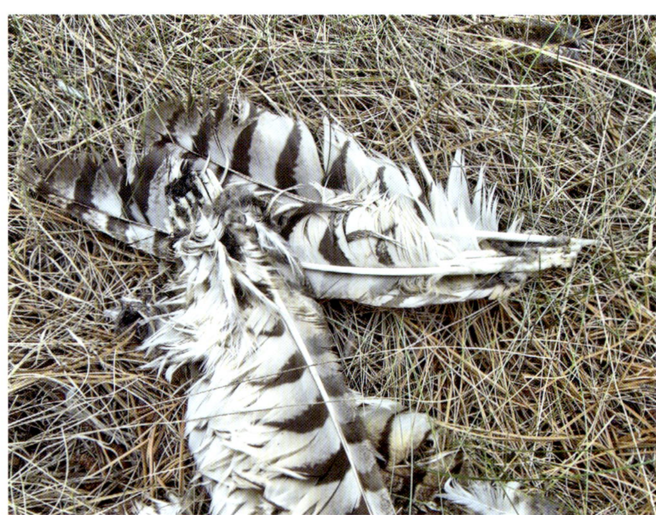

This owl was killed by a mammal. The feathers are clearly taken off in clumps. Mammals rip the feathers off in clumps whereas birds pluck individual feathers.

Chapter 8

REHABILITATION OF GREAT HORNED OWLS

Ever since I was a young boy, I was amazed by Great Horned Owls. It wasn't until 1986 when I was able to hold a live owl. At that time I had just graduated college and was living in Stevens Point, Wisconsin. A bird-bander friend, Chris Cold, was given a young Great Horned Owl that was found on the ground. He knew of a Great Horned Owl nest that was in a large white pine north of town. The nest had two owlets in it. These owlets were about the same age as the one he had. We drove to the nesting area and walked to the nest tree with the owl in a box. While Chris was climbing the nest tree, I was able to hold the owlet. When Chris reached the nest, he banded the two owlets that were in the nest and lowered a basket down to me so I could place the owlet in. He raised the owlet to the nest and added it to the family, then returned to the ground. The mother accepted the new youngster and raised it to fledging as she did with her own owlets.

After having moved to northern Colorado and becoming a bird rehabilitator, I've received over twenty Great Horned Owls — all of which were either injured or orphaned. Fortunately for me, I was able to spend several days volunteering at the Birds of Prey Foundation early in my rehabilitation career, which enabled me to work with these large owls. Before this opportunity, I was very intimidated by them. It wasn't until I had the chance to work directly with these birds that I realized they aren't as scary as I was making them out to be. On the first day of my volunteering, my job was to clean the cages of the birds in the intensive care area. These birds were in plastic pet carriers of assorted sizes. Depending on the bird and its injury, some cages had perches and others did not. All of the cages had a small bowl of water inside, usually at the front of the cage.

The way I learned to clean cages with a live wild bird of prey inside was to place a large folded towel in one hand and open the door with the other. Slowly, I would move the towel towards the bird and then slowly remove the water dish, food remains, and towel from the bottom of the cage and replace each with fresh ones. If you're lucky, the bird will remain on its perch as you do this. If not, the bird will, most often, move to the back of the

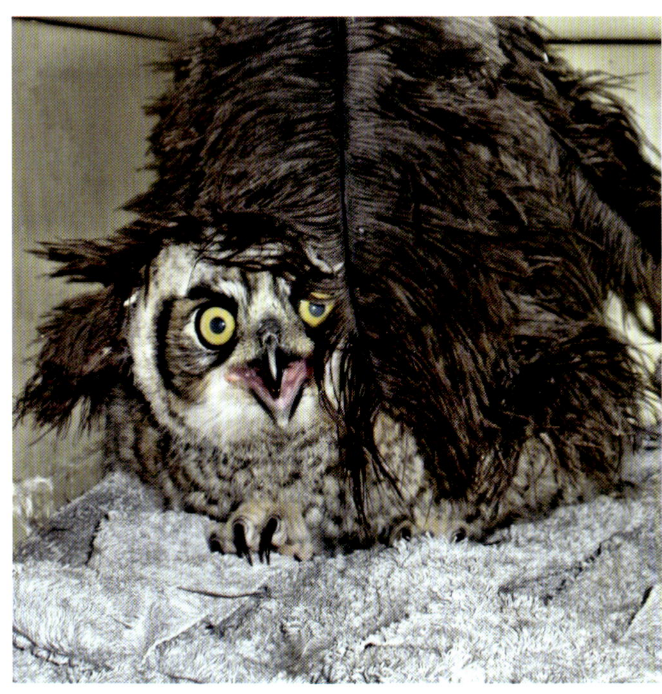

When I received this young owl, I gave its mother back to it by using a feather duster as a surrogate mother.

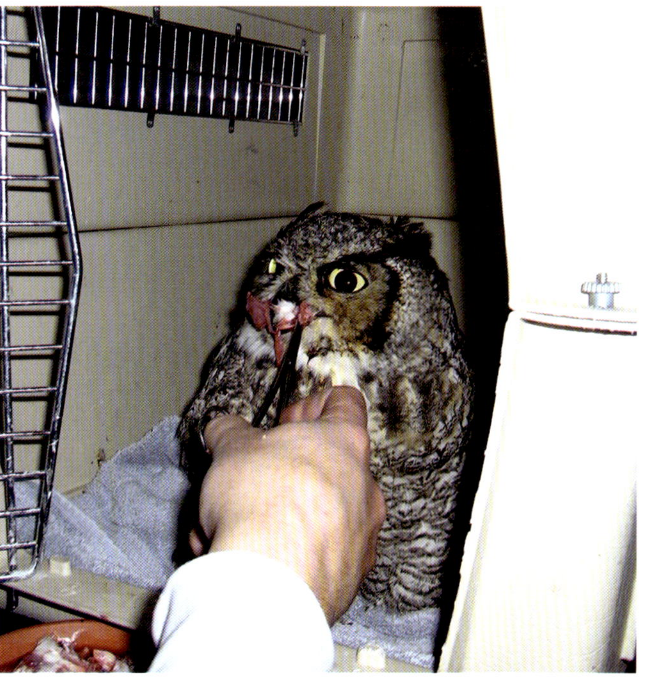

At times I am able to hand-feed hungry Great Horned Owls. *Photo by Susan Rashid.*

cage and wait until you're finished. In the worst case scenario (usually if the cage has an accipiter such as a Sharp-shinned Hawk inside), the bird will fly out of the cage and you have to catch it and put it back in the cage without it injuring it or yourself.

Having the opportunity to clean cages with these large owls inside gave me the ability to learn to be in close proximity to these birds of prey without being afraid of them. I quickly learned to respect them, but also lost my fear of them. They're actually more afraid of you than you are of them.

Most of the Great Horned Owls that end up in rehabilitation facilities are fledglings found without their parents around. I've received several young owls, of various ages, over the years. The youngest was about three weeks old and the oldest was about eight weeks. Whether a young owl is brought to me or I go to retrieve it, the procedure is always the same: I first introduce myself to the bird and let it know that I am here to help him/her. I then slowly reach down with a towel and place the towel around the bird, picking up the owl to see if it has any injuries. When picking up a young owl, there is little to be afraid of because most young owls are too young to know what their feet and talons can do. The young birds most often will look at you and snap their bills. This bill snapping is a sign that the bird is afraid.

When young owls are in my care, I place a feather duster in the bird's cage along with a water dish. The feather duster is wired to the inside of the carrier so it hangs a few inches from the bottom, leaving room for the owl to lie under the feathers as it would if it was under its mother. The owls all seem more content when they have some feathers to hide under. The feather duster represents the bird's mother and the owl readily lies under the feathers. The only problem with this is that the owl doesn't have the warmth of its mother, but it is much better than nothing.

In most cases the young owls will readily accept food from me. To feed the young birds, I use a small forceps and tiny pieces of meat, usually rat or rabbit. I dip the meat in water and place it on or in front of the owl's bill and it doesn't take long before the owl begins eating. Once

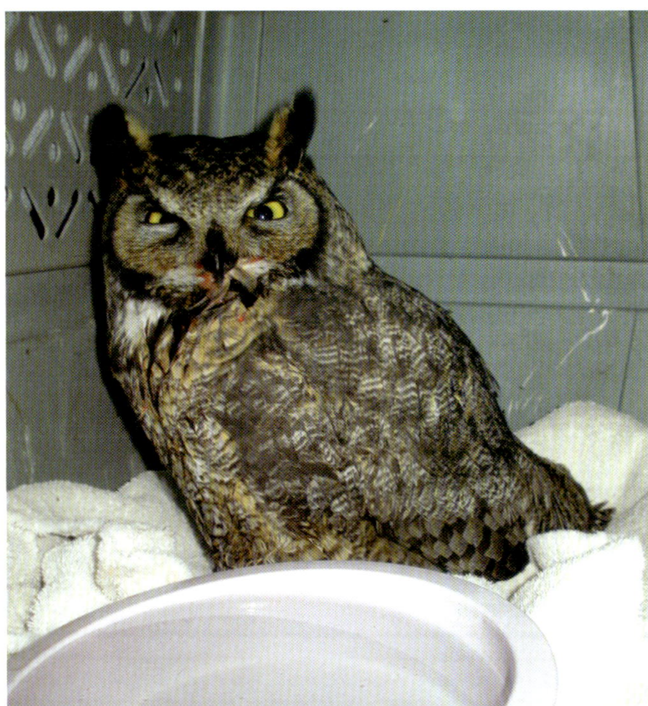

A Great Horned Owl that came to me emaciated. I named him Sutton after the road he was found on.

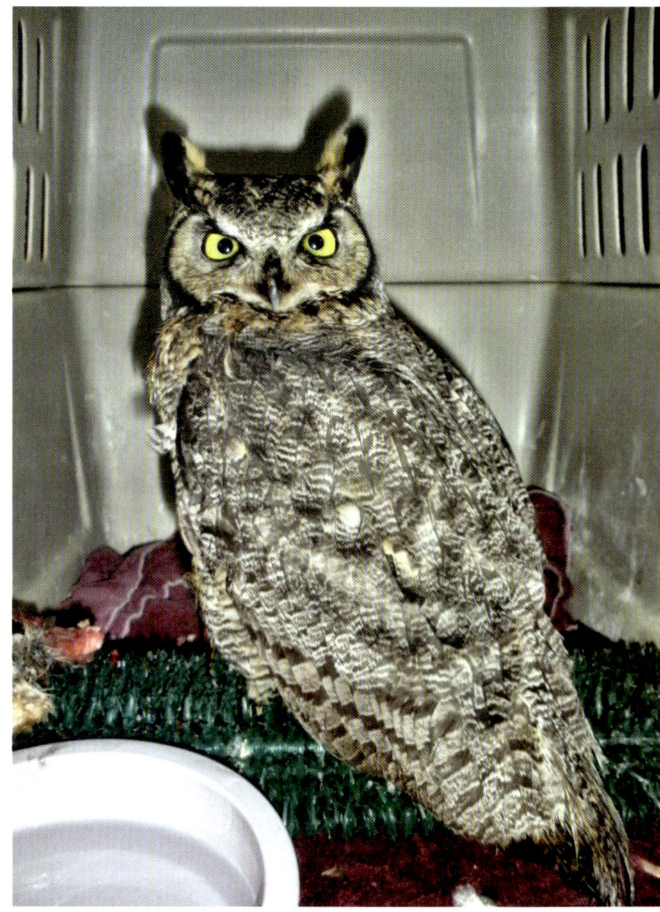

The same owl after he had several healthy meals.

the bird begins eating, it doesn't stop. At about six weeks of age, the young owls will pick at food and often begin eating on their own. I have yet to have a young owl that did not readily accept food from me. As with most young birds, at one point, they may look at their captor as their parent and begin to become imprinted on their captors. At this stage, it is important that you take the owl to a foster parent so the young bird can recognize others of its own species.

Once the owlets eat on their own, I like to take them down to foster parents at the Birds of Prey Foundation, so they can be raised by owls rather than people. This way there is no chance of the birds being imprinted on humans. The foster parents are a pair of owls named Nina and Pom. I remember the first young owl that I brought to Nina. She already had four or five young owls in her care as I entered her flight cage. As soon as she heard the clicking of the young owlet's bill, she began hooting. As I entered the cage and she saw the owlet, she began hooting at the owlet. I placed the owlet in a large box in the front of the cage, or on the ladder leading to Nina's nesting box, which is high off the ground in the back of the flight cage. It only takes about one day before the new owlet is sitting with its new mom. When the owls are about ten to eleven weeks of age, they are placed in a large flight cage for prerelease training, which consists of what is called "live training": We release live mice and rabbits in the cage with the owls, enabling the young owlets to capture and kill their own food. The young owls need to be proficient at this prior to their release.

I have received many injured adult Great Horned Owls over the years as well. The injuries that these owls incur are quite remarkable and wide-ranging. The latest owl was found just at sun-up on January 6, 2012, perched on a rock. The homeowner was alerted to the owl by scolding Black-billed Magpies and American Crows. He called me, explaining that he had a large owl in his front yard that appeared to be injured. I made the short drive to his house and found the owl still perched on a rock. The bird showed me no interest as I slowly moved toward it and placed a towel over him and picked him up. As I was carrying the owl to my truck, the homeowner came

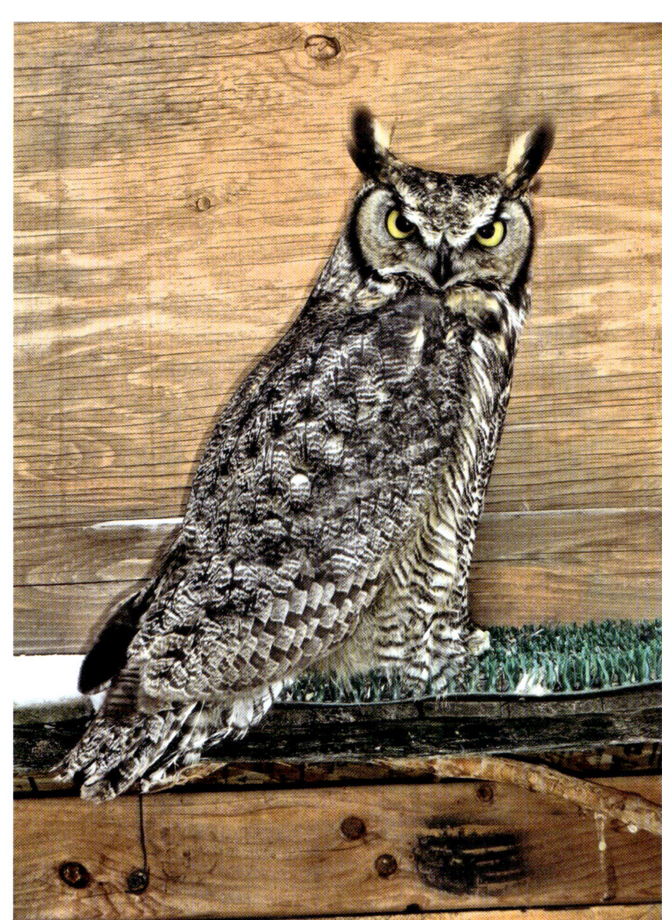

Sutton in my flight cage before being released.

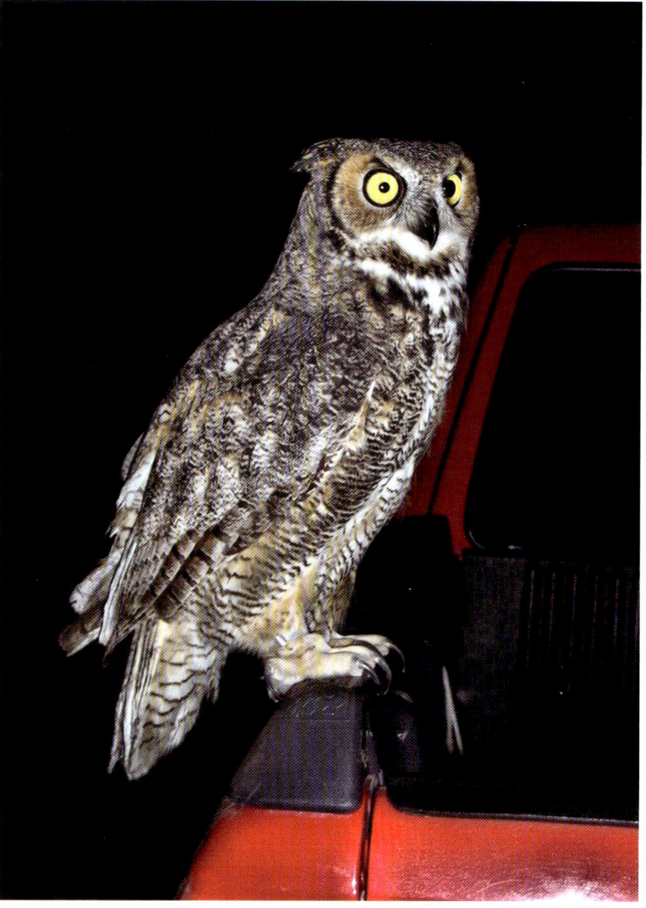

Sutton perched on the back of my truck before flying away. It is important to release nocturnal birds at dark.

out to see the owl up-close. I looked at the inside of the owl's mouth to find it was very pale, almost white, which is a sign of dehydration.

I palpated the owl's wings to see if it had a wing injury, (to palpate the wing, I hold the bird by the legs with my hand and run my fingers up and down the inside of the bird's wing bones with the other), but as luck would have it, the owl was fine in that regard. I then palpated his breast bone to find how well the owl had been eating — that owl was very thin. A bird that is in good shape or even fat will have a breast that feels like that of a chicken — very well rounded. When feeling the breast of a thin bird, you will feel the breast bone and very little muscle on either side of it. He was a young owl that was out on his own, apparently searching for a territory to claim. He must have been searching for several weeks; however, due to the high winds and snow that winter, he was most likely unable to do so. This is why he ended up thin and unresponsive. He most likely hadn't had a good meal in several weeks. It was fortunate for him that he ended up in an area where someone could find him.

I took the owl home, placed him in a large pet carrier with a water dish, and cut up a few mice and fed them to him using a forceps. I use a forceps instead of my fingers because often times I need to place the food behind the owl's tongue so he will swallow the food instead of regurgitating it. I fed the owl every half-hour that entire day until about 7 p.m., when he regurgitated everything that I had previously fed him. Evidently, I had been feeding him pieces that were too large for him.

I then began to feed him very small pieces of food for the next few hours. I stopped feeding him at about 11 p.m. and went to bed. The following morning I checked on the owl to find that he had digested all of the food from the night before. I continued to feed him for the next three days and nights. On the fourth day, I decided to leave his food in his pet carrier with him to see if he would eat on his own. I went to work and came home eight hours later to find that he had eaten all his food. For the following three days, I left cut up food for him and he readily ate, day and night.

After ten days, I placed the owl in my flight cage so he could move around a bit. My cage is only 8 x 8 x 16 feet (2.44m x 2.44m x 4.88m). I kept him there for three days until I was able to take him to the Birds of Prey Foundation, where he could fly in a much larger cage with several other Great Horned Owls. He was released in the spring when the weather was mild enough for an inexperienced owl to find a territory of his own. I banded the owl and have yet to hear back from him, so I am hopeful that he found a nice area to live and raise his family.

The most disheartening injured owl I was ever called about had to be the one that was stuck in a barbed wire fence. On the morning of May 15, 1995, I received a call from Robert Pollock, a professional photographer living in Allen's Park, Colorado. He explained that he had a large owl impaled in barbed wire behind his house and the poor bird was being harassed by American Crows and Black-billed Magpies. When I arrived at his house, I saw the owl in his backyard, hanging between the four stands of wire. I cut the fence to get the owl free, leaving small pieces of barbed wire in the bird's wing, so as not to cause any more damage to the poor bird. The magnificent owl had struggled so much that the barbs of the fence had torn all of the feathers, skin, and muscle from the ulna and radius bones of his right wing. I placed the owl in a pet carrier and rushed him to the veterinarian in Estes Park, so he could put the owl out of its misery. Unfortunately, that owl had to be euthanized.

Over the years, I've received hundreds of calls about "injured owls." I remember receiving a call late one evening. The man on the other end told me that he found a Great Horned Owl that couldn't fly very well. I asked him if the bird had anything in its talons (claws) that were making it unable to fly, such as prey; sometimes the prey will be too heavy for the owl to carry off. He told me that the owl was definitely injured and not carrying prey. I made the 22-mile (35.20km) drive to the area where the owl was and met the fella who called me (I have since forgotten his name). Using our flashlights, we made a short hike through the trees. Before seeing the owl, I found a headless drake Mallard lying on the ground. As I had suspected, the owl had killed an adult Mallard and tried to carry it away, but because the duck was too heavy, the owl couldn't get off of the ground with him. We never did find the owl, but I am sure he wasn't far from his duck dinner.

Fledgling Great Horned Owls are quite lazy and often end up near homes or even on porches and decks. On several occasions, I have been called to remove young Great Horned Owls from the ground around homes and businesses, as well as decks and porches of homeowners. On June 15, 2005, I received a call from a homeowner near the Wild Basin area of RMNP; he told me a large owl was on his back porch. The homeowner was afraid to walk past the owl and called me. I arrived at the home in question to find a fledgling Great Horned Owl on his porch next to a shovel. The little guy really had an attitude, looking at me as if to say, "Don't even think about coming near me." I walked up to the little guy and placed a towel over the owl and removed him from the porch, placed a leg band on the bird, and placed him in a nearby ponderosa pine. As I was doing this, his mom was flying all around, hooting at me. When the homeowner returned home, the owls were nowhere to be seen.

Years ago, as I was out birding at Lake Estes, my pager went off. I called the number on the pager. It was the owner of the restaurant I mentioned earlier asking if I could come and move a young owl that was perched on his railing next to the front door because it was scaring his patrons as they entered the establishment. Not having a net or even a towel to catch the owl with, I had no idea how I was going to catch the bird without getting hurt. I drove into the parking lot and saw the young owl perched on the cement wall. I looked behind the seat of my Ford Ranger® and found a baseball cap. I put the cap on and walked to the owl. When I was within reach of the owl, it began to snap its bill at me. I introduced myself to the bird and then asked the bird how he got to the wall and where his parents were. In a few steps, I was within reach of the bird. I lowered my left hand and moved it rapidly as the owl watched it. In a second, I grasped the bill of my cap, took it from my head, and covered the owl's head, grabbing it and picking the large bird from the wall all in one move. I took the owl to my truck where I placed an aluminum Fish and Wildlife Service leg band on him and placed him in the back of the restaurant on the branch of a ponderosa pine.

On June 10, 2008, Steve Thompson, an employee at the YMCA of the Rockies just south of Estes Park, called me to tell me of a young Great Horned Owl that was laying on the side of a dirt road on the YMCA's property. After several minutes, I arrived and was directed to the owl. I walked to the owl, which was indeed lying on the side of a dirt road, and placed a towel over it and picked it up. I checked the young owl for any apparent injuries.

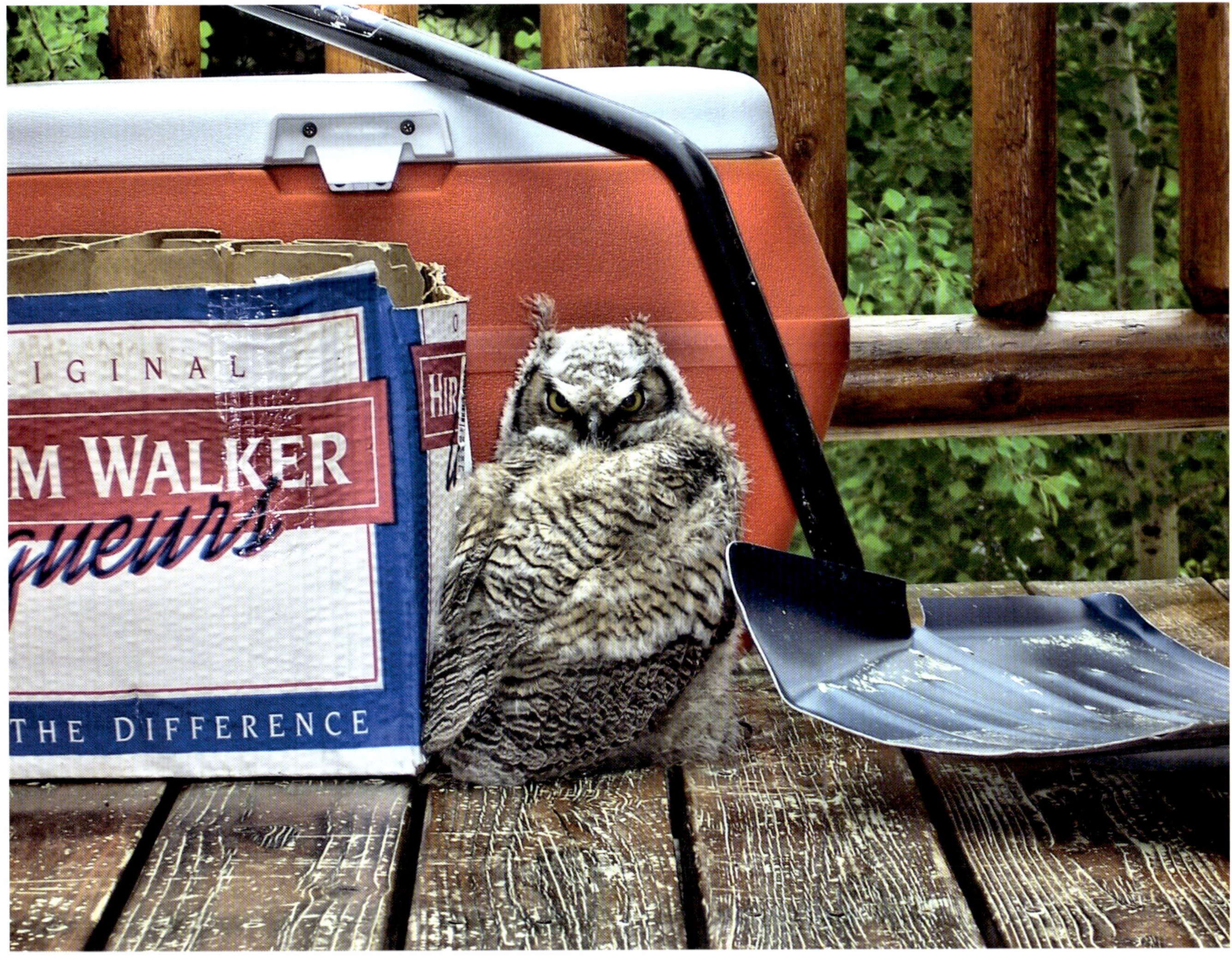

A fledgling Great Horned Owl that decided to perch on someone's back porch. Notice how even at such a young age, it tries to conceal itself by perching between the box, the shovel, and the cooler.

Finding no injuries, I put a leg band on the bird and placed the owl on the branch of a ponderosa pine and moved off. I returned two hours later and the bird had flown off. At times, young owls just don't want to perch on a branch and feel more comfortable lying on a platform or other flat surface. In this case, the platform was the ground.

On May 15, 2004, a little after 5 a.m., I received a call from the manager of the Estes Park health club, who told me there was a large owl perched on the ground floor at the back of the club. After a few minutes, I arrived, walked in, and met the manager. She pointed to the room where the owl was and I made my way to the room with my butterfly net to find the large owl perched on the ground along the back wall. I slowly moved to the owl and got as low as I could. When I was close enough, I quickly placed the net over the bird and picked it up. As I did with the other owls, I put a leg band on the bird and placed him on a branch of a Ponderosa Pine near the parking lot. The owl sat for a moment and then flew off.

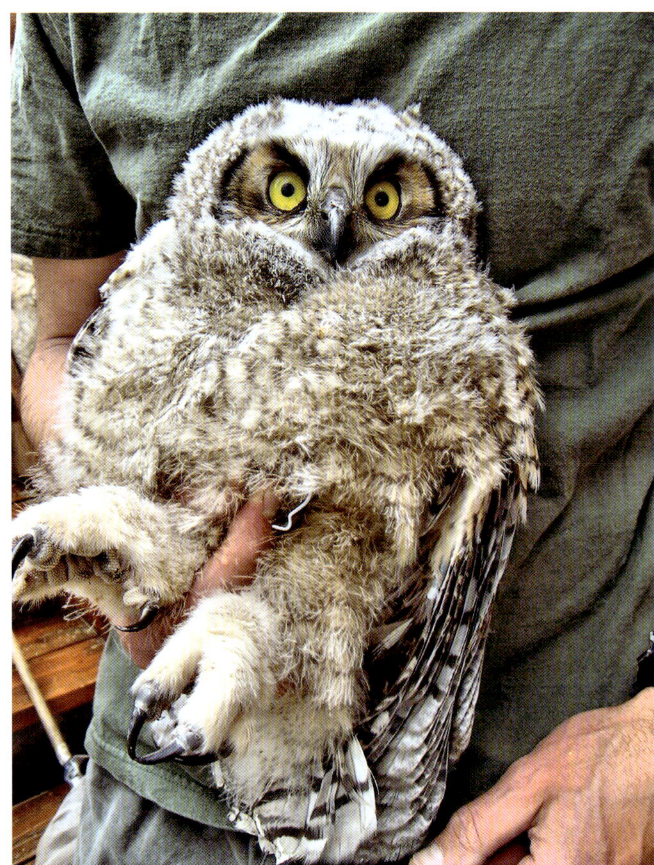

That same owl after I picked it off the porch.
Photo by Susan Rashid.

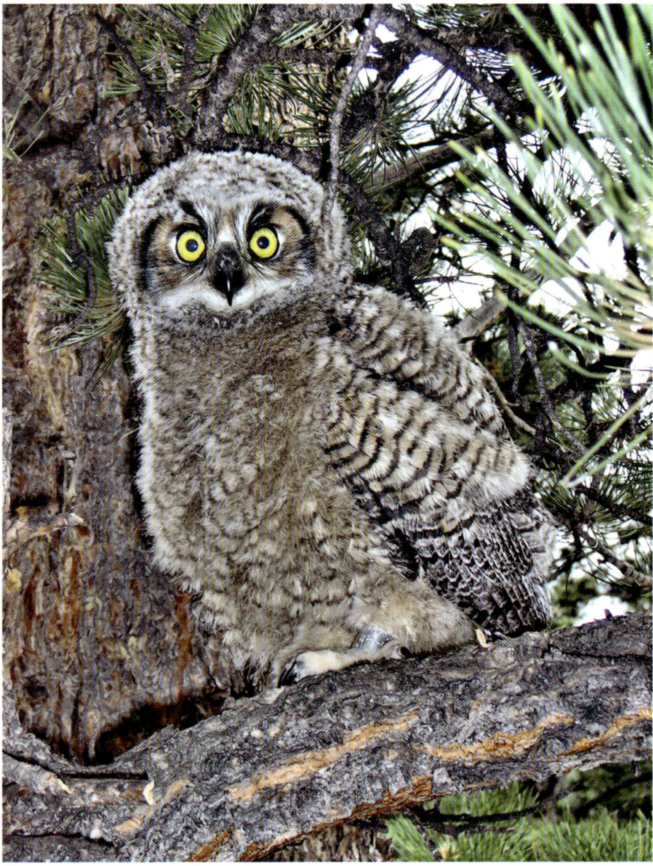

After taking the owl from the porch, I placed it on the limb of a ponderosa pine, where it would be safe.

Later that year, I received a call from the owner of the Best Western® motel just a few miles down the road from the health club. They have an outbuilding with clothes washers and dryers for patrons to do their laundry. The owner explained that there was a large owl perched on one of the washing machines and their patrons were afraid to enter the building.

My wife, Susan, and I arrived at the motel, parked the car, and walked to the office. Upon entering the office, I explained to the girl at the front desk that we were there for the owl. The girl directed us to the building where the owl was. As Susan and I entered the laundry building, we found the bewildered owl perched on top of one of the washing machines. I walked to the owl, asking it how it got into that building, and quickly covered it with my net. I picked up the owl and walked out of the building with the owl in hand, as my wife brought my bands to me. I placed a leg band on the owl and positioned it on a branch of a large ponderosa pine near the parking lot of the motel. The owl perched for a moment and then flew away.

Two interesting owl captures both occurred at the YMCA of the Rockies. The first was in 2004, when some of the wait staff in the dining hall heard what they thought was a raccoon in the chimney above the fireplace. This fireplace has a piece of metal at the top, which covers three-quarters of the top of the fireplace from the back to the front. There is a small opening at the top front of the fireplace for the smoke to flow into the chimney. This opening is barely large enough to reach my arm into the chimney and touch the top of that metal covering. Apparently, things were quiet during the day, but after dark they would hear noise in the chimney above the fireplace.

After a week, the staff heard the owl hooting from inside the chimney and called me. I arrived at the dining hall after lunch, when there wouldn't be anyone in the room that might be bothered to see an owl. I reached into the covering above the top of the fireplace and slowly reached around until I could feel the bird's legs. I grasped both legs and pulled the owl out of the chimney legs first.

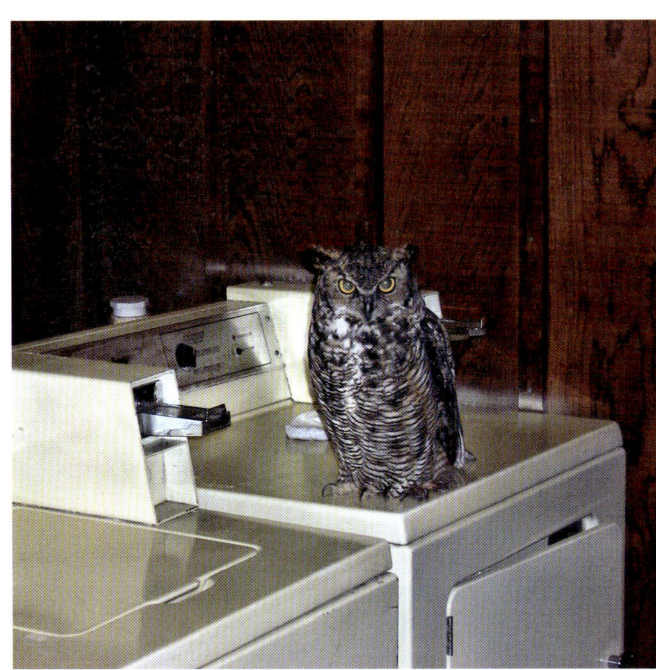

After being called about an owl perched on a washing machine, I arrived to find just that.

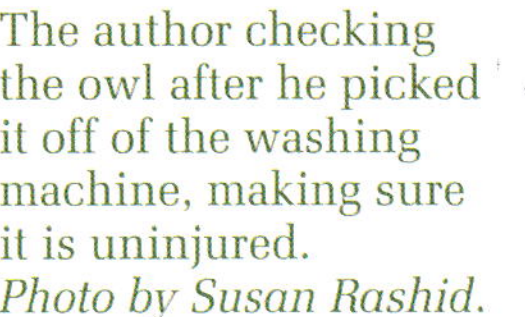

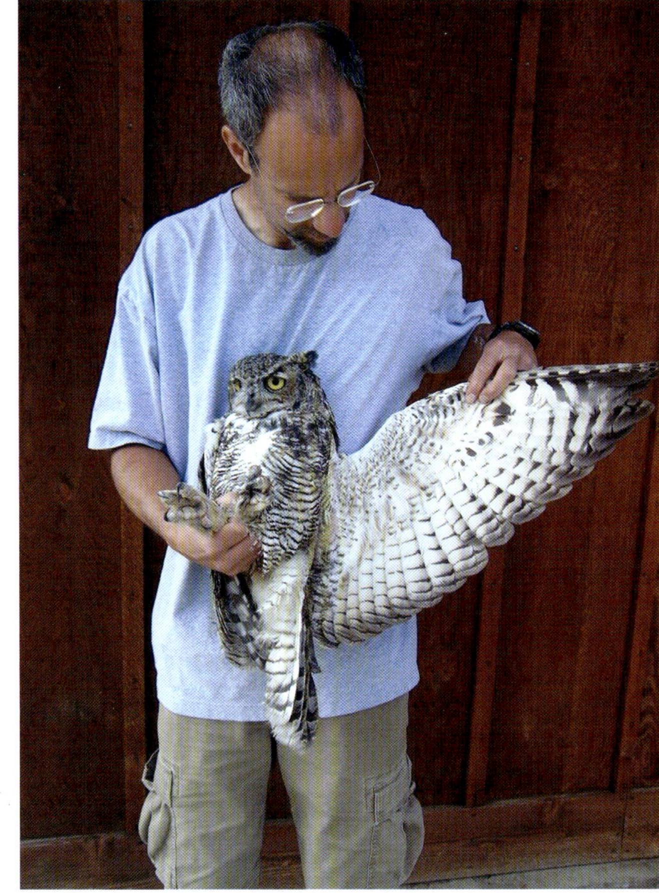

The author checking the owl after he picked it off of the washing machine, making sure it is uninjured. *Photo by Susan Rashid.*

As you could imagine, the owl was covered with soot and dehydrated. It was a young bird that had recently begun flying. It had apparently perched on the top of the edge of the chimney and fallen down into the chimney, landing on the metal covering above the fireplace, and then it couldn't get out. I took the owl home and washed the soot off the bird the best I could and placed him in a pet carrier for a few days with food and water. On the fourth day, I took the owl to the Birds of Prey Foundation to make sure the bird could fly well enough to be released. The bird was in captivity for eighteen days. When I took the bird back to the YMCA, it was just after dark. It is important to release nocturnal birds just at dark so they have the entire evening to find a place to roost during the day, so not to be detected by potential predators.

I pulled into the parking lot near the dining hall. There were dozens of people walking throughout the property that evening. When I got out of the car, I heard and saw the adult female Great Horned Owl perched on the pinnacle of the dining hall, with a young owl perched on the top of the ponderosa pine next to the hall. I knew the ages of these birds because of the sounds they were making. The young bird was making food-begging calls while the adult female was hooting. I took the pet carrier out of my car and placed it on the roof and opened the carrier door. The adult owl began hooting as the young owl walked out of the carrier and onto the roof of the car. Due to being so large and heavy, when Great Horned Owls take off, they often swoop low and gain elevation as they flap, which is exactly what this bird had done. The young owl flew from the top of the car and landed next to his mom. The owl that I had just released and the adult touched bills, almost as if they were kissing hello. The adult flew off and the two young owls followed. It was quite the eye-opener, seeing that even after more than two weeks apart, these owls could recognize one another. If someone would have told me about that, I'm not sure I would have believed it. However, actually seeing it is another story.

When I began rehabilitating Great Horned Owls, Sigrid Ueblacker told me that it is extremely important to release Great Horned Owls back where they came from, because they are so territorial that they will do whatever it takes to get back to their territory. After seeing those two owls interact, it really made an impression on me about how the owls are able to identify each other, even though to us they all look alike, as well as how important it is to release the birds back where they came from. Reading about nature and actually seeing it in action are two very different things.

My wife and I are cat owners and have had cats for over twenty-five years. Yes, cats and birds in the same house. Most of the cats don't even mind the birds, but I had two that found the birds very interesting. One was a striking Himalayan called Little G. My cats would routinely sit in the office with me while I painted. My drawing table is against the window so I can paint with natural lighting during the day and watch the birds at the feeders just outside my window. I received an injured Great Horned Owl that I had placed into a large pet carrier and put the carrier on the top of the roll-top desk in my office. Unbeknownst to Little G, there was now a Great Horned Owl in the room that wasn't in the room a few hours earlier; G walked into the room as she always had, but this time the owl instantly began snapping its bill, raising its wings up over its back, and stomping its feet on the perch. Little G froze for a few moments and stared at the cage — and then ran out of the room and hid under the couch and didn't come out for about a half-hour.

When scared, owls often look as if they are in a catatonic state and appear to be unable to see. After the incident with Little G, it occurred to me that placing a live cat near an owl would be a great way to find out if the owl was blind or not. If the owl can see, it will either look directly at the cat, or go into a hiding posture, hoping the cat doesn't see the owl. Occasionally, when a bird has crashed into a window, they are temporarily blinded. Pressure builds up on the optic nerve and the bird can't see until the pressure is released. It often takes a few days for the swelling to diminish, after which the bird can see.

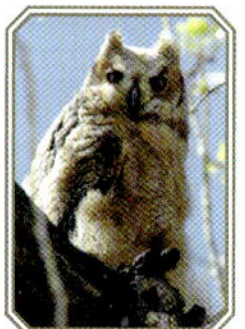

A FEW FINAL THOUGHTS

As you have most likely figured out, I have an incredible fascination with and respect for the Great Horned Owl. It has fascinated me longer than any other avian species. I remember talking to a friend in 1998, as I was beginning my Northern Pygmy-Owl research. He told me that there was barely enough information published about the tiny Northern Pygmy-Owl to fill a three-ringed binder, yet there is enough information on the Great Horned Owls to fill an 8 x 8-foot (2.44 x 2.44m) room from floor to ceiling! That intrigued me. That is when I really began paying serious attention to Great Horned Owls. My thought was: if the species is so widely studied, there must be something to Great Horned Owls that warrants all of the attention.

One thing that is so fascinating about Great Horned Owls is that they're found in virtually every habitat in North America. I've found Great Horned Owls in the center of large cities and in the woods far from human habitation. Therefore, whatever species I'm researching, whether it is Northern Pygmy-Owls, Northern Saw-whet Owls, or even the Northern Goshawks, I inevitably find Great Horned Owls at some point during my research. The diminutive Northern Pygmy-Owls and Northern Saw-whet Owls can often be heard vocalizing within the territories of the larger Great Horned Owls. However, I've yet to identify any interaction between the species. I've found Northern Saw-whet Owls and Northern Pygmy-Owls nesting within a few yards of one another and several hundred yards from a pair of Great Horned Owls.

Great Horned Owls begin nesting in the winter, which often makes nesting owls easy to locate as the female's head and ear tufts protrude above her nest. Due to their early nesting activities, Great Horned Owls can pick the best nest sites within their territories to raise their families. These owls can nest virtually anywhere, from abandoned nests of other birds and animals, to caves, cliffs, and even man-made structures.

Being such a large and powerful owl enables them to feed on a variety of species, which includes virtually any small- to medium-sized creature that craws, walks, flies, or swims. They're often the most powerful avian predator within their territory, enabling them to kill and carry creatures that weigh more than they do. This has gained them the nickname "the flying tiger."

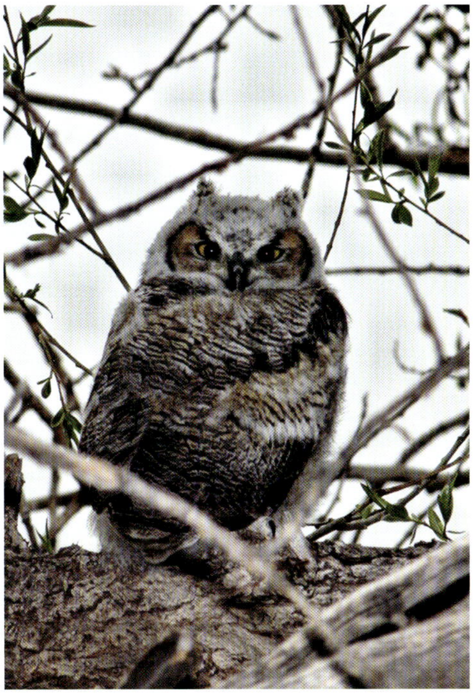

A fledgling Great Horned Owl.

For years, I was intimidated by these large owls. It wasn't until I began rehabilitating them that I realized my intimidation was completely unwarranted. In many cases, as soon as the owls realize that I'm just trying to help them, they often relax enough to eat in front of me. I've been able to hand-feed certain ones minutes after they were brought to me. I had one young owl that enjoyed being in captivity so much that when I tried to release him, he didn't want to leave. When I released the owl, it was in a pet carrier which I placed on the top of my car. I opened the carrier so the owl could fly out. The bird just walked to the back of the pet carrier and stood against the back wall. I then lifted the back of the pet carrier a few inches, hoping the owl would fly out due to the awkward angle. The owl still didn't come out. Using a towel, I reached into the carrier, placed my hands around the owl, brought him out of the carrier, and held him, enabling him to fly off at any time. He still didn't fly off. It wasn't until I gently tossed him into the night sky that he finally took flight.

That is one of the many reasons that I love these owls so much. Great Horned Owls have a reputation for being a large and aggressive predator. Yet at times, they can be easily intimidated. I would not have believed that such a large and powerful bird would be afraid to leave its human captor. With every Great Horned Owl that I'm fortunate enough to handle, whether it is during a banding operation or handling an injured owl, I get an indescribable feeling of excitement.

GLOSSARY OF SCIENTIFIC NAMES

BIRDS:

American Crow *(Corvus brachyrhynchos)*
American Kestrel *(Falco sparverius)*
American Robin *(Turdus migratorius)*
American Woodcock *(Scolopac minor)*
Araucana Rooster *(Gallus inauris)*
Bald Eagle *(Haliaeetus leucocephalus)*
Band-tailed Pigeon *(Columba fasciata)*
Barn Owl *(Tyto alba)*
Barred Owl *(Strix varia)*
Barred Rock Chicken *(Gallus domesticus)*
Black-billed Magpie *(Pica pica)*
Black Duck *(Anas rubripes)*
Black Tern *(Chlidonias niger)*
Blakiston's Fish Owl *(Bubo blackistoni)*
Blue-winged Teal *(Anas discors)*
Bonaparte's Gull *(Larus philadelphia)*
Boreal Owl *(Aegolius funereus)*
Broad-winged Hawk *(Buteo platypterus)*
Broad-tailed Hummingbird *(Selasphorus platycercus)*
Brown Fish Owl *(Bubo zeylonensis)*
Burrowing Owl *(Athene cunicularia)*
California Gull *(Larus californicus)*
California Quail *(Callipepla californica)*
Cassin's Finch *(Carpodacus cassinii)*
Cave Swallow *(Petrochelidon fulva)*
Chipping Sparrow *(Spizella passerina)*
Common Eider *(Somateria mollissima)*
Common Goldeneye *(Bucephala clangula)*
Common Grackle *(Quiscalus quiscula)*
Common Nighthawk *(Chordeiles minor)*
Common Poorwill *(Phalaenoptilus nuttallii)*
Common Raven *(Corvus corax)*
Common Yellowthroat *(Geothlypis trichas)*
Coopers Hawk *(Accipiter cooperii)*
Coot *(Fulica americana)*
Dark-eyed Juncos *(Junco hyemalis)*
Double-crested Cormorant *(Phalacrocorax auritus)*
Downy Woodpecker *(Picoides pubescens)*
Dusky Grouse *(Dendragapus obscurus)*
Eastern Meadowlark *(Sturnella magma)*
Eastern Screech Owl *(Otus asio)*
Elf Owl *(Micrathene whitneyi)*
Eurasian Collared Dove *(Streptopelia decaocto)*
Eurasian Eagle Owl *(Bubo bubo)*
European Pygmy-Owl *(Glaucidium passerinum)*
European Starling *(Sturnus vulgaris)*
Ferruginous Hawk *(Buteo regalis)*
Ferruginous Pygmy-Owl *(Glaucidium brasilianum)*
Flammulated Owl *(Otus flammeolus)*
Forester's Tern *(Sterna forsteri)*
Franklin's Gull *(Larus pipixcan)*
Golden-crowned Kinglet *(Regulus satrapa)*
Gray Jay *(Perisoreus canadensis)*
Gray Partridge *(Perdix perdix)*
Great Gray Owl *(Strix nebulosa)*
Great Horned Owl *(Bubo virginiianus)*
Greater Green Heron *(Butorides virescens)*
Greater Roadrunner *(Geococcyx californianus)*
Greater Yellowlegs *(Tringa melanoleuca)*
Green-tailed Towhee *(Pipilo chlorurus)*
Hairy Woodpecker *(Picoides villosus)*
Harris's Hawk *(Parabuteo unicinctus)*
Harris's Sparrow *(Zonotrichia querula)*
Hermit Thrush *(Catharus guttatus)*
Herring Gull *(Larus argentatus)*
Horned Lark *(Eremophila alpestris)*
House Sparrow *(Passer domesticus)*
House Wren *(Troglodytes aedon)*
Killdeer *(Charadrius vociferus)*
King Rail *(Rallus elegans)*
Leach's Storm-Petrel *(Oceanodroma leucorhoa)*
Lesser Goldfinch *(Carduelis psaltria)*
Lesser Yellowlegs *(Tringa flavipes)*
Long-eared Owl *(Asio otus)*
MacGillivary's Warbler *(Oporonis tolmiei)*
Malay Fish Owl *(Bubo ketupu)*
Marbled Murrlet *(Brachyramphus marmoratus)*

Mountain Bluebird *(Sialia currucoides)*
Mountain Chickadee *(Poecile gambeli)*
Mountain Quail *(Oreortyx pictus)*
Mourning Dove *(Zenaida macroura)*
Northern Cardinal *(Cardinalis cardinalis)*
Northern Flicker *(Colaptes auratus)*
Northern Goshawk *(Accipiter gentilis)*
Northern Harrier *(Circus cyaneus)*
Northern Mockingbird *(Mimus polyglottos)*
Northern Pintail *(Anas acuta)*
Northern Saw-whet Owl *(Aegolius acadicus)*
Northern Shrike *(Lanius excubitor)*
Northwest Crow *(Corvus cairinus)*
Ovenbird *(Seiurus aurocapillus)*
Passenger Pigeon *(Ectopistes migratorius)*
Peregrine Falcon *(Falco peregrinus)*
Pharaoh Eagle Owl *(Bubo ascalaphus)*
Pigeon Guillemot *(Cepphus columba)*
Pileated Woodpecker *(Dryocopus pileatus)*
Pine Grosbeak *(Pinicola enucleator)*
Pine Siskin *(Carduelis pinus)*
Purple Gallinule *(Porphyrula martinica)*
Purple Martin *(Progne subis)*
Pygmy Nuthatch *(Sitta pygmaea)*
Red-breasted Nuthatch *(Sitta Canadensis)*
Red Crossbill *(Loxia curvitostra)*
Red-napped Sapsucker *(Sphyrapicus nuchalis)*
Red Shouldered Hawk *(Buteo lineatus)*
Red-tailed Hawk *(Buteo jamaicensis)*
Red-winged Blackbirds *(Agelaius phoeniceus)*
Ring-necked Pheasant *(Phasianus colchicus)*
Rock Eagle Owl *(Bubo bengalensis)*
Rock Pigeon *(Columbis livia)*
Rock Ptarmigan *(Lagopus mutus)*
Rosy Finch *(Leucosticte species)*
Rough-legged Hawk *(Buteo lagapus)*
Ruby-crowned Kinglet *(Regulus calendula)*
Ruffed Grouse *(Bonasa umbellus)*
Rusty Blackbird *(Euphagus carolinus)*
Sharp-shinned Hawk *(Accipiter striatus)*
Short-eared Owl *(Asio flammeus)*
Snow Owl *(Bubo scandiacus)*
Spotted Eagle Owl *(Bubo africanus)*
Spotted Owl *(Strix occidentalis)*
Spotted Sandpiper *(Actitis macularia)*
Spruce Grouse *(Falcipennis canadensis)*
Stellar's Jay *(Cyanocitta Stelleri)*
Swainson's Hawk *(Buteo swainsoni)*
Swainson's Thrush *(Catharus ustulatus)*
Swamp Sparrow *(Melospiza Georgiana)*
Three-toed Woodpecker *(Picoides tridactylus)*
Townsend's Solitaire *(Myadestes townsendi)*
Varied Thrush *(Lxoreus naevius)*
Veery *(Catharus fuscescens)*
Virginia Rail *(Rallus limicola)*
Western Tananger *(Piranga ludoviciana)*
Whip-poor-will *(Caprimulgus vociferous)*
White-breasted Nuthatch *(Sitta americana)*
White-crowned Sparrow *(Zonotrichia leucophrys)*
White-faced Ibis *(Plegadis chihi)*
White-tailed Ptarmigan *(Lagopus leucurus)*
Williamson's Sapsucker *(Sphyrapicus thyroideus)*
Willow Ptarmagan *(Lagopus lagopus)*
Wilson's Snipe *(Gallinago delecta)*
Yellow-rumped Warbler *(Dendroica coronata)*

TREES AND SHRUBS:

American Beech *(Fagus grandifolia)*
Balsam Poplar *(Populus balsamifera)*
Black Birch *(Betula lenta)*
Black Spruce *(Picea mariana)*
California Black Oak *(Quercus kelloggii)*
Common Juniper *(Juniperus communis)*
Cottonwood *(Populus sp.)*
Douglas Fir *(Pseudotsuga menziesii)*
Engelmann Spruce *(Picea engelmanni)*
European Larch *(Larix decidua)*
Gamblles Oak *(Quercus gambelii)*

Juniper Tree *(Juniperus scopulorum)*
Lodgepole Pine *(Pinus contorta latifolia)*
Mountain Alder *(Alnus tenuifolia)*
Oak *(Quercus sp.)*
Paper Birch *(Betula papyrifera)*
Ponderosa Pine *(Pinus ponderosa)*
Poplar *(Populaus sp.)*
Quaking Aspen *(Populus tremuloides)*
River Birch *(Betula nigra)*
Russian Olive *(Elaeagnus angustifolia)*
Sub Alpine fir *(Abies lasiocarpa*
Sycamore tree *(Platanus wrightii))*
Wax Currant *(Ribes cereum)*
White Cedar *(Thuja occidentalis)*
White Spruce *(Picea glauca)*

ANIMALS:

Bobcat *(Lynx rufus)*
Deer Mouse *(Peromyscus maniculatus)*
Douglas Squirrel *(Tamiasciurus douglasii)*
Eastern Chipmunk *(Tamias striatus)*
Elk *(Cervus elaphus)*
Fisher *(Martes pennanti)*
Flying Squirrel *(Scuiriopterus scuriopterus)*
Golden Mantled Ground Squirrel *(Spermophilus lateralis)*
Gray Jay *(Perisoreus canadensis)*
Harvest Mouse *(Reithrodontomys sp.)*
Hispid Cotton Rat *(Sigmodon hispidus)*
House Mouse *(Mus musculus)*
Least Chipmunk *(Eutamias minimus)*
Long-tailed Vole *(Microtus longicaudus)*
Meadow Vole *(Microtus pennsylvanicus)*
Montane Vole *(Microtus montanus)*
Mountain Lion *(Felis concolor)*
Northern Bog Lemming *(Synaptomys borealis)*
Northern Flying Squirrel *(Glycomys sabrinus)*
Northern Pocket Gopher *(Thomomys talpoides*
Northern Pygmy Mouse *(Baiomys taylori)*
Pack Rat *(Neotoma cinerea)*
Pine Martin *(Martes americana)*
Raccoon *(Procyon lotor)*
Red-backed Vole *(Clethrionomys gapperi)*
Red Squirrel *(Tamiasciurus hudsonicus)*
Short-tailed Shrew *(Blarina brevicauda)*
Shrew *(Sorax species)*
Smokey Shrew *(Sorex fumeus)*
Snowshoe Hare *(Lepus americanus)*
Southern Red-backed Vole *(Myodes gapperi)*
Texas Kangaroo Rat *(Dipodomys species)*
Weasel *(Mustela species)*
Western Jumping Mouse *(Zapus princeps)*
White-footed Mouse *(Peromyscus leucopus)*
Woodland Mouse *(Peromyscus leucopus)*
Wyoming Ground Squirrel *(Urocitellus elegans)*

REFERENCES CITED

Aigner, P. A., M. L. Morrison, L. S. Hall, and W. M. Block. "Great Horned Owl Food Habits at Mono Lake, California." *The Southwestern Naturalist.* Vol. 39, no. 3.286, 1994; 288.

Armstrong, W. H. "Nesting and Food Habits of the Long-eared Owl in Michigan." *Michigan State University Museum Biological Series* 1:61-96. Vol. 1, no. 2. 1958.

Austing, G. R. and J. B. Holt, Jr. *The World of the Great Horned Owl.* Philadelphia, Pennsylvania: J. B. Lippincott Company, 1966; 13-153.

Baumgartner, F. M. "Courtship and Nesting of Great Horned Owls." *The Wilson Bulletin,* 1938; 274-285.

"Territory and Population in the Great Horned." *Auk.* Vol. 56, 1939; 274-282.

Belthoff, J. R. and G. Ritchison. "Natal Dispersal of Eastern Screech Owls." *Condor,* 91, 1989; 254-265.

Bent, A. C. *Life History of North American Birds of Prey* (Part Two). Dover, Delaware: Dover Publications, Inc., 1938.

Bloom, P. H. and S. J. Hawks. "Food habits of nesting Golden Eagles in Northwest California and Northwestern Nevada." *Raptor Research* 16 (4), 1982; 110-115.

Bluhm, C. and E. K. Ward. "Great Horned Owl Predation on Short-eared Owl." *Condor,* 81; 1979; 307-308.

Burkholder, G. and D. G. Smith. "Great Horned Owls (*Bubo virginianus*) nesting in a Great Blue Heron (*Ardea herodias*) Heronry." *J. Raptor Research* 22 (2), 1988; 62.

Bull, E. L., M.G. Henjum, and R. S. Rohweder. "Nesting and foraging habitat of Great Gray Owls." *J. Raptor Research* 22 (4), 1988; 107-115.

Cade, T. J. "Ecology of the Peregrine and Gyrfalcon populations in Alaska." *University of California Publications in Zoology,* 63. California: University of California Press, 1960; 151-290.

Cameron, F. S. "Birds of Custer and Dawson Counties, Montana." *Auk* 24, 1907; 260-269.

Craighead, J. J. and F. C. Craighead, Jr. *Hawks, Owls and Wildlife.* Harrisburg, Pennsylvania: Stackpole Company, 1969.

Devine, A. and D. G. Smith. "Great Horned Owl nesting in Monk Parakeet Colony in Suburban Connecticut." *J. Raptor Research* 26 (4), 1992; 267.

Dixon, J. B. "History of a pair of Pacific Great Horned Owls." *The Condor,* Vol. XVI, no. 2, 1914; 47-54.

Eakle. W. L. and T. G. Grubb. "Prey remains from Golden Eagle Nests in central Arizona." *Western Birds,* Vol. 17, No. 2, 1986; 87-89.

Elder, W. H. "Early nesting of the Great Horned Owl." *Auk,* Vol. 52, No. 3, 1935; 309-310.

Errington, P. L. "Food Habits of Southern Wisconsin Raptors. Part One: Owls." *The Condor,* 1932; 176-186.

"Studies on the behavior of the Great Horned Owl." *The Willson Bulletin.* December 1932; 212-220.

Errington, P. L., F. Hamerstrom, and F.,N. Hamerstrom. 1940. "The Great Horned Owl and its Prey in North-Central United States." *Iowa Agriculture Experiment Station Research Bulletin,* 277; 759-850.

Franks, E. C. and J. E. Warnock. "Great Horned Owl nesting in a popular area." *The Willson Bulletin,* Vol. 81, No. 3, 1969; 332-333.

French, T. W. "Great Horned Owl Predation on Leach's Storm Petrels in Maine." *Auk,* Vol. 96, No. 1, 1979; 202.

Guillion, G. W. "Horned Owl Preys on Cooper Hawk." *Condor,* Vol. 49, No. 6, 1947; 244.

Hamerstrom, F. O. M. "Food of Central Wisconsin Horned Owls." *The American Midland Naturalist,* Vol. 22, No. 3, 1939; 700-702.

Henry, C. J. "Golden Eagle takes wounded Great Horned Owl." *Auk,* Vol. 56, No. 1, 1939; 75.

Holt, D. W. and S. Drasen. "Early Nesting by Great Horned Owls in Montana." *J. Raptor Research* 35 (1), 2001; 66-67.

Houston, C. S. "Eggs of other species in Great Horned Owl nests." *Auk*, Vol. 92, No. 2, 1975; 377-378.

"Brood size of the Great Horned Owl in Saskatchewan." *Bird Banding*, Vol. 42. No. 2, 1971; 103-105.

Houston, C. S., D. G. Smith, and C. Rohner. "Great Horned Owl." *The Birds of North America*, No. 372, 1998; 1-28.

Jehl, J. R. Jr. and B. G. Murray, Jr. 1989. "Response: Evolution of Sexual Size Dimorphism." *Auk*, Vol. 106. 155-157.

Johnsgard, P. A. *North American Owls*. Second Edition. Washington, D.C. and London: Smithsonian Institute Press, 2002.

Latham, R. "The food of predaceous animals in northeastern United States." Pennsylvania Game Commission, Final Report, P-R Proj. 36-R Rept., 1950; 1-69.

Mader, W. J. "Notes on Nesting Great Horned Owls in Southern Arizona." *Journal Raptor Research*, 7 (3/4), 1973; 109-111.

Marti, C. D. "Feeding Ecology of Four Sympatric Owls." *The Condor* 76, 1974; 45-61.

McGillivary, W. B. "Size, sexual size dimorphism, and their measurement in Great Horned Owls in Alberta." *Canadian Journal of Zoology*, 63, 1985; 2364.

McMillian, M. A. "Food-Hunting Behavior by a Great Horned Owl." *Florida Field Nat.* 26(3), 1998; 91-93.

Minor, W. F. and M. Minor and M. F. Ingraldi. "Nesting of Red-tailed Hawks and Great Horned Owls in a central New York Urban/Suburban Area." *J. Field Ornithol*, 64 (4), 1993; 433-439.

Morse, D. H. "Great Horned Owls and nesting seabirds." Auk, Vol. 88, 1971; 426-427.

Mulaik, S. "An early nesting date of the Great Horned Owl." *Auk*, Vol. 52, No. 2, 1935; 187.

Mysterud, I. and H. Dunker. 1979. "Mammal ear mimicry; a hypothesis on the behavioral function of owls horns." *Animal Behavior* 27, 1979; 315.

Newton, I. *Population Ecology of Raptors*. Vermillion, South Dakota: Buteo books, 1979.

Olmster, R. O. "Feeding Habits of Great Horned Owls Bubo virginianus." *Auk*, Vol. 67, No. 4, 1950; 515-516.

Packard, R. L. "Great Horned Owl attacking squirrel nests." *The Willson Bulletin*, Vol. 66, No. 4, 1954; 272.

Palmer, R. S. *Handbook of North American Birds*. Vol. 4. Diurnal Raptors (part 1). New Haven, Connecticut: Yale University Press, 1988.

Rashid, S. *Small Mountain Owls*. Atglen, Pennsylvania: Schiffer Publishing, Ltd., 2009.

Reed, B. P. "Growth Development and Reactions of Young Great Horned Owls." Auk, Vol. XLII, 1925; 14-31.

Reynolds, R. T. and E. C. Meslow. "Partitioning of Food and Niche Characteristics of Coexisting accipiter during breeding". *Auk*, 101, 1984; 761-799.

Reynolds, R. T., S. M. Joy, and D. G. Leslie. "Nest productivity, fidelity, and spacing of Northern Goshawks in northern Arizona". Stud. *Avian Biol.* 165, 1994; 106-113

Rohner, C. and F. I. Doyle. "Method of Locating Great Horned Owl Nests in the Boreal Forest." *J. Raptor Research* 26 (1), 1992; 33-35.

"Food stressed Great Horned Owl Kills Adult Goshawk: Exceptional Observation or Community Process?" *J. Raptor Research* 26 (4), 1992; 261-263.

Schemnitz, S. D. "Notes on the Food Habits of the Great Horned Owl in Western Oklahoma." *The Condor*, 1962; 328-329.

Seidensticker, J. C. "Notes on the food habits of the Great Horned Owl in Montana." *The Murrelet*, Vol. 49 (1), 1968; 1-3.

Seidensticker, J. C. and H. V. Reynolds. "The nesting, reproductive performance, and chlorinated Hydrocarbon resides in the Red-Tailed Hawk and Great Horned Owls in south-central Montana." *The Willson Bulletin*, Vol. 83, No. 4, 1971; 408-418.

Sharp. W. M. 1"An Unusual Nest of the Great Horned Owl." *Wilson Bulletin*, Vol. 54, no. 2, 1942; 141.

Shoemaker, F. H. "Peculiar Nest of the Great Horned Owl. *Auk*, Vol. 14, No. 3, 1987; 318.

Sibley, D. A. *The Sibley Guide to Birds*. New York, New York: Algred A. Knoft, 2000.

Smith, A. P. "Diurnal Activities of the Great Horned Owl." *Auk*, 1912; 240-241.

Smith, D. G. "Great Horned Owl." *Wild Bird Guide*. Harrisburg, Pennsylvania: Stackpole Books, 2002; 1-95.

Smith, D. G. and B. A. Smith. "Hunting Methods and Success of Newly-Fledged Great Horned Owls." *Journal of Filed Ornithology*. Vol. 43, No. 2, 1972; 142.

Swenk, M. H. "Great Horned Owls Dying in the Wild from Diseases." *The Willson Bulletin*, 1932; 180.

Terres, J. K. *The Audubon Society Encyclopedia of North American Birds*. New York, New York: A.A. Knopf, Inc., 1982.

Toops, C. *The Enchanted Owl*. Stillwater, Minnesota: Voyager Press, 1990.

Vaughn, T. A. "Diurnal foraging by the Great Horned Owl." *Wilson Bulletin*, Vol. 66, no. 2, 1954; 148.

Voous, K. H. *Owls of the Northern Hemisphere*. Cambridge, Massachusetts: MIT press, 1988.

Wells, D. E. *100 Birds and How their got their name*. Chapel Hill, North Carolina: Algonquin Books, 2002; 103-105.

West, S. "Great Horned Owl Predation on Cave Swallows." *Western Birds* 18, 1987; 125.

Wiley, J. W. "Relationship of nesting hawks with Great Horned Owl." *Auk*. Vol. 92, 1975; 157-159.

Wolhuter, B. R. "Second Report of Great Horned Owl Preying on Short-eared Owl." *Journal of Field Ornithology*. Vol. 36, No. 2, 1968; 319.

ABOUT THE AUTHOR

Scott Rashid is the founder and director of the Colorado Avian Research and Rehabilitation Institute in Estes Park, Colorado (www.carriep.org). Members of the institute research species including Northern-Pygmy Owls, Northern Goshawks, Northern Saw-whet Owls, and American Kestrels. They also rehabilitate the injured birds in and around Estes Park and Rocky Mountain National Park.

Scott has been drawing and painting birds since childhood. Working primarily in watercolor, he has depicted many North American bird species. His art is in numerous private collections throughout North America and Europe.

Since 1997, Scott has been operating a permanent bird banding station at the YMCA of the Rockies south of Estes Park. During the banding sessions, he has trapped and banded a variety of avian species, including warblers, finches, sparrows, along with hawks and owls. In 2014 he banded is 10,000th bird there.

The author with a nestling Great Horned Owl.
Photo by Susan Rashid.

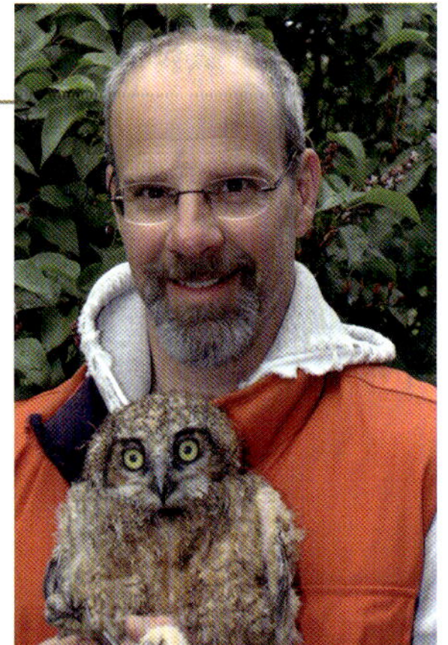

MORE SCHIFFER BOOKS

by the author

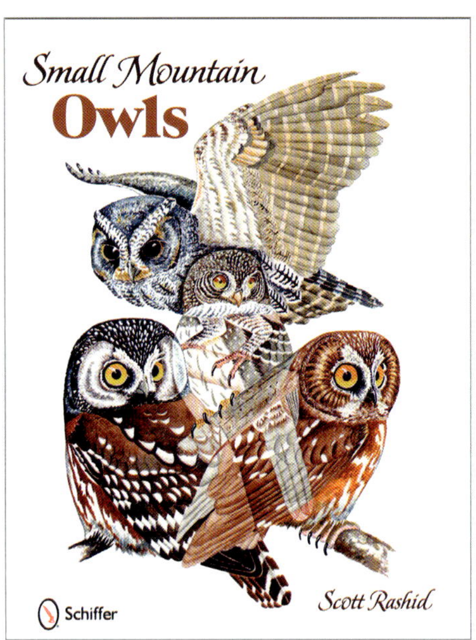

Small Mountain Owls. Scott Rashid. This guide provides detailed information and over 160 photos and drawings of four species of small mountain owls: the Flammulated Owl, Northern Pygmy-Owl, Northern Saw-whet Owl, and Boreal Owl. Detailed information about these owls includes their ranges, anatomy, coloration, vocalizations, ranges, courtship, nesting behaviors, egg laying, fledgling raising, hunting habits, diets, mortality, longevity, and more.

Size: 8 1/2" x 11" 166 images 160 pp.
ISBN: 978-0-7643-3282-1 hard cover $39.99

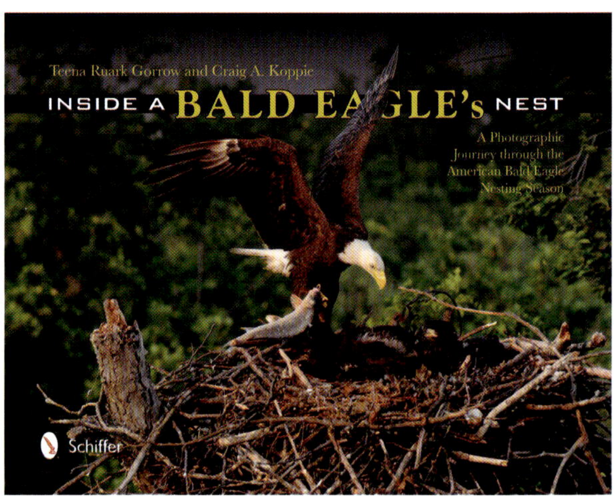

Inside A Bald Eagle's Nest: A Photographic Journey through the American Bald Eagle Nesting Season. Teena Ruark Gorrow, Ed.D,.and Craig A. Koppie. A photographic documentary of American Bald Eagles during nesting season, offering a rare glimpse into the behaviors of America's national symbol as it prepares a nest, mates, lays eggs, and raises its young. Observe how eaglets grow from hatching to fledging and experience first flight.

Size: 11" x 8 1/2" 160 color images 112 pp.
ISBN: 978-0-7643-4464-0 hard cover $24.99